THE WISE HOURS

The Wise Hours

A JOURNEY INTO THE WILD AND SECRET WORLD OF OWLS

Miriam Darlington

TIN HOUSE / PORTLAND, OREGON

This is a work of nonfiction, except for a handful of names and
identifying details changed to respect individuals' privacy.

Image credits: p.1 Barn Owl (John James Audubon), p.38 Tawny Owl
(John Gould), p.82 Little Owl (John Gould), p.125 Long-Eared Owl
(John Gould), p.159 Short-Eared Owl (the von Wright brothers), p.187
Eurasion Eagle Owl (the von Wright brothers), p.231 Pygmy Owl
(the von Wright brothers), p.265 Snowy Owl (John James Audubon), p.303
Feather (Rawpixel)

First US Edition 2023
Printed in the United States of America

Manufacturing by Lake Book Manufacturing
Interior design by Beth Steidle

Library of Congress Cataloging-in-Publication Data

Names: Darlington, Miriam, author.
Title: The wise hours : a journey into the wild and secret world of owls /
Miriam Darlington.
Description: Portland, Oregon : Tin House, [2023] | Includes
bibliographical references.
Identifiers: LCCN 2022047721 | ISBN 9781953534835 (hardcover) |
ISBN 9781953534842 (ebook)
Subjects: LCSH: Owls. | Owls—Behavior.
Classification: LCC QL696.S83 D36 2023 | DDC 598.9/7—
dc23/eng/20221012
LC record available at https://lccn.loc.gov/2022047721

Tin House
2617 NW Thurman Street, Portland, OR 97210
www.tinhouse.com

Distributed by W. W. Norton & Company

1 2 3 4 5 6 7 8 9 0

For Wendy
the wisest owl of all

A wise old owl lived in an oak
The more he saw the less he spoke
The less he spoke the more he heard.
Why can't we all be like that wise old bird?

—ANON.

Contents

Beginnings

MY SON BENJI SAW THE OWL FIRST. SHE WAS PERCHED like a silky totem pole, talons grasping the gloved hand of her keeper. At first, too busy with getting a place in the queue for artisan bread, I walked straight past the owl man as he stood quietly holding his charge. How was it that they were barely visible? They blurred into the humdrum busyness of the townscape, as if there was something self-effacing—a kind of greyness, an owl-camouflage that both possessed. I learned then that the mind does not easily register things that we are not expecting to see.

The owl relies on the cryptic facets of its colours, markings, and posture to shield it from the gaze of others. But something about the plumage flared on the edge of my vision and perhaps my deep-seated fascination with owls made me turn, and when I saw her I lost all interest in buying fresh bread.

Benji was already right there. Together we stared. The Great Grey Owl, *Strix nebulosa*. Grail of the boreal forest.

Keenly aware, she gripped that leather glove tight as her head swivelled from side to side and her eyes settled on each and every distraction. I drifted closer, not wanting to startle her, but longing to be within reach of those smoky, brindled feathers. Could I touch?—Yes, it was important to get her used to people, he said. She was only a few months old.

Her softness took my breath away. Deadly beauty. She turned her face towards me and I noticed its astounding circumference. There is a narrow area that falls between pleasing and preposterous, I thought, and this owl's circular face and bright yellow eyes fitted into it with perfect grace. The massive facial disc, the owl man, Pete, explained to me, produces a funnel for sound that is the most effective in the animal kingdom; she had the most sensitive ears known to humankind. The owl didn't miss a word.

Pete told us that he had known about the batch of three large, cream-coloured eggs (which had been laid in this country by a captive owl) and once they hatched he had chosen this owlet at two weeks old and raised her. She had needed constant supervision and care, and was now, as with all young birds on seeing their first carer, "imprinted" upon him. They were inseparable. I watched as he repeatedly leant his cheek on her feathers, closed his eyes, and spoke to her with such tenderness that I felt as though I was intruding on a private conversation.

"I want an owl," Benji said, his hand on my shoulder. "Can I have an owl?"

He must have known what I'd say. This is a wild creature. Shouldn't it stay in the wild? We wrestled with ourselves, with our consciences, with our hearts.

When she was fully mature, Pete was planning to show his Great Grey Owl at the local rare-breeds sanctuary. My mind filled with a strange concoction of feelings. She's a captive,

I thought. A pet. She'll be an exhibit, a misfit, unable to do what she has evolved to do, dependent on her enemies.

She could be bred, Pete added, noticing my expression, and her chicks could be taken and released into the wild. Again he laid his face against her feathers and closed his eyes.

Could they be released? The laws around captive breeding are very strict on these matters, surely? The magnificent foreigner turned her head and looked past me with her lemon-coloured eyes.

"The yellow eyes," Pete said, "mean that she hunts in the daylight."

Of course, in her native Lapland, during the summer months, there is no night-time. And in the winter, she must rely on her ears for the months of darkness. In spite of all the qualms, I was captivated.

Then, something startled her. For a split second she tottered on her tethers and I felt the breeze from her spreading wings. I must have closed my eyes, and when I opened them again, in front of me a striped grey haze of staggering silence and softness was rising; a giant butterfly, a god of the tundra. As her wings filled the air, I heard nothing but the whisper of snow falling in thickets of spruce and pine.

This owl's origins were in the far north, in the boreal forest. To somebody out shopping for food at the market on a Saturday morning, from the cosy shires of England where at worst it is just wet in the winter, the very word "boreal" released an aromatic dream of resiny spruce forests, the whiff of wildcat, the pocked tracks of wolverine ghosting through the snowy tundra.

But this owl was on a leash. She bated again, tethered by jesses. Her wings worked, but she would never fly free. She righted herself, folded her wings, and settled, neatly doing what she was trained to do.

The joy of an encounter like this is always woven with an uncomfortable undercurrent. Owls, like so many species, no longer exist purely as astonishing, innocent, wild beings. They are emissaries from an imperilled ecosystem, rare representatives of natural freedom and abundance. Once we were conscious of being surrounded by wild things—they shaped who we were. Without their presence we feel, as poet John Burnside perfectly described, a sense of homesickness. Surely, to be fully human, we still need their wild company, even at a distance?

So what can a writer do, faced with a world whose wildness appears to be unravelling? The first thing perhaps is to get to know the wild, experience it, and pay attention to it. By giving our attention in this way we might avoid the blandification that happens, especially to so many "cute"-faced animals. As we "cutify" the natural world it is at risk of becoming tame and ornamental. Once we have encountered the wild face to face, been brushed by the downdraft of its phantom swoop or been awoken by that spine-shivering nocturnal cry, it becomes real, embedded in our minds, a subtle but vital part of our being. Perhaps with this kind of attention, we can come to fully care: a word that derives from the Old English *cearu*, which means "to guard or watch," "to trouble oneself." Facing up to our scars and losses, taking the trouble and the time to explore the ecological details of some of the most fragile species and to record them accurately on the page, is the least we can do.

This is the story of my journey to explore those ecological details, paying attention to the incremental shift owls have experienced, and still are experiencing, from wildness to a kind of enforced domesticity. I wanted to immerse myself in their world, from the wild owls to the captives that are kept in aviaries and sanctuaries and beyond, to look into the mythology, kinship, otherness, and mystery that wild owls offer. I hoped that during my search some wider truths would rise to the surface. I would try to find all of the wild owl species in Europe, to extend the limited baseline of the six British species that I knew lived on my patch and might survive extinction here during my own lifespan.

In his book *Biophilia*, biologist E. O. Wilson explains: "We are human in good part because of the particular way we affiliate with other organisms. They are the matrix in which the human mind originated and is permanently rooted." Losing sight of the natural world in which the brain was assembled over millions of years is a risky step, Wilson says. Offering a formula for reconnection, he urges: "Mysterious and little known organisms live within walking distance of where you sit. Splendour awaits in minute proportions."

My manifesto was an exploration of the nearby, then, accepting my part, my own implication in it all. To try to regain some balance, I would invite in some sanity for myself and for others, and along the way a sprinkling of enchantment might seep in. I would scour the twilit woods, fields, and valleys of my home archipelago and then reach further afield, learning about the ecology and conservation of these night-roaming raptors, about their presence as well as their absence. What was their place in our ecosystem; how and why have we made them into stories, given them meanings, wrapped them with all the folklore and superstition that we could muster? And why was it that owls were becoming semi-domesticated, kept as pets in aviaries and shown in "owl-displays," like a new kind of surrogate kin, when so many of their kind were threatened in the wild?

I would rise at dawn and follow the flicker of the white Barn Owl near my home; I would drift along the leafy Devon lanes at dusk to find the Tawny Owls I had heard calling. I wanted to track down the species I hadn't ever seen: the irascible, yellow-eyed Little Owl, the rare Long-eared Owl, and the elusive, migratory Short-eared Owl. I might even be able to see one of the feral Eagle Owls that I had heard were living wild in northern England, and perhaps, if I were lucky, a vagrant Snowy Owl might appear.

The plan was to unveil each of these species in their wonder, amongst their forests, meadows, moorlands, and marshes. But no sooner had the owl scheme spread its wings in my mind than my son Benji fell seriously ill. I knew I had a choice; I could accommodate his illness and work my owl search around him, writing up my findings as and when I was able to, or I could put the whole thing on the shelf. It felt wrong for our lives to be stopped in their tracks, and so slowly, with an open mind, I began. Difficulties repeatedly muscled their way in. Every parent's fear is that our young might be struck by injury or illness. How could I hide the frightening personal drama that was invading our life? The line I had read in Dante's *Divine Comedy* years earlier while studying as an undergraduate student was suddenly very real: "Nel mezzo del cammin di nostra vita / mi ritrovai per una selva oscura / ché la diritta via era smarrita," Dante says. "Midway along life's journey, I found myself in a dark wood, and the path was lost."

If I had known my year of owls was to be so permeated with my son's illness I might have faltered. But alongside the challenges the owl research slowed and deepened and Benji came under its wing. Alongside the fears and challenges my owl research slowed and expanded. Unexpected opportunities arose—invitations to Finland to see Eagle Owls; to Lapland to see Hawk Owls, Great Greys, and Ural Owls; to Serbia for Long-eared Owls; Scops Owls in France; and more Eagle Owls in Spain. In the end I managed to travel the length and breadth of Europe, finding commonalities just as my own country was breaking away from the unity we'd known for many years. Going in search of all thirteen species of owl that inhabit our vast, multilingual, many-owled corner of the world, I found uniformity in a shared devotion to our wondrously varied wildlife. And far from distracting me from my family and my roots, my journeys deepened my sense of home and my ability to listen to what was near. As I learned from one of my wise-beyond-her-years undergraduate students at the University of Plymouth, adversity leaves you both a stronger and a softer human, and it is underwritten with a strange kind of joy, even at its worst moments.

Carl Jung said "fear seeks noisy company and pandemonium to scare away the demons." I endeavoured to slow down and forgo many of my modern-world distractions. The clamour of gadgetry is as distracting from our purpose as it is sometimes helpful—and it disturbs the owls. For the owl years I abandoned my smartphone and gadgetry, staying with the quieter insights of my senses and notebook.

Women habitually remain silent about their personal lives for fear of repercussions. The honest inclusion of my family's small truths might add up to a bigger truth. For better or for worse, raw life had butted in. Again and again, I found myself living with hope when it seemed as if there was no hope. And so, my story became braided with two ecologies—the ornithological and the personal.

)

FOR MORE THAN 60 million years owls have roamed the night sky—*Homo sapiens* have only been here for a fraction of that time, less than two hundred thousand years. And just as our ancestors might have done, in some ways we still struggle to understand these birds. With the aid of genetics and taxonomy we have made progress, and distinguished owls into two ancient families: the *Tytonidae*, those large-headed owls with a tall, narrow skull, asymmetrical ears, a heart-shaped facial disc, and long, feathered legs (this group includes *Tyto alba*, our Barn Owl); and the *Strigidae*, the owls with shorter, asymmetrical skulls—this group includes all the other European species. Both have particularities that no other bird has, adaptations for nocturnal activity and predation. The flat facial disc, large eyes, and downward-turned beak lend the owl its wise, human-faced quality. The familiar face provides a contrast to the bird's eerie ability to turn its head up to 270 degrees. This unique, uncanny feature—and the fact that owls were difficult to see and to know in the dark with their noiseless flight, when all other birds fly with more obvious sound—disturbed and intrigued our ancestors, and produced a fear and fascination that have never quite disappeared.

Owls have a complex attraction for humans. Their loose, soft feathers, rather than the stiff, rigid plumage of other birds, can give them an attractive "fluffy" effect. The gentle contours are not for cuteness, however; they are solely evolved to insulate, and to cloak this predator in invisibility. Their patterning produces visually confusing camouflage that breaks up a silhouette beyond any hunter's wildest dreams. Their feathers are silencers, meant to mask themselves but also designed not to drown the subtle sound of their prey. While our ancestors may have been in awe of the owl's fearsome abilities as a nocturnal predator, these days we can have a tendency not to see beyond the fluffiness. But the hooked, sharp-edged bill, unlike that of the majority of other birds which have a horizontal bill, is for ripping flesh. The acute hearing and the stealth-swoop are for murder by momentous, feathered eruption. The ferocious raptorial talons are for striking and gripping—these are zygodactyl talons: instead of three toes facing forward and one behind, the outer digit has a joint that enables it to swivel backwards so two toes can be placed at the front and two behind. The prodigious strength of its grip is vital. The Eurasian Eagle Owl's deceptively velvet-feathered feet act as boxing gloves. This giant owl deploys its thunderous punch to grasp, snap, and puncture. Blakiston's fish owl, of a similar size and weight to the Eagle Owl, has spines called "spicules" on the underside of its toes to enable it to grip dicey aquatic prey.

But perhaps what also attracts us humans to owls is admiration, particularly that they have the skill to fly at night. This bird is feathered perfection; grace and beauty with talons. Just as a poem is the best words in the best order, this bird must be the best night-hunter in the best kit. Even without the glamour, we can't fail to envy the finely honed precision that is compressed here. The owl is made for one thing only: to survive, and to do so by stealth. For this reason, over time our suspicious minds have wondered whether it also has any supernatural qualities: Hidden in its cloak was there the capacity for evil, for instance? For if *Homo sapiens*, the wise humans—who in general do not appear always to have entirely mastered their own baser instincts—possessed the same set of abilities, it would surely make a potent concoction. And so by projection this mysterious night creature has gained human meanings that meant nothing to it.

In Egyptian, Celtic, and Hindu cultures, the owl's symbolism was involved with guardianship of the underworld. The owl was revered as the winged keeper of souls after death. In Malaysia and Indonesia it is *burung hantu*, the "ghost bird." The ancient Greeks associated it with wisdom and courage; the Romans with foreboding and fear. Wise or evil, the owl was a porous receptacle for all of our chosen meanings. But why all this mythologising? Perhaps we need and enjoy a story with a good fright in it, to bond us, to explain ourselves to ourselves, to remind us on some level of our origins. That "sweet sense of horror, the shivery fascination with monsters and creeping forms" that E. O. Wilson confirms is wired into our minds. The human brain is configured to be wary of predators and their movements, and as predators tend to stare at their prey, the large-eyed owl provokes that trigger, the age-old possibility of threat. Humans were kept awake and alive by that possibility, whether it was perceived to be supernatural or natural, a spirit, a bear, an owl, a wolf, or a lion.

In order to survive, humans learned to outsmart dangers; the domestication of dogs and cats may have been one way of doing this. Storytelling may also have been another way we learned to do it. To think about, predict, and prepare for danger with a story was to teach our vulnerable young how to do the same. Perhaps we love the owl for its spookiness because it reminds us to be on the lookout. Literature has never failed to embolden our fascination for nocturnal ghostliness and its creatures: in Sylvia Townsend Warner's haunting novel *Lolly Willowes; or the Loving Huntsman,* the heroine longs for something shadowy and menacing, "a something that lurked in waste places and that was hinted at by the sound of water gurgling in deep channels and by the voices of birds of ill-omen."

In Japan, on the other hand, the word for owl is *fukuro,* which means "good fortune," and so the owl is lucky. In Aboriginal Australia, Eerin the grey owl is a protector, sleeping by day and flying by night to keep watch and to warn if danger approaches. In South Australia the Nyungar tribe protects a standing owl-stone, Boyay Gogomat, a creator, healer, and destroyer. The Wardaman tribe in Northern Australia believes that at a unique rocky outcrop that overlooks the outback dwells Gordol, the owl who created the world.

Owls have been part of our landscape, psychological context, and emotional ecology from the moment *Homo sapiens* became self-aware. When the daily soundtrack of birdsong died down, we noticed the owl's voice in the dark and felt puzzled and unsettled. The human brain is primed for curiosity and story, so owls invited in our myth-making. Now it is impossible to see these animals without clouding them with what anthropologist Franz Boas described as our *Kulturbrille*, a cultural lens that automatically colours the way we perceive everything. We observed owls' hunting skills, noted their powerful sensory capacities, and coveted their silent mastery of the air. They would have been and still are part of our spiritual system, that expanded along with our sense of identity as a species, our sense of our place in the world. Owls have found their way into our mythology, art, literature, and religion and so appear to be polarised. On one side, the imaginary owl of the mind, the human-created spirit bird, the familiar, the icon, the owl as commodity. Looking at any of these, we are really only looking at ourselves. On the other side, the real, live animals that breathe and fly and hunt, and this owl is so often beyond our reach. However much we taint them with our own meanings, in art, in story, in photography, and on screens, they still remain beyond us. Until relatively recently, the more we have tried to understand them through the prism of our own experiences, the more we have obscured their true nature.

I wanted contact with the true nature of these birds. Encounter was what interested me, to observe the birds in the wild. To see some of the more elusive owls I needed specialists to guide me. I went in search of the people who could help. Unexpected friendships grew. My guides helped me find my owls—but they also taught me something else. I found that in the end any encounter between a wild owl and a human must always be tentative, aware of the assumptions we might wrongly make. Just as I would only ever be a small fragment of the owl's landscape, I could only ever partially come to know owls. Learning that was a whole journey in itself.

IN THE FIRST century AD, Pliny the Elder wrote in his *Natural History*:

> The eagle-owl is thought to be a very bad omen, being as it is a funereal bird. It lives in deserts and in terrifying, empty and inaccessible places. Its cry is a scream. If it is seen in a city, or during the day, it is a direful portent, though several cases are known of an eagle-owl perching on private houses without fatal consequences.

I love that Pliny covers himself, carefully stating that some homes might occasionally be spared the fatal consequences.

The irony is that most of the 250 species of owl on the planet evolved as forest birds, and since humans depend upon the planet's forests to maintain our atmosphere, as we continue felling and burning we are spelling our own doom.

Once we lived much more consciously within the eco-system. Our lives were sensitive to the wild, entirely embedded amongst predator–prey relationships, and animals were respected as part of our lives in ways which it is difficult for Western humans to remember or imagine. In December 1994 a group of three spelunkers, or cavers, were following an old mule path beside a cliff face along the Ardèche river in southern France when they came face to face with an astonishing reminder of our connection to the animal world. They found a narrow slot in the rock of the cliff, and climbing inside they felt a tiny current of air emanating from some rubble. The subtle breath from the rock could mean only one thing: there was an unexplored cave inside. They cleared the rubble and scrambled in. By the light of their lamps they found that the cave, larger than any they had seen before in the region, was scattered all over with bones, scratch marks, and wallows, all from one extinct animal: the cave bear.

Moving through the chambers of what came to be known as the Chauvet cave—named after one of the explorers, Jean-Marie Chauvet, who later wrote about it jointly with the other cavers—they found astonishing paintings. It began with red ochre dots and smudges made by the hands of Palaeolithic artists, and as the chambers of the cave stretched out for over 240 metres, they found each chamber contained new wonders. The red ochre was replaced by black, and these turned out to be the earliest paintings. In some places horses and bison had been engraved in the soft surfaces of the cave walls, perhaps scratched with a human finger. Small fragments of charcoal were lying about where they had been knocked from the artists' torches, as if they were still fresh. A mammoth, a leopard, and soon a whole pantheon of animals danced across the walls, and their forms felt vibrant enough to be recent. The artists had used the uneven surface of the rock as if the animals were emerging from it.

"Suddenly our lamps lit upon a monumental black frieze. It took our breath away. There were shouts of joy and bursts of tears. We felt gripped by madness and dizziness," the cavers later wrote in their book *Dawn of Art: The Chauvet Cave*. They were staring at a panel that had been scraped clean and worked into a scene of a dozen hunting lions, their heads deftly shaded, their eyes alive and intelligent, their bone structure and musculature clearly delineated. These were familiar, intimate portraits. The expressions of the lions as they stalked were varied and well observed. Carbon dating showed that the first of these paintings had been begun around 36,000 BC. They were far older than anything previously discovered. The bears, bison, reindeer, cave lions, rhinoceroses, horses, and mammoths had been depicted by artists who were skilled and attentive. The graceful depictions were accurately and lovingly rendered and showed that the artists must have worked calmly and reverently. Were these devotional images? Returning from the deepest part of the cave where the lions reside, and looking back into it, in a place where the floor had collapsed so that it was now unreachable, the cavers noticed that on the ceiling there was engraved a striking solitary figure of a Long-eared Owl.

The Chauvet owl is the oldest known depiction of an owl in the world. It is 45 centimetres tall—close to the size of a large Long-eared Owl, *Asio otus*. It has clearly etched ear tufts, and is perched on a downward-drooping rock pendant. Most interestingly, its back is shown facing outwards, wings folded, with fifteen streaks to demarcate the densely lined plumage. This closely observed owl is depicted as if swivelling its head 180 degrees backward to peer into the dark, its face turned to look out into the cave and meet the gaze of the people walking towards it. To portray it thus, the real animal must have been watched many times and its skill noted. In view of the sophistication of the other drawings, the deliberate positioning of the bird suggests the artists understood something of the Janus nature of the owl, its troubling liminal status on the boundaries of light and dark. This owl captures a strange suggestion, its ability to face both ways, both out into the cave and back into the body of the rock and whatever that was thought to be concealing, as if the rock were merely a veil.

We cannot know exactly what the owl meant to those artists, only guess that they perhaps trusted that it would be meaningful—a helpful companion perhaps, or a guardian in these deepest reaches of the dark. Humans are the loneliest of creatures amongst all the earth's species, self-consciously and visibly a species apart. But when they hunted for food every day for their survival, our ancestors must have known their prey intimately. They would have gazed into the anatomy of their prey animals and experienced the resemblance. On the outside we may look different, but on the inside it is clear that in some way we are related—there is a common ancestor, somewhere way back—and in peering into the entrails and skeletons of the birds, early humans may have felt recognition. The organs, the spine, the ribcage, the breastbone; the arm-like wings with fingery tips; the hips joined to the legs, the toes; all, at their core, relate to and reflect our own human structure.

This unspeaking kinship with animals may have drawn us, or certain of us, more companionably into the dark unknown recesses of the caves, as well as into the deepest recesses of our imaginations. Looking at the Chauvet cave masterpieces, where animals appear to spring from clefts and cleaves in the rock, perhaps here was a place where we felt we could call them up out of the ground. We can never know for sure, but it might be here that humans started to fit these animals with symbolic thoughts and began to use them as metaphor. They became useful as a way of explaining the world. Was it from this point onwards, with the slow appropriation humans excel at, that the exploitation of animals began? At first they might have been respected as unspeaking companions and beings that were meaningful in ways humans have forgotten now. They would have seemed magical, both mortal—as they could die—and immortal, as new identical members of their kind seemed to reappear and carry on. Later they were raw material to be used, subjugated, and also silenced.

With the advent of medieval Christianity, animals became fair game for teachings that justified religious beliefs. Owls were dirty and slothful, according to Benedictine abbot Hrabanus Maurus in *De Rerum Naturis*, written in the year 847 AD. He intended this encyclopedia as a handbook for preachers, stating that owls cry out when they feel that someone is going to die: "He flees from the light, in the sense that he does not look for the glory of human praise," Maurus tells us. Unpleasant, antisemitic connotations abounded in the illustrations of his owls. During this period, strange images of owls in religious artworks such as illustrated bestiaries and sculptures were often given a human face with a prominent hooked beak to denote the supposed long, hooked nose of the Jews. Scenes of the owl being mobbed by other birds were common in the medieval manuscripts—and in reality wild birds do call in alarm and mob owls as they threaten to predate their nestlings. To some medieval minds the mobbing was punishment for being a night-creature that shunned God's light. The owl was often carved on misericords in medieval churches and monasteries. Here too they were portrayed as being attacked by other birds as if they were sinners condemned by righteousness. As monks sat down on these misericords they would be doing Christ's work by robustly squashing the evil.

Owl symbols abound in the darkly imaginative Renaissance paintings of Hieronymus Bosch (1450–1516). There are very few paintings by this artist that do not contain a hiding owl. Bosch's owls might not be malevolent, however, and are sensitively depicted. It is as if they are merely supervising the action in the paintings, not taking part in it. As the owl is a creature that can see in the darkness where others are blind, for Bosch it might in fact be seen as bringing light to darkness, contrary to medieval Christian views about the bird. His tiny owls often peep out, watching wherever there is a human committing a sin or misbehaving in any way. In *The Garden of Earthly Delights* and many of the other paintings, owls appear embroidered in some item of clothing, hidden in a pocket, sitting in a basket, peering from a windowsill, in a tree, fountain, or vase, everywhere and anywhere, ubiquitous watching eyes. Art historians have been discussing the meaning of Bosch's owls ever since. Far from symbols of wickedness, they seem to be symbolic observers, meditative representations of the esoteric teachings Bosch was party to, representing mystery and meditation, a consciousness or conscience bigger than our own.

None of the critics suggest that these owls are whimsical; they seem to be deliberate. The Pygmy Owl and the Barn Owl—the varieties Bosch most often depicted—were known to be frequently out in daylight, and were looked upon more favourably at the time. The Pygmy Owl, often diurnal, has a pleasant flute-like hoot, and in France it was said to be benevolent, and especially lucky company for travellers. The Barn Owl had domestic aspects, and was a familiar companion that lived close to our dwellings and destroyed vermin. The ingenious Bosch was evoking complex thoughts about the solitary contemplator. The clear-sighted, meditative, wise bird that remained in its quiet nook in the brickwork (or cell) all day was like a monk. The owls were thoughtfully placed to bear witness to the human misdemeanours happening elsewhere in the paintings.

Albrecht Dürer's melancholy portrait of a deep-eyed young Tawny speaks of a surge of sympathy in his 1508 depiction *The Little Owl*. This delicate watercolour sensitively traces something of how the artist feels about the captive owl. Instead of dissecting it or using it as a Christian vessel, in fine detail he catches particular aspects and distils an elusive essence of owlness. The large eyes with fathom-dark pupils and the sharply hooked claws, the soft, brownish-grey camouflage, all show well-observed traits of this young nocturnal predator. Fragile lines trace the long primary feathers and the softer down on the owl's breast. The fierce young bird is captured in an alert yet thoughtful moment, and with its claws spread wide on a man-made surface, its wings furled, it poignantly suggests that this young owl has all his life ahead. The wild creature's isolation from nature in a captive environment suggests that Dürer felt the potential of the creature yet disapproved of the cultural appropriation or caging of it, and cared about more than the simple appearance and received ideas of owls. It is caught in a poignant, vulnerable pose, and its predatory power appears locked up, as if it cannot wait to be its simple, natural self and fly free.

As our representation of owls proliferated, we continued to cage them with our human ideas and misconceptions, and now in the twenty-first century they are often literally caged. Since the phenomenon of Harry Potter, where owls were often depicted as glamorous companions, they are increasingly popular and often desired as pets. In Britain their breeding in captivity is regulated and they are sold by falconry specialists, but increasingly second-hand owls are easy to come by online. Across the world an unintended effect of Harry Potter has spread with the books' fame. With its translation into many languages and vastly popular films, and alongside the rise of social media, special interest pet owl groups have proliferated. In Java and Bali where bird markets are widespread and owls are not protected, wild-caught owls are commonly sold as pets. The Pramuka market, the largest in Jakarta, may often have up to sixty owls for sale, with eight different species on show at a time. In Indonesia it is traditional to keep birds as domestic pets, but previously *burung hantu* or "ghost birds" were feared and avoided. Now the ghost bird is called a

"Burung Harry Potter" and prices are rising for the rarer owls as more and more people wish to own one. The loss of these unprotected apex predators from the wild must be interfering with fragile ecosystems, imperilling the conservation of rare species, as well as causing distress to the captive owls. A 2017 research survey by the Oxford Wildlife Trade Research Group found many species now being sold freely in the Far East: the Javan Owlet, the Bornean Wood Owl, the Buffy Fish Owl, the Australasian Barn Owl, and many Scops Owls were noted, and still more species were unidentifiable due to poor light conditions, feather damage, or the owls being sold as chicks or juveniles.

Framed in cages, in high resolution on our TV screens or in closely filmed nature documentaries, owls present a paradox. The binary distinction between owls as cute and owls as sinister can make them appear as ferocious as they are fascinating. While the reptilian burn of their gaze still seems to suggest that our mortal existence is of little significance, in Hollywood films their chill call foreshadows some ghoulish turn in the plot. At the same time, in the world of consumerism the owl has been reduced to an item to collect, sequestered for a companion, a cutesy fashion accessory, or printed on crockery and clothing. Owl toys are obsessively hoarded and displayed. The owl has become an "experience," a collectible, a postcard, and a pin-up.

Where, amongst all this, is the real owl?

ONE AFTERNOON IN MARCH I walked away from the houses of our suburbia and into the overgrown green lane in the next valley. It was windy, the eye-watering wind that bites, but the downward drift pulled my feet into a steady rhythm. The undulating ground felt like a great sleeping animal, and there was some energy rising out of it that lent the mind some balance. Common polypody, ivy, and hart's tongue ferns covered the banks and clattered in the breeze; above my head crows tumbled and flapped and the wind tossed all the sound up like flotsam. In the mud there were badger tracks, then some fox prints, and after that, the slim slots of a roe deer. I began to feel the deep humanness of the track, a thousand years of passage, all the human and animal feet that had weathered it into this eroded way opened by roots and water and footfall.

I thought of the huge lone oak standing in the middle of the field, still dignified, squeezed between the tremendous mounds of earth that would soon be marked on the map as the new development being built close to our house: "The Camomile Lawns." Somehow, long ago, in the midst of the rough pasture of the field, in spite of the grazing noses of cattle, its acorn managed to take its chances and sprout. My mind ranged through its elephantine stature and its gnarly bark, imagining its thousand dependants: its fungal, algal, and plant inhabitants; its ferns, beetles, wasps, and lacewings; its birds, bats, shrews, and other small mammals. We live in the company of intricate and complex systems.

"The Camomile Lawns." My trust wavered each time I walked back past the sign, its veneer created by some faraway corporation. The field is being developed as I write, earth moved in tremendous heaps, sifted and flattened. By the time you are reading this, the town will have grown, and one hundred houses been built for human families. The whole town is expanding, quite suddenly, and hundreds of homes are being built in different locations all around its edges. People need homes, and they need the green amongst them. The same developments are happening in many places. But neon glow and street lighting will rise at night where before there were pools of darkness. Unless it is provided for, the wildlife will have to adapt, or leave.

Tyto alba

BARN OWL

In spindrift mist a white owl sits
on the barn's storm-wrecked hull.
Moon-faced she takes the last midnight watch,
talon-tight on the listing deck of oak.
In place of the nest, a squared-up show boat,
no space for quilted flight,
no cobwebbed corners,
no mothy, fathomless dark.

—JENNIFER HUNT, "Barn Conversion"

WE HAVE A LONG ENTANGLEMENT WITH THIS SPECIES, tethered by a story more complex than our simple admiration for its beauty, its super-senses, and its formidable hunting skills. Our association is important for the owl, too. It has adapted to live alongside, even among us. Our closeness has developed over time, like a marriage, but perhaps not an altogether happy one.

As a vole hunter the Barn Owl was attracted to the dense rodent populations that inhabit our man-made rough pastures and meadows. But while in the early twentieth century this owl was a common sight in the fields of lowland Britain, it is no longer the case. The Barn Owl Trust tell us that the causes of the owl's current decline are the result of human activity: changes in agriculture, loss of nesting and roosting sites, the increased use of lethal hazards such as rodenticide, and the proliferation of trunk roads all have combined to impact on the sensitive Barn Owl. It is likely that there are fewer than five thousand pairs left in Britain.

To begin at the beginning. These raptors were on the planet long before us. Fossil remains of owls have been dated from 65 to 56 million years ago. In the Pleistocene, *Ornimegalonyx*, giant Barn Owls, ranged across the Mediterranean area. They stood over a metre in height, weighed twice the heft of today's Eagle Owl, and preyed on large rodents such as capybara. Our human ancestors may have noticed these hunters and been fascinated by their nocturnal powers and haunting cries; unable to explain the owl's uncanny skills without the benefit of science, they might have believed these creatures were party to some knowledge that eluded us.

The Barn Owl's long, lightweight wings evolved for grassland hunting, not dense forest like some of the short-winged owls. It came from the plains and scrub of warmer, drier climes. But as the ice sheets retreated from Northern Europe between ten and twenty thousand years ago and humans spread north in greater numbers, so followed this wraith-like owl. It was drawn by the pasture that small-scale farming created, and later found the protective nesting cavities that were offered by some of our cliff-like structures: farm buildings, attics and haylofts, churches and homesteads all mimicked the owl's native cliff-scapes and provided the perfect place to breed. So from our early history *Homo sapiens* and *Tyto alba* began to share both feeding grounds and housing. While some of the owl's northerly movement may have been due to climate and habitat change, much of this was human-made. The owls came to depend on our shared habitat, where it could easily find shelter: drifting low above scrub and floating over meadow grasses, it uses its acute hearing to hunt in prey-rich portions of grassland, its super-sensitive ears pinpointing small rodents with ease even in the faintest glimmer of moonlight.

Our lightly grazed pasture was thick with native grasses perfect for the tunnels and nests of small rodents, particularly field voles, the owl's main food source. For over a thousand years our clearings, meadows, and summer pastures have made a dense and diverse thatch—velvet grass, sweet vernal-grass, false oat-grass, red fescue, rough meadow-grass, smooth meadow-grass, false-brome, wood false-brome, upright brome, and cocksfoot—all useful species that when left un-mown or un-grazed decompose so slowly that they form a "litter layer" providing protection for small mammals. Fields with such ecological niches were perfect foraging ground for the owls, but this once-common farmland is under threat—from increasingly intense agriculture, mechanised farming, and more aggressive use of rodenticides and pesticides.

But it is not all bad news. The agricultural relationship between humans and Barn Owls has taken on a new aspect in recent years. It is accepted that the Barn Owl actively removes vermin; but could Barn Owls remove as many if not more rodents from our fields and barns than a chemical intervention? To address this question and raise sympathy for the Barn Owl, in 2011 Mark Browning dreamt up the Barn Owl/Rodent Project. This flash of inspiration was set up in California to investigate whether it was more sustainable to deal with an infestation of rodents by owl or by rat poison. A 100-acre vineyard had been overrun by a voracious American rodent named the pocket gopher. These prolific nibblers were causing huge economic damage to valuable vines. For the project, Browning designed owl nest boxes and placed them at 500-metre intervals along the perimeter of one vineyard. By the following year, twenty-five Barn Owl nest boxes had been erected and these had attracted eighteen pairs of Barn Owls that fledged sixty-six young. Browning calculated that if each adult owl needed one rodent per day and the growing young double that, a conservative estimate was that in 2011 the owls consumed 9,576 rodents in total. In 2012, the growing population of owls consumed approximately 15,204 rodents: by any account, a prodigious number of rodents was being eliminated. The owls were shown to be targeting the vineyard where the gophers burrowed, and the level of gopher damage was considerably reduced.

Even with the initial investment, the owls would pay for themselves within two to five years: for the Californian study the original cost of twenty-five nest boxes, poles, mulch for bedding, and installation labour was approximately $6,000. By the end of the second year, the rodents harvested by the owls came in at a cost of $0.24 per rodent. And as the study rolled on, the cost per rodent declined year on year until, after a five-year period, it was all but negligible.

In contrast, some landowners use strychnine pellets to control their rodent infestations. Strychnine costs hundreds of dollars per application, and the process is lengthy and time-consuming, requiring days of labour—only for the whole process to be repeated once the rodent population recovers. Who could argue? The Barn Owl was the victor!

In Jordan and Israel similar Barn Owl projects have taken place, and the owl is now celebrated for its uses in terms of farming sustainability. In such pioneering conservation schemes these useful raptors are replacing pesticides.

Coupled with the loss of its traditional habitats, here in Britain the Barn Owl is on the northernmost edge of its range. In the highlands and far north it is too cold, too wet, and too blowy to be comfortable for the delicate, warmth-loving Barn Owl. Its plumage is not waterproof, and with no oily defence against heavy rain, if it becomes waterlogged it cannot fly. If it cannot hunt, it may quickly starve or die of exposure. Frost and frozen ground in winter, heavy rains in autumn, flooding, high wind; all extreme and unpredictable weather threatens the ability of the Barn Owl to feed. As a lightweight bird it has so little body fat that it needs the warmth and shelter of beams, the insulating thatch of our old barns. But recent bad winters have made it increasingly difficult to find food; rain makes it impossible to hunt, snow and ice send prey scurrying underground or affect vole populations so severely that the owls have simply starved. As a vole specialist the Barn Owl is especially vulnerable, its prey subject to huge fluctuations. It is also extremely site-faithful and so doesn't have the option of simply abandoning a site that is no longer hospitable. A home bird, almost without exception it remains in its own patch all its adult life and nests consistently in the same place. It does not migrate, and may only vary its roosts occasionally. Many generations of Barn Owls might stick to the same site. Amongst unsympathetic conversion of its sheltering roosts, loss of mature trees, and ever-more intensive farming, along with encroaching roads and faster-moving traffic, the Barn Owl is not well adapted for survival.

IN MARCH I'D STARTED to find owl pellets. Between the size of a conker and a champagne cork, these undigested, regurgitated remains had been cast along with whitewash splatters beneath the old oak near my home. These were signs that indicated only one thing: the presence of an owl. As the days lengthened, my interest deepened. Barn Owls begin to pair up in late winter and might settle on a roost that will be a good potential nesting site. In the privacy of their nest cavity or a hidden roost high within the beams of an old barn there will be much courtship bonding. All through the spring, mutual face-preening and cheek-rubbing are interspersed with the male bringing the female gifts of voles. If they can get into breeding condition and the food supply is good, around 75 per cent can breed any time between March and August, but eggs have been found in January, and it is possible that if the owls are in the right condition they could breed at any time in a good year. If it is a bad year, and their habitat does not provide enough voles, mice, or shrews, breeding is more likely to fail, or even not take place at all.

I watched the roost. Sometimes in the tree an alert whiteness was perched, watchful, occasionally uttering nervous calls. Around the same time as my owl-watching, out of the bedrock of our home a series of tremors happened. One of our own young got sick. It was an illness that was so unusual, so difficult to diagnose and then to treat, that its unfolding had a seismic effect on us. Perhaps illness is always like this, from the common cold to cancer, all of them jostling somewhere on a Richter scale of life change. It was around April when we noticed the first signs. My nineteen-year-old Benji and I were sitting by the river, where the crepuscular soundscape of bird chorus was heightening over the marsh. For Benji, on the cusp of moving into the adult world, this was time off before his final year in college, where he was learning to design and build houses. I relished his quirky end-of-teenage company sitting next to me, close and content. I knew that there would not be much more of this. Soon he might be away at university and things would never be quite the same. When he tipped awkwardly sideways, shivered for a few moments, and slowly righted himself, I thought nothing of it. He was quiet for a moment and then he said: "Do you ever get that thing where you start twitching?" I turned to look at him, puzzled.

We didn't know it, but somewhere in the invisible pathways of Benji's brain, some synapse was misfiring. Amongst the millions of neurons inside his head, messages were going awry between nerve and nerve, from pathway to pathway.

We would often come down to the reed beds like this to hear the owls. It's hard to write this in hindsight and accept that, at that point, we had no idea of what was to come for Benji. At that moment, our attention was all on one owl, and now it was calling across the reeds to another: a screech, then a reply, as if they were throwing lightning bolts to one another, as if each was catching the other's cry in its craw and lobbing it back.

"Look," Benji said, feeling better again. He touched my arm and we watched a white owl lift free of the reeds and emerge to glide across the river. Its body was reflected in the caught light of the water.

IN MAY AND early June I always left our window wide open to catch the height of the dawn chorus. Some nights, and very early mornings, I was woken by the owl's disembodied cry, a shriek that jangled the nerves. It reached right into that place where once long ago we might have shivered at the ill omen. The cry would draw me out of my bed, and dawn walks down the green lane, through the gap, and into the field, had become ritual. Each time, it would take a while for my senses to attune. Shadowy leaves, roots and earth, uncanny darknesses, the strata of animal habitations, weasel runs, vole ways. Leaves dripped, bird wings flickered. Usually, Benji was safely asleep and his younger sister Jenny tucked away in her world too.

The cry, when it came one morning, was so piercing that I leapt out of bed and scrambled for my binoculars. Leaning out in the half-lit air I caught the mothy wings, the buoyant turn as the sensitive ears captured every minute sound: the twitch of insect legs, the drone of power lines, the rasp of fescue stems. The feathered radar of its face tilted to block out interference, to capture the wisp of light paws: *prey—right there*. Wings folded so they were streamline-smooth, talons outstretched, silently it dropped.

I leant further out of the window. The field curved over the horizon, and I could just make out not one but two shapes moving. My owls were a pair, their long, light wings carrying them over swathes of grass. The screech of the male ripped the air again and seemed to be answered by the female. The scratchy calls had been pressing into my inner ear for weeks and now their urgent voices simmered, fingernails on sandpaper.

When the owl is hunting, it quarters the field, back and forth, and a strike may grasp nothing. Only a small percentage of attempts end with a kill and this means that Barn Owls live on a knife-edge. This is a predator that has to be light enough to drift silently over tall grass, long-winged and elfin enough to float, then to dive in and grasp what might be hiding there. As well-evolved for the task as the Barn Owl may seem, there are stiff challenges: it has a "low wing loading" that means it is so light it can glide buoyantly and effortlessly, but it has a body mass index so precarious that if an owl does not make a kill for more than a few days it can quickly starve.

I skipped a shower and dressed in a vest, jumper, long trousers, and socks. It could be cold and damp in the fields this early; I pulled on wellington boots and left my husband, Rick, just woken, his face blue-lit as he blearily tapped at the screen of his iPhone. I trotted out, refreshed by the washed air, the blue sky filled with a yawn of plane-sound. Towards the field, along the edge of suburbia, prickles, ferns, and nettles lined the way. Then the sign, sprouting up: "Site Acquired for Development." The announcement of "stunning new homes" had been there for a week or so, jutting out of the hedge and into my thoughts. I wanted to pace out this place, to watch over it a little. This rough-edged bit of land housed dwellers far more sensitive than its new owners would see.

In the hedge, thick, sappy Spanish bluebells had broken out of the nearby gardens on the edge of town and taken over sunny parts of the banks. They were going over now, and pale; some were swollen with seeds. Just as my head was down in the flowers and seed heads something flickered on the edge of my vision. That sylph-quiet movement of wings. It quartered the field, this way and that, catching the light.

It came again, swivelled, saw me, and veered off. I took a few steps forward, keeping my silhouette within the shade of the hedge. And then it stooped, diving down on to something.

Brief sightings like this reveal fleeting glimpses of these creatures, so I tried to listen harder, engage all my senses, walk more softly; to close in without encroaching. I waited for the cry but none came, so I spun my binocular focus to where it dropped into the grass: and there it was, rising up, weighted with prey. The close-up visual framed chunks of the bird as it flew. I held my breath at its smooth white breast. No speckles. It could have been the male? Where was it taking its catch? When it hovered briefly, the perfect fan of tail feathers shone and light fell through its wing tips.

An adult Barn Owl can swallow a whole field vole in one go. Owls cannot chew, so within a few minutes the prey is crushed and dissolved in the bird's ventriculus, or stomach.

ONCE THE FLUID and soft tissue in the vole's body have been liquefied, the fur and harder parts pass into the gizzard. This muscular stomach is an organ that birds have instead of teeth. It retains the indigestible bits—the bones, teeth, claws, and fur—crushing them into a compact, gizzard-shaped pellet. The pellet will remain there for a period of hours until it is regurgitated and dropped to the ground. It is very tempting if you find one to take it home and try to identify what the mystery parts are. Fur and bone dissected with tweezers under a lamp through a hand lens become field vole jaws with incisors and molars. The species of vole or mouse is indicated by the colour of the molars: Are they pinkish? Or rotated? There might be meadow pipit feathers, rat skulls, each pellet a map containing all the grizzled drama of the owl's nocturnal predation. And the Barn Owl breaks the rules. When it is under pressure from breeding and needs to catch more voles, or if it is unsuccessful in the night, it often hunts in the day, preying on different species, but primarily here in the UK on the variety of small mammals that inhabit our grasslands.

It began to rain softly, and seeing the apex of a barn roof and an ivy-clad gable end I scuttled into the lee for shelter. The barn was half-ruined. When I got further inside, something alive was there, a presence beyond any mice or jackdaws.

I stepped further in, my feet grating on the dusty floor, and the quiet was broken by a rattlesnake hiss. It bubbled up from nowhere in particular, making my skin prickle. Hunched in a corner, a small, downy face and two dark eyes stared at me.

A fallen owlet.

And higher up, the source of the hissing; a small snowdrift of siblings, calling from their high ledge. I had thought the owls might nest in a cavity in the old tree, but of course they preferred this rickety but reliably dry human-made space instead.

How quick we are, to want to come to the aid of fallen things. This tumbled chick wouldn't last a night on the floor while the foxes had cubs to feed.

It's so easy to be preoccupied with the guilt of it all: climate chaos, the loss of species, the Pacific Garbage Patch. Here was something to save. I had heard news that the owls were in trouble that year. While we suffered our own weather patterns, outdoors the other tribe, who still have to live on their skills and their wits, who take their chances and don't always make it, had survived all through that stormy, wet winter. They had survived well enough to produce young.

I scanned the wall for handholds. I could try to climb up and put it back and then quietly withdraw, hoping the parents would soon return. So I approached, and the owlet wobbled, but it didn't flee. I placed my hands around its warm, tickly body. I checked the thinly muscled wings. Some of the adult feather shafts had begun to come through, encasing what might one day be flight feathers if it survived the summer. Before it reached maturity its extravagant body-warmer of soft, white down would insulate its back, head, and belly. It was way too small to fly yet. How old? Three weeks, perhaps four?

Its feet wriggled at first, but soon its feather-weight settled into my grip. I expected it to smell like a kitten but its alien stink of rotting mouse, vole blood, and acrid ammonia hurt my nose. There was something part-reptile there: I looked into its wincing face, felt its scaly feet, and at their tips, whetstone-grey talons, already gripping fiercely. Millions of years of evolution, honed for predation.

What would it be like, to have bones filled with a mesh of air, wings that could spread and float the body out onto miles of nothing? Neither the owlet nor I knew anything of this.

With one hand grasping it I started to climb, my fingers stretching for holds in the stone. I dropped back down; I needed two hands. The owlet fitted inside my shirt along with a suspicious, parasitical tickling. Perhaps I needn't have plopped it down next to my skin, but sometimes you just have to keep going. With both hands free I could get up there more easily. At the ledge, I undid the tangled claws from me, pushed the fallen owlet back with the others, and let go.

I stepped quickly away from the hissing owls and all the stories of hauntings rose in my mind. You can see how the superstitions grew: the owl was a night bird, it came upon you silently, startling out of the mist or moonlight. Its white wings seemed to magnify its size and weirdness. Its appearance must have felt like a visitation. Above all, its awful screech around church towers, belfries, and graveyards must have frightened the life out of people. But right now it just seemed as though the poor creature needed help. I withdrew rapidly. All an owl wants is to be left in peace, to make its living, to bring up its young safely and without disturbance, to continue the bloodline. Not so different from us, really.

But any sentimentality or cutesy image we might harbour today for this heart-faced killer can be dismissed with a look into the habits of those hissing youngsters. When they are first born, they are bald and bristly, the most unattractive babies that only a mother could love. Even after two weeks, when they have grown down, these snowy, powder-puff bundles have been witnessed—thanks to the nest cams we inquisitive humans have set up—standing on a cache of slaughtered voles that the devoted parents catch ceaselessly and pile up in case of lean times. Worse still, the parents have laid their eggs at intervals, so when there is little to eat, the larger chicks may pick on and bully the smaller ones. Sometimes, if there is not enough food forthcoming, they might devour their weaker, more recently hatched siblings, swallowing them down whole.

SEPTEMBER ARRIVED WITH cool air and departing swallows. My teaching was about to begin. Lectures planned and papers written, my own taken to school and to college; the dog walked, the washing-up mostly done, the emails answered. It should all have been fine, but there was the niggling worry about Benji. While I had been out owling, commuting, living, Benji had been going downhill.

The family was seated around the kitchen table. It was Saturday lunchtime and I was serving spaghetti. There was fresh parmesan and chopped parsley. Jenny brought a jug of iced water. She had cut a chunk of lemon and dropped it in. We had made a salad of lettuce with toasted pine nuts. Everything was just right. Benji held out his plate, then put it back down before I had time to fill it. I stood, spaghetti spoon in hand, and watched his head drop and his body list to one side. Everything goes into slow motion. Benji is listing, like a ship going down. I shake his shoulder but his face is odd, as if he's lost all motor control. Is he breathing? His head is twitching, but he is still breathing normally. Before we can do anything, he begins to slide out of his chair and drop to the floor.

In the time it took for us to work out that Benji was not fooling, Jenny's chair scraped on the floor as she fled the room in fright.

Benji's eyes swivelled. He couldn't speak, or move. A thin line of saliva came from the corner of his mouth. His breathing was laboured. His lungs were being crushed. Suddenly I was trying to remember the first-aid class we did when he was a tiny baby. Which way was the recovery position? How do we move him? Do we call an ambulance? As a nervous new parent, I had taken first-aid courses. But that was long ago, when Benji seemed so frail that I still feared at night that his breath might simply stop. Now he was a muscular six foot, and weighed in at sixteen stone.

We got him into the recovery position, and then we noticed he could blink. Could he communicate with blinking? We crouched to see into his eyes. Are you comfortable? One blink, obviously meaning "No." Is there anything you need? Two blinks: "Yes." Do you want an ambulance? Two blinks.

Benji lay on his stretcher and his powers of movement slowly returned. Any fuss would send him back into the seizure. Was it epilepsy? Early-onset narcolepsy? While we waited for the tests, for the MRI scans and the EEGs and then later the sleep-deprived EEGs, his head and shoulders wired with a dizzying array of coloured wires and nodes, I needed to hear something solid, over the flapping inside my head. Beside the perma-drone of worries, I needed to slow down. We needed to slow down.

On the good days, we tried to carry on as normal. When we went out, I took an emergency foil blanket with me to wrap around Benji just in case. It wasn't epilepsy, they told us, even though that was what it looked like. We stopped the driving lessons in any case because of course they were not safe any more.

We could still go together on foot to look at the owls. Sometimes when there were two we tried to tell them apart. From our bird books we found that females often have darker markings, but that's not always true—these creatures can frequently challenge our wrong-headed assumptions. So often, an assumption becomes an anecdote, and then it becomes fact, which of course it is nothing of the sort. Owl feeding habits had once been the subject of much speculation and debate, especially amongst gamekeepers and landowners with a living to protect. Speculation became knee-jerk reaction, and owls were shot. That was until the evidence, in the form of pellets, was dissected—owl stomachs are less acidic than other birds of prey, so contain more concrete evidence of their "savagery" than other raptors. These were useful birds, it turned out. The pellets were full of rodent bones. They were controlling vermin as effectively as a cohort of cats.

While Benji stayed at home through the winter I conversed with my students on how and how not to become better writers, answered their questions, commented on their essays, but in the background, a small chasm had opened up, and it was deepening. Benji could have various treatments, but he had had to permanently give up his house-building and carpentry plans. Scaffolding was not a safe place to be any more, and using power tools was not recommended. Sometimes what you thought was solid begins to melt away. No more college; Benji was staying at home.

In the months that followed the advent of Benji's unpredictable illness, the family gained a new attentiveness, a kind of listening sensitivity. When I slept, vertiginous moments took hold; I shocked myself awake and lay in a cold film of sweat. For a moment before I opened my eyes, just for a second I had thought that I could control my descent with feather-light wings. Light sleeping, and then full-blown insomnia, crept into my nights: in the twilight hours I was becoming owl-like.

Benji's seizures came every day now. While we fussed about what to do, he wasn't recovering. He fell at the slightest thing. We were living in a strange state of continual alert. For a moment we might not notice anything, then one of us would perceive the quiet from his end of the room, or a thump, and he was gone. We needed to remain calm and focused, to listen to the medics, and to him, but while none of us fully understood what was going on, I was living with a ball of barbed wire in my stomach.

THE BARN OWL'S HEARING is so accurate it should be called "earsight." Deploying what science calls its "enhanced auditory-spatial awareness," some of the areas of the owl's brain that process sound and the parts that process visual information are interconnected. The resolution and topographic precision produced in Barn Owls exceed those of any other species studied. This super-powered owl aids its earsight by bobbing, dipping, and turning its head so that its sound scanner—the facial disc—can capture sound waves and transport the faintest of whispers to the hearing apparatus—the asymmetrical ears. Cute YouTube films of young owls performing this dance are actually demonstrating how owlets learn to use their prodigious hearing. With the head-bobbing an accurate picture of what is around can be created in the owl's brain and the bird can decide what action to take. I knew that owls' auditory accuracy was almost as precise as bats' echolocation, but I still wanted to find out more.

In order to establish the precise powers of the owl's hearing, humans have experimented with measuring exactly how the birds can orientate their sound sense. The stiff feathers of the facial disc can move and be directed towards the site of any sound, and in total darkness, Barn Owls' enhanced senses can amplify and precisely locate their prey. Like humans the owl has a pre-aural flap in its ear, the operculum, but owls can swivel theirs at will, unlike us, directing them towards sound.

Even more impressive, the Barn Owl's outer ear cavity reaches from the top of the cranium all the way down to the lower jaw. Inside the cochlea, the hairs that receive sound are longer than in other birds, and are frequently replaced—unlike in humans, who consequently go gradually deaf with age. Then there is the owls' final secret weapon: the ability to hear the higher-frequency sounds made by the movements of small prey better than the lower-pitched sounds of their voices. One set of experiments revealed that the most high-pitched sounds rodents make apart from squeaking are rustling and chewing—the mouse can be innocently nibbling, not uttering a squeak, and still be caught.

Once a sound is detected, this super-sense achieves such precision due to the asymmetrical placing of the ears behind the facial disc. One of the Barn Owl's ears is larger and orientated downward, and the other smaller and higher on the skull, so sound reaches them at fractionally different moments, enabling the owl to triangulate the sound's exact position. Scientists have tried blocking one ear and found that the owls cannot locate prey in darkness without the use of both ears. It is not surprising that the owl once developed a reputation for possessing a dark side; its skills must have seemed skin-creepingly powerful. But where owls and Satan were once synonymous, we now explore these birds more sympathetically, with a scientific approach, and our ignorance has been replaced by a little more understanding.

WHEN IT TAKES HOLD, my curiosity usually gets the better of me. And so after a long, wet winter, when the days began to brighten and it felt like the edge of spring once more, I hatched the next stage of my plan. In order to get closer to the object of my fascination, and perhaps be allowed to peer into an owl's actual ears to see for myself, I took my research to the next level. I volunteered to work at the Barn Owl Trust.

Luke, the Barn Owl Trust's new survey officer, was far from irritated by my request to hang out asking bothersome questions in order to find out more about Barn Owl conservation. He was delighted. The reason for the delight was that my timing was perfect. This year happened to be the ten-yearly survey of the Barn Owl population in the southwest, and the Trust needed all the help they could get with the huge volume of conservation work that this required. Apart from enthusiasm, reliability, and honesty, you do not need any particular special skills to be a Barn Owl volunteer. So on my very first day, after my briefing, we would (I hoped) get our hands on some real live wild Barn Owlets in order to count and measure them.

The Barn Owl Trust was conceived in the early 1980s when David and Frances Ramsden became concerned that due to changing farming practices there was less food for Barn Owls, and less habitat for wildlife in general. They began by putting up nest boxes and helping farmers to conserve Barn Owl habitat on surrounding land, and by 1988 the Trust was established. Now, the Trust is a fully fledged charity and the main source of Barn Owl information in the UK, all still run by David and Frances Ramsden and their team. The Trust's work has grown and grown; under its slogan, "Conserving the Barn Owl and its Environment," the aim is to restore the land for wildlife and to protect owls. Their beautiful 26-acre nature reserve has blossomed out of a piece of heavily grazed farmland bought with a legacy donated by a lady called Vivian Lennon. It is now established as the location of one of Britain's foremost charities working for Barn Owl conservation.

Counting nesting Barn Owls is a precarious and risky procedure, often up very high ladders, at the tops of creaky old barns and other inaccessible places where the owls choose to nest. Luke needed an equipment holder, a map-reader, and most importantly, I think, a ladder "footer." That was me. Luke and I would travel in the Owl Mobile (one of a small fleet of sturdy vehicles specially embossed with the Barn Owl Trust's logo). Since the nest sites are sensitive to disturbance I signed an agreement to be discreet. I would change the names of the nest sites and not disclose any locations or give away any nesting grid references.

Kitted out in hiking trousers and the Barn Owl Trust's logo shirt and fleece, Luke looked as if he would be as at home abseiling down a cliff to find precariously perched nests as repairing a Barn Owl box high in a roof (his previous profession was in building oak-framed houses). Before we left in the four-by-four we had to kit me out too, and Luke found me a logo shirt so that farmers would feel at ease when they saw me approaching. Then we stacked the boot with survey equipment: a large toolbox for fixing broken owl nest boxes, torches, binoculars, boots, waterproofs, gloves, helmets, ladders, climbing harnesses, and safety equipment; first-aid kit, collapsible poles on which to fix strange cuboid foam plugs (for blocking up nest holes); packed lunches, flasks of tea and large water bottles, pellet collecting bags, and finally the emergency mobile.

Luke showed me how to load and unload the ladders from the roof of the van. I would be lowering them and carrying them about while he spoke to the landowners. A great deal of the Trust's work is about encouraging farmers and landowners to care for their Barn Owls and teaching them how best to protect and conserve the birds' habitat. Some landowners can be very protective, Luke told me; they love their owls and are not always keen to have them bothered by helmeted people wishing to climb up to the peace and privacy of their beams. Only five foot two, I clambered up to the roof of the truck for the first time by putting my foot in the wheel arch on top of the back tyre and hefting myself up so that I could reach to fix the ladders to the roof. If I found that my legs were a little short for the scramble it took some effort to stretch my arms and reach the catches that fixed the ladders on to the roof rack, but Luke's safety check (wobbling the ladders vigorously enough to shift the whole vehicle) left me pleased to see my fixtures did not budge.

At last we climbed into the van and Luke handed me the OS map we were to use for the day, and the clipboard with the list of Barn Owl sites we would be surveying. Excited about actually finding nesting Barn Owls, I forgot for a crucial period of the drive that I was in charge of the map-reading, so for a while, nobody was navigating. My job was to guide us to the hidden sites, whose coordinates I had to precisely locate. Once Luke reminded me which part of the map we were on, and I finally found it on a fold and managed the coordinates the correct way around, and he explained it all again, we were all set. We left the main road and branched off into deepest Devon, June sunshine pouring down on the bushiest and most flower-filled hedgerows and most sinuous network of lanes imaginable.

Just as we turned into the lushest jewel of a valley that I had ever seen and the Owl Mobile was teetering on the steepest edge, I risked taking my eyes from the map for a moment to peer out.

"Is it this turning, do you think, or the next?" Luke said patiently.

"This one, this one," I hazarded, unable to see round or through a towering thicket of cow parsley and meadowsweet that did not match up in any way with anything I had on my map. I had a fifty-fifty chance of being correct.

I don't know how he managed it, but Luke maintained a neutral expression at my slapdash attitude to map-reading. All our time together—and there were many hours and days of it—his professionalism never wavered. We plunged onward into a narrowing drive winding through a forest of ferns, spires of foxgloves, hawthorn, honeysuckle, and hazel. I wound my window down: everywhere in the green light the air was vibrating with birdsong: rooks, swifts, thrushes, finches, robins, wrens, and warblers. Finally the hedges opened out on to a wide, cobbled yard belonging to a thatched sixteenth-century farmhouse. Scents of hay floated on the air and I felt as if we had slipped into another dimension.

We pulled up on the cobbles. "I need some food," Luke said.

I looked at my watch. It was 10:15 AM. He backed the van around and parked up the hill next to a surf of seeding grasses and swifts swooping and skimming down to a reedy valley beyond.

Luke got his binoculars out in an instinctive gesture that over our next outings became a familiar habit.

"Two o'clock. Buzzard."

I got my binoculars out to search where he was pointing.

"No, down there."

We watched birds for a few minutes. Luke had now seen my Leica binoculars, the single most expensive item I have ever bought myself. This one brilliant piece of kit has moved me into the silent conversation that happens between all birders about your position on the spectrum of seriousness. It has smoothed situations that I will not go into now, but let's just say that the binoculars are useful in more ways than I expected when I made the purchase.

Through our lenses we watched a group of four or five swifts dipping and shrieking over the reeds, shooting up into the sky, their flight paths like twizzling streamers.

Luke put his binoculars down and looked at me with a piercing blue gaze. I attempted to return it with a worthy expression.

"Lunchtime," he said, and reached for the packed lunch stowed on the back seat. This, I learned, was almost as serious a part of the day as our research. Luke's packed lunch was more of a luxury hamper organised by Ratty, the famous picnic aficionado in *The Wind in the Willows*. First Luke ate a pear, three or four crackers, then an apple and a banana, followed by a flapjack. This was first lunch, so he left the Mars bar and the baguette bursting with salad, chutney, and cheese for later.

"When I used to build houses," he said, through a second muesli bar and a slug of tea from his jumbo thermos, "we used to eat a lot—you know, you need it, working outside all day, but I still get really hungry and have to eat about every two hours."

I stared at my meagre Marmite sandwich, making a mental note to bring something more substantial tomorrow. We sat and looked some more through our binoculars and the conversation turned to his great interest: raptors. We ranged from goshawks and hobbies to the most important of all, peregrine falcons. In between telling me about his study of coastal peregrines and watching another buzzard, Luke started on an orange and then after some thought finished with the Mars bar.

"Peregrines," he said, stowing peel and wrappers and cores in the lunch bag, "are naturally birds that hunt and nest on the coast and cliffs. This year, out of the eight nesting sites I've been watching, all but one have failed, which is potentially of serious concern." The orange peel had filled the vehicle with its scent. Luke carried on. "While peregrines seem to be thriving in some towns and cities, and have a remarkable ability to adapt to urban cliff-scapes such as church towers and old industrial chimneys, and have a huge following amongst birders, in their natural habitat they are not doing so well. It could be just a bad year, or it could be something more serious, we just don't know. We need more data."

"That sounds like what's happening with urban herring gulls," I suggested, and there followed more discussion about the habitat loss of both species, questions arising from species adapting to live in towns and cities, and finally how people see some of these enterprising gull varieties as pests while not always realising that they are in serious decline. With all the shared concerns and interests I was thrilled at having so much to talk about, but it was time for the job in hand, which was the Barn Owls down in the valley.

The land was already baking in the late morning sun, and the potential owls were no doubt cosily shaded and cool inside the dark recesses of their hidden barn. Having made extra sure that we tidied everything away, we checked the map again, drove back into the yard, and the owners appeared, right on time for our rendezvous. While I eased the ladders down, Luke jumped out to speak to them for a few moments. I found him frowning over the OS map at the route we would have to take through the fields to get to the traditional barn where the pair of Barn Owls was thought to be nesting.

A minute square on a field boundary, the site was hidden away, three or four fields up a hill and down a valley. "That looks like a long way uphill to carry the ladders," Luke muttered. "Let's just take one section. I think we can risk it."

We put on our helmets, and packed torches, gloves, and some tools in case the nest box needed any repairs. We were all set.

"Your helmet is on back to front," Luke told me.

We carried the ladder together, me at the back, sweating but determined to keep up with Luke's stride. The sun was beating down. It took me a significant amount of trotting to keep up with the muscular pace. As we approached a copse, Luke stopped, put the ladder down, and reminded me to be very, very quiet. No chatting from now on.

"The owls will already know we are here," he whispered, "and they may be extra sensitive if they are on eggs. The owners have told us they regularly see the pair of owls and the last thing we want to do is scare them off if they are nesting. Barn Owls have some of the highest levels of domestic protection, and you can be fined for 'recklessly' disturbing them whilst nesting," Luke explained.

I deployed my best stealth walk and tried not to breathe, a challenge after all the exercise and the heat.

We arrived at a jungle of brambles and hawthorn trees. Luke motioned with his hand in a downward movement to be quiet, then made a thumbs-up to signal that we were there. I noticed with admiration that he was not in the least bit sweaty. Beneath the hot helmet my face felt as though it had turned into a tomato.

The owls had made a good choice of dwelling. From under the rim of my visor, I could see it was fortified by a menacing barricade of stinging nettles. Maybe there were walls and a roof in there, but you couldn't be sure.

"It's going to be hard to get in quietly without disturbing them," Luke said.

We put the ladder down and peered into the undergrowth. Every part of me felt as if it had been challenged. This was only our first site visit; ahead was an apparently impenetrable thicket. Were all the sites going to be like this? We still had four more to find after this one.

"I think I can see a way in," Luke suggested. "You're smaller than me—can you get in that way? The door should be on the other side if you can get round."

I flattened the nettles in my path as silently and softly as I could. After a few moments the walls of the old barn came into focus. The whole structure appeared to have grown up out of Devon mud rather than been built. Its camouflage was something to behold. Mud-made, pockmarked walls sat atop layers of hefty local stone and an ancient oak-beamed doorway. Above was a roof that looked decidedly untrustworthy. I ducked beneath twigs, stepped over branches, and unhooked brambles from my legs. Luke followed in my tracks, carrying the ladder easily on his shoulder with his arm threaded nonchalantly between the rungs.

We stood silently inside, our eyes adjusting, scanning the cool dark. I could not have dreamt a more owlish place. I looked up to the beams and wall edges; this is where the owls would be, if there were any. How would they find their way inside here in the first place? I wondered. I added this to my mental list of notes and questions. Later Luke explained that because Barn Owls evolved to nest in cliffs and trees they are programmed to investigate any dark cavity in their search for safe, dry roosts and nesting places.

Inside, muffled darkness breathed a sense of something watching us. In the dark, our other senses become more acute, and I could smell something sickly-sweet, as if a feathered presence was secreting itself into the air. Luke gently lowered the ladder down and leant it against the wall. The old barn was silent as a crypt, straw strewn around, a stillness smelling of old sheep wool, hay, and manure. I could see why an owl might like it: it was airtight and entirely private. Swallows were flitting in and out of the doorway into what appeared to be absolute darkness. As our eyes adjusted, Luke gestured for us to look up into the eaves and scan the high beams. Quietly we shone our torches around. One beam had telltale splatters of what looked like white paint around it. Owl whitewash! A perch? Luke swished the beam of his torch down over the barn floor. Pellets, hundreds of them! Along with the droppings, this was the source of the smell. It was a regular roost.

Then something bright in the darkness caught my eye. Standing tall with its eyes clenched tightly shut, perched in the corner, close to the apex of the roof. Our first Barn Owl. And there beside it was the nest box that the Trust had put up two years before. Luke had still not seen the owl, looking instead straight at the nest box with his carpentry eye, judging what part of it might need repairing.

I moved quietly towards him, touched his shoulder, and pointed. As he turned, something about the bird altered. Was it losing its nerve, getting ready to take flight? We stood immobile and looked up at the shy creature that was now trying to make itself as cryptic and narrow and unobtrusive as it possibly could. All three of us were statues, trying not to draw attention to ourselves, but the elephant in the room was that we, the humans with shiny helmets and torches, were intruding into this shy creature's sanctuary. Our sudden appearance and sweeping light must have felt to the owl like the most abominable threat.

I swear the owl was pretending to be asleep, the way a small child might do, but it was obviously not asleep. Its eyes were not perfectly shut; there was a crack of darkness that discreetly watched out from under the pale lashes. Below the box, Luke gestured with a sweep of his torch, lay another mountainous heap of black pellets. My job was to collect some to take back for research.

As we looked down, suddenly, the Barn Owl took flight. Its silence was absolute. It flew up and down in the still, cool air of the barn, white against black, uncanny as a negative photograph, elegant, yet vulnerable. Too unsure to fly over our heads and out into the sunshine, it fluttered, panicked, this way and that, confused, frightened that it had made itself obvious, still trying to escape. We crouched down so as to be less obtrusive, and straight out it went, gliding on a cushion of warm air over our heads and into the sunlight.

"Damn," Luke said. "That's the last thing we wanted to happen."

I felt mortified.

"OK, it's not too bad," he reassured. "At least it's sunny and dry. It won't be in any danger. It'll find a perch nearby and come back any minute, so we'll have to be quick."

Luke hoisted the ladder up. "If it was raining or windy I'd be more worried. Barn Owls are a bit crap in bad weather but it's fine today."

We listened; if there was a hissing noise we would know they were breeding and that there were young in the nest box, but disappointingly, there was no sound. Barn Owlets constantly call for food by hissing in the manner of rattlesnakes, and I wonder if this is a residual evolutionary tactic. When the Barn Owl inhabited warmer places, dry mountains and deserts and such, where there would have been real rattlesnakes, this call could have served as a threatening mimicry to deter owlet-eating predators.

Luke showed me how to plug the nest box in case there was a female inside. Now I properly understood what the extendable pole and the foam plug were for: if there was a female owl sitting on eggs we would need to stop her fleeing the box and potentially abandoning her eggs, which would defeat the whole point of the exercise. Nervously holding my plug in place I looked on while Luke donned some climbing gear. He fastened on a harness, took a coil of rope, and climbed the ladder. This was so high up that my heart was in my mouth. I was footing the ladder and plugging the hole all at once.

WHAT IF HE FELL? By the time Luke reached the top of the ladder and hooked the rope onto a beam my neck was hurting from looking up at him. He manoeuvred up to the nest box, and with a slight struggle and the use of a screwdriver managed to open it. I watched, holding my breath as he peered in. Would an owl fly out? What was in there?

"One dead owlet," Luke reported. "And an addled egg. Hold your nose!" He cleared the debris, which came raining down around me, fixed the lid back on, and, as he came back down, passed a pile of feather and bone on a ledge. A dead adult owl. He brushed it to the ground and we looked at the corpse, its long wings drooping. The legs were surprisingly long, tipped with grasping toes and their prodigious talons evolved for diving into long grass. Everything about the owl's form was adapted for hunting from the air for small mammals in tall grass. Its rough facial disc was stiffer than I had imagined, as if it had been starched like a choirboy's collar. I parted the feathers to peer in and find the asymmetrically placed ears. I immediately regretted that. The ears were fathomless, with a bristly-pink, fleshy flap of skin, and frankly not very nice. Why or how this owl died, we couldn't know, but it would not have been because it couldn't hear well. "It may have starved," Luke said. He took the owl. "They're pretty wimpy really," he admitted. "Not like peregrines."

I knew that Luke would be leaving the Trust soon, when his survey was done, to go and pursue his peregrine research. He would be going on to study conservation biology at university, and I would be back working full-time. Before I had time to feel too down about this, he gave me the dead owl to borrow for my research. It lay in my hands, head lolling, perfect wings half-folded as if it had just fallen asleep, its eyes not quite closed. Under the lids I could see shadowy slivers of blackness. The feathered ruff of its facial disc frowning into a tight heart shape as if it was wincing, its body so light it might have died of starvation. Gently we placed it on the scales to weigh and yes, 214 grams, that was far below normal: this was starvation weight. A healthy male might weigh around 330 grams, a female slightly more, even up to 360 grams.

"It's probably inexperience," Luke said. "Often, young adults don't know how to feed themselves properly—maybe it couldn't hunt effectively enough. Many newly fledged young die because they are not really skilled yet. Look at its middle talon—that's a clue to the age. If there's no ridge there—" he showed, with his index finger carefully uncurling the front middle toe—"it shows that it was very young, and still in its first year."

Mature adult Barn Owls have a serrated inner edge to their middle talon, probably for grooming, and it was not there in this owl. It could have been from a late brood the previous year, so less than a year old.

I wondered aloud whether it was male or female. The darker plumage, the speckles on the breast, the dark bars on the primaries and tail feathers, and the golden brown feathers around the throat all suggested, Luke said, that it might be a young female, but we couldn't be sure. I wrapped my unhappy gift carefully in a bag to take home.

Back with the family, I showed my find. Jenny spent some time gazing at its face. She held it in both hands and examined the wings closely, opening them by the window so that light shone through them. This way, they looked like angel wings.

We stored the owl in the freezer. Later I found Jenny had sellotaped handwritten labels to the freezer drawers to warn interlopers about the less-than-savoury contents: Food, Food, Food, Dead Owl etc. My specimen collection went unappreciated by Rick, whose stash of curries and other delicacies now had to be eaten up, or stowed elsewhere.

"Can we have this drawer back yet? There isn't enough room," Rick suggested after a period of strained patience.

"Will you have it stuffed?" Jenny asked.

"You could boil it and get the skeleton," Benji said.

I didn't want to do any of this, so there it remained, encased in its cold mausoleum, until one day I couldn't stand it any more and decided to get it out.

I placed the owl on the table to thaw, and when it was ready I began to examine it. When fully flexed, the wingspan measured just over 107 centimetres. There were ten primary flight feathers and on the upper side they were clearly barred with chocolate brown against a buff background; on the leading edge they were golden brown and the soft, tapering trailing edges faded into a creamy-white softness. Underneath, they were paler. This must have been to conceal their silhouette against the sky, so that any prey would be less likely to see them coming. On the first primaries, a stiff comb-like fringe lined the leading edge of each feather. This is what breaks up the air and dissipates the sound of the Barn Owl's flight so effectively. Of all the owls the Barn Owl is the quietest, and looking closely I could see how.

With a hand lens I examined the rest of the primaries and began to see the pattern and order within. All the flight feathers had a subtle velvety fringe on the windward side, the leeward vane trailing into nothing, so soft I couldn't tell by touching where the feather surface ended and the air began. Wind farm manufacturers and aeronautical engineers covet the silence of the owl's flight, attempting to mimic the design and maximise stealth in fighter jet wings and wind turbine blades.

Each feather became more fascinating the closer I looked. The keratin shaft is like a trunk where tines—or to use the correct term, "barbs"—of feather fork away into little branchlets, a forest of barbules, wind silencers meshed together by tiny hooklets of astounding regularity. This complex arrangement is strong but light enough to create an aviation tool that manipulates air currents with absolute perfection. Now the wings became things of wonder in my hands. From this perspective, still attached to the owl's lighter-than-light body, they seemed as wind-honed as larger formations across the Earth. The dunes of Namibia, the blasted rock sculptures of the desert in Arizona; wind-blown curves and feathered crests of snow atop alpine mountain ranges.

I took a sharpened pencil and selected a sheet of thick paper of the sort that seemed worthy. The graphite was just right for the ashen cobweb of silver that shawled the wheat colour of the owl's back and head. On its breast, a few irregular graphite flecks suggested again that it might be a female, as males often (but not always) have a pure white front. The legs were startlingly long and lanky, designed for making a strike for prey in tall grass. The talons had a mean, tapering sharpness that suggested serious business. This may be a light bird but its violence and power are hefty. As I drew, the owl began to fasten itself in my mind. Why is it that humans are constantly trying to create representations of things beyond our own experience? We try to possess them in some way. But these creatures can never be truly possessed by anything other than the wind and the grass.

Again, the graphite made for a good talon-grey, even though I am not very skilled at drawing. The dark rotation of the pencil, in the simple act of contact with paper, with a fleck of white for a curve of light, did a fair job. There is a kind of intention in drawing, and I was seeing things that I would never have noticed or understood without this close looking, without this lens that focused my attention. The white petals of the eyelids, with their slivers of black pressed just beneath; the pale skin of the cere—the skin around the top of the beak— fading into the nostrils; and a hooked bill that was both raptorish and human-like. The soft golden bib cupped the face, the wings slipped open and closed like the bloom of a windflower.

SINCE THE SECOND World War much of British farmland has changed, in some places almost beyond recognition. It is thought that the loss of old pastures and rough grasslands due to more intensive agriculture might have caused a decline of 70 per cent in the Barn Owl population. With the proliferation of dual carriageways the low-flying Barn Owls have been victims again; they do not have the resources to avoid fast cars. Finally, the increased use of rodenticide may be the final straw for some owls. Eating poisoned rodents can build up toxins in a bird's system, weakening and possibly killing it eventually. We cannot know how it feels to regularly ingest such poisons, or what the effects are, but nausea, weakness, lack of appetite, coordination problems, and decreased resistance to disease may result. Nearly 90 per cent of Barn Owls found dead and subsequently tested have very high levels of rat poison in them. Is it the poison that kills them? We don't know for sure, but its build-up in their frail bodies is likely to weaken them.

The good news is that many farmers are delighted still to have Barn Owls on their land. Old superstitions in rural areas have long been replaced by increased sympathy, and now the Trust's special nest boxes are often lovingly watched over by the landowners. If owls come to nest, it can be like a badge of honour.

After Luke had gone to deepen his specialisms by studying conservation biology at university, I stayed on as a helper. My next Barn Owl man, Tim, was the Barn Owl Trust's permanent conservation officer. Like Luke, Tim appeared to be tremendously happy for the company, and he was equally tolerant about my map-reading. When we arrived at our first site of the day the farmer stopped work as soon as he spotted the Owl Mobile, and quickly came to chat to us. When he saw that we would be ringing the birds, he called his son on his mobile, and soon the whole family arrived on an assortment of quad bikes and on foot, all in their welly boots. They had put up a nest cam and so already knew there were four owlets in this box, and this was their opportunity to see them up close.

We assembled to watch Tim ascend the ladder, and waited to see the owlets as he lifted them one by one from the nest and gently posted each into a small white cotton pouch to be lowered down to my waiting hands. Each warm, wriggling packet would be examined, then weighed by being inserted upside down in a most undignified way into an owlet-safe transparent plastic tube. Under the watchful eye of the farmer and his family, each would be quickly measured and ringed so that we could record as much data as possible. The rings mean that we can track the owls, keeping a record of how far they disperse, and where and when they perish—if they are found and handed in, that is.

After ringing around twenty owlets from four different sites in this way, I began to tire of them. Just as I felt I could not go on, Tim suggested stopping for lunch. We found a shady verge, pulled up, opened our packed lunches, and got out to listen to the birds. Straight away, Tim identified the various songs:

"Listen to that: a sedge warbler! That's a whitethroat!"

Then I noticed something magical. Tim was standing with his head tipped to one side.

"Can you hear that?"

"Which bit?" I asked, still in awe that he could separate the different voices and identify them.

"It's a redstart. Look, on that branch there. No—up—top left!"

We watched the redstart bobbing nervously on its twig, its tail flicking while it called. Tim closed his eyes to listen more intently. "That note! When it gets to that note—it rips your heart."

That moment I realised with a lump in my throat the great secret of volunteering: it is the giver who gains, and it is a gain through the soul, not the pocket. And with each newly learned birdsong, each gently weighed owlet, the heart grows a little more.

When we arrived at the final site and I looked wearily at the map, I noticed the name. We were at a spot marked Dead Man's Bottomcoombe.

I turned to look at Tim, who was twinkling. He'd saved this one deliberately, barely suppressing a giggle.

"*Dead Man's Bottomcoombe?*"

Ahead was a dell of ferns, ash fronds, and hazel trees, and hidden amongst columns of cow parsley and hemlock, the barn was so organic and so pockmarked with insect burrows, birds' nests, and bee holes, it could have sprouted from the underworld. Or an old Devon man's bottomcoombe.

The walls appeared to be entirely made out of red Devon mud, and the roof was grown over with ivy. The entrance gaped onto a blackness only an owl could be attracted to. I stood back as Tim entered, and after a moment an adult Barn Owl flew so silently over his head that he was totally unaware of it. I stood watching as it swooped around, looking for a perch. When the owl settled in a nearby tree I followed Tim inside, and another flew over our heads, trying to flee our intrusion. Tim set up the ladder and ascended as the adult owl darted out to join its partner. Immediately we could hear the familiar rattlesnake hissing. Again we had to quickly weigh and ring each owlet. Astounded by Tim's continued stamina at this point in the day, I steadied myself and got ready to take each owlet in my hands as it came down. One by one he inserted each into a soft cloth bag and ever-so-gently lowered them down to me. Four this time, and as I stood and waited, a pair of owlet papooses dangling from each hand, staring up at Tim at the top of the ladder, he exclaimed: "Aha! I didn't see you in that corner!"

He gently lifted out a last reluctant owlet, crooning: "Look at you! Look at that tummy! You'll be too fat to fly." Owlet number five was the tubbiest owlet you had ever seen, and weighed in at nearly 400 grams with Tim admonishing it: "You'll have to go on a diet or you'll never get going!"

Tim noted all the details of the final brood along with the little fatty, which I agreed must have consumed an extraordinarily large vole at its last feed. Wing length, body weight, tummy size, and ring details all went into the meticulously kept notebook. All of this information was important, all of it needed so we can continue to monitor how the owls are doing. If this work was not carried out, we might miss something, and the owls could falter without our realising.

My period volunteering with the Barn Owl Trust was nearly over. It was a kind of time out of time, when you get your heart swelled again and again, as you engage in your favourite pastime with some of the most devoted, knowledgeable, generous, and good-humoured people ever. If I could distil the joy of learning it would be that moment, counting owlets and being taken by surprise, again and again, by how inspiring, satisfying, and real this work could be. And I learned that we have come a long way: from its earliest inkling as an overgrown hobby in the 1980s, to its fledging in 1988 as a charity, to the present day as the twenty-first-century Barn Owl Trust. Today it not only gathers and collates national data on Barn Owl populations, but also educates and inspires children in schools and trains international groups of experts, consultants, and conservationists from all over the world.

It strikes me that despite the ups and downs of our shared history, in this particular instance humans might be making some progress. When we get it right, and work with nature rather than against it, we can achieve the most extraordinary things.

Strix aluco

TAWNY OWL

"Who'll dig his grave?"
"I," said the owl, "with my pick and shovel,
I'll dig his grave."

—ANON., "Who Killed Cock Robin?"

AT MY DESK, A MESSAGE POPS INTO MY INBOX: "BENJI collapsed on the bus on the way to college."

Imagine you're on a bus to work: it's early, and as the bus jiggles along the road you notice a young man—his head is lolling, and he appears to be falling out of his seat. His eyes are closing. You think: he could be drunk, or worse. What do you do? Then the young man begins twitching and slowly collapses off his chair. Each time the bus goes over a bump or rounds a corner, he slips a little further. His legs fold under him, the seat scrapes his back. Most step around him when it's time to get off at their stop.

One final passenger is left with Benji on the bus as it reaches the depot. Pushing her buggy and toddler past, she pauses, nervously: "Are you OK?" But he can't reply. She sees the line of drool, the glazed eyes; confused, she informs the driver, and flees.

Back from the hospital, Benji is recovered, and remarkably positive.

"The bus driver found me," he explains, "when we got to the depot. He picked me up and put me back in the seat."

"That's amazing—he must be strong!"

"Yes, he was! He had masses of tattoos, said he'd been in the . . . what was it . . . SA . . . ?"

"The SAS."

"Then, when I couldn't speak, he called the ambulance."

"Didn't anybody else help you before that?"

"One woman asked if I was OK."

Benji usually remains conscious during his seizures, so he was aware of everything, but could not speak or control his movements.

We decide that we should find out who that driver was, and write and thank him. In that moment our gratitude was beyond measure. Angels look like ordinary people, but just sometimes they appear and catch us when we fall. Perhaps many of us have it in us, that capacity as humans to be at our very best. Empathy becomes compassion becomes kindness. I have seen it again since, a hand held, an arm round a shoulder, something beyond words.

Benji was tested for epilepsy and also for narcolepsy, and still no cause could be found. In the meantime he couldn't be prescribed any medication in case it was the wrong one, and we had to wait. But we contacted the bus company online to thank them, and I returned to my owl studies.

The Tawny Owl is one of the most nocturnal of all owls. With its cryptic brown patterning and silent flight it is rarely seen, and its unsettling cry in the dark must have seemed to our forebears to be the voice of night itself. It still awakens deep-seated ancestral memories. The disembodied shriek, the black eyes that seem to stare into your soul, and the ghoulish swoop can combine to bring the darkest regions of our imaginative superstition and folklore to life. For a thousand years and more the Tawny's wavering hoots were portents of death; in Chaucer's long poem *The Parliament of Fowls* we are told that amongst all the birds the owl is the one laden with doom: "The owle eek, that of deth the bode bringeth." The most common and widespread woodland owl in England, the Tawny must be the one Chaucer was thinking of, but to find the roots of these beliefs we can look beyond literature into the earlier evolution of human culture. In the traditional nursery rhyme

"Who Killed Cock Robin?" many birds lament the murder of the robin and plan the funeral ceremony together. Each of the birds is positioned with an anthropomorphic role according to its physical or perceived attributes. It is the owl who has the most lugubrious of jobs:

> "Who'll dig his grave?"
> "I," said the owl, "with my pick and shovel,
> I'll dig his grave."

Human thinking appears to be predisposed, by history, education, and culture, to associate this animal with death. But there is also some relish in the shadowy aspects of the twilit owl, and we come back to it time and again, as if there is something about it that is wired into stories that we do not want to forget. Peel back the linguistic layers of the Cock Robin nursery rhyme-cum-murder story, and beyond its medieval resonances of Christian burial ritual it might be riddled with far more ancient beliefs than we might at first notice.

Among the different theories about the origins of the Cock Robin story is one that stems from the old hero Robin Hood, who stole from the rich and gave to the poor. This one suggests that it is a political tale about all of nature turning to stand in support of Robin Hood (represented by Cock Robin).

But the poem has older resonances even than this, in which the birds of the rhyme have become vessels, metaphors compressing and carrying myth onward, used to tell a story that was convenient to current thought. It has been suggested that embedded in Cock Robin is a story of ancient seasonal rites that celebrate the moment in the Celtic calendar when summer is conquered and replaced by winter. Cock Robin may in fact represent the Celtic sun god Lugh. In the ancient tale of the battles between the seasons, Lugh is seen wielding his lightning spear, fighting for the love of a goddess representing Nature, and is murderously slain by a spear thrown by his shadowy counterpart, the persona of winter. Some mythographers believe that Lugh was commonly known as Coch Rhi Ben and that he would have been involved in rites each year as midsummer came and went, as harvest took place and winter came. Might this name have been anglicised to Cock Robin from its Celtic origin? Other suggested sources are from Nordic culture, whereby Cock Robin is based on the figure of Baldr, again an ancient personification of day or spring, once more brutally murdered. The more we dig, the more it seems as if the same story about a ritual sacrifice or killing of a king figure could have interwoven different tales through time.

But where does the owl stand amongst all of this? In Cock Robin the owl is the holder of the darkness associated with death and burial. To this day, these repeating associations and stories remain a current that flows through our language. Etymologists suggest that the pronunciation needed in order to rhyme "owl" with "shovel" does point to a very ancient origin, possibly in Middle English. So if the old sonority of the words brings messages from the dim and distant past, today the sound of the Tawny's hooting call is still used to chill us. In cinema it indicates that evil is afoot. The cliché scare-factor has dwindled perhaps, but some age-old suspicion remains. That eerie sound, coupled with the *Exorcist*-like head-twist of the real owl, does appear unnatural and can still evoke a certain primeval response. The poor owl suffers from a concoction of all this mythologising, but on some level, humans are longing not only for the spooky mystery of enchantment, but also the reminder of our own mortality.

Considered to be more "musical" than other owl calls, the male Tawny Owls' wisp-like, fluting voices are the ones we hear most often. There is a small peak in their calling from

August to October when the youngsters disperse from their parents' territory, and then they become more audible again at the end of the winter, when breeding begins—this is the most night-bound owl, echoing through our dreams and night-time experiences. In the past was this sound perceived to be the voice of the triumphing darkness of winter?

After the young owls have been driven out by their parents and are forced to assert their own territories in December and between Christmas and New Year, when the weather is still and windless, I often rise before dawn to listen to them. I sit in an armchair by the balcony and watch the gradual rise of the winter light through the glass. If it is not windy or wet (Taw-nies seem not to bother to hunt in bad conditions as the sound of rain disguises the pattering feet of their prey), I usually hear one. Tawny Owls are territorial and appear to get into breeding mode around January and, if they do not have one already, they will attract mates by calling regularly through the night. In February they are usually all set up with a partner and settling on a nesting spot, normally a sheltered nook high in a mature tree. Sometimes they will take over an old nest; other times they will start to excavate their own nests in a hollow tree.

In winter, every time a hoot wavers through the mist I stand outside and listen to the strange hoarse note some of them have. Every time, I hope to spot one perched close by on a leafless tree at dawn—when the weak sun comes up you can sometimes see them, feathers ruffled and relaxed, warming themselves beside the trunk or on a south-facing branch. They sit quite still, confident that their mottled camouflage will act as concealment. Usually I only hear them, and rarely do they appear. But one crisp morning, I got very lucky.

One minute I was sipping my tea by the window. There was nothing but the palest edge of grey light and a wisp of steam from my cup—and then a shadow swooped out of the air. With the lightest of scratches, as if the dawn light was solidifying into life, there it was, perched like an exclamation mark on the balcony: a Tawny Owl, come to my home.

Its softly feathered feet and black talons were curled on the balustrade as if I had called it in, as if what I had been thinking had just made itself manifest. But there it was, right in front of me, and it turned its head and stared in at me as I stared out at it. It fixed its two dark eyes on mine. Its brown camouflage was exposed against the mist: the rust-tinged facial disc, the tree-bark beige and cream flourishes, the ambrosia-pale, flecked breast, the streaked back and the short, stubby tail. I was transfixed. The symmetry of its face seemed to reclaim all its unnerving, eerie mystery as it rotated and returned repeatedly to pierce me through with those huge eyes.

A little more steam rose from my morning mug of tea. My mind tumbled down the generations, struck by magical thinking. Thousand-year-old ancestors would have made this moment an omen. But this owl was just an owl, not a sign, and I was just lucky. But still . . .

The owl tipped its face downward to eye the twenty-first-century mealworms scattered for the starlings. It looked at me, gazed over the lawn, viewed the unruly hedge. It seemed in no hurry to leave. As it paused a while longer I stood up, moved toward it, touched the glass. Could it really see me or was I just another meaningless form? The movement triggered the owl's reaction. In one fluid movement it opened its wings and tipped off the balcony, drifting away as silent as the wash behind a wave.

Regaining my composure I ran outside to interrogate the chill air. Where had it come from? Where did it go? Tawnies, I knew, have small territories, but to find out how small, to investigate how close to my house this creature could be living, I first headed for my shelf of books. The Tawny Owl,

Wood Owl, or Brown Owl as it used to be known, is Britain's commonest owl and it is the only one that has efficiently adapted to survive in urban areas. With the park nearby, as well as a children's play area and the closely mown football pitch, the town had a range of habitats interlinked together. The closest was a patchwork of woodland with scrubby areas, many trees, some huge mature oaks—I guessed that's where it was roosting. There were un-mown grassy banks for voles and mice, bramble patches and hazel trees; a stream and damp, reedy areas, so plenty of hidden, overgrown wild places.

In the absence of extensive woodland, many places in our towns must in fact be great for Tawnies. If it has been raining, and they have been unable to catch mice, they can wait for earthworms in our lawns, and hunt for frogs and other amphibians around our ponds. And when my friend's goldfishes kept repeatedly disappearing, and she put up a camera trap, she caught the culprit; no more fish left, but an opportunistic Tawny, cloaked by the night, paddling about, brazenly bathing on camera. Perhaps it wouldn't have been so exuberant if it had known its evening bath was going to be put up on YouTube. Tawnies need to bathe, and are frequently behind whodunnit mysteries in people's gardens such as opportunistically disappearing pet fish, for which cats normally get the blame. People do not expect owls to come to their gardens, but it's commoner than you might think. In May 2017, Michael Hilton of Harpur Hill near Buxton reported his most senior goldfish missing. Aptly named Fish, the victim became famous on Michael's blog "Buxton Weather"—and two thousand readers were mystified. There had been no storm surge; what had happened to Fish? Could it have been a heron? A fox? An otter, or even a cat?

"Fish was a seven-year-old goldfish—originally when bought, gold—but had turned pure albino white over the years and grown to around 180 millimetres," Michael told me sadly. "He was our favourite." The CCTV had only been recently installed but it was a good investment. Using the footage Michael was able to identify the perpetrator. At precisely six minutes past midnight the cameras showed a very large bird drop down from its rooftop perch to seize poor Fish who must have been highly visible due to his albinism. In the film, with Fish barely able to struggle in the tight grasp of its razor talons, the Tawny exits the water and pauses on the side of the pool. Evidently the owl was not in the least bit fooled by the life-size plastic decoy badger sitting next to the pond. After a minute to allow its feathers to drip dry and to look around and check the pond for any relatives of Fish, the owl flies off nest-wards with its prize—since it was May, and breeding season, presumably to feed the waiting wife and owlets.

Where mature trees and hedges are threaded between the houses and roads of our suburban places, conditions are per-fect for Tawnies. They can perch and wait for small mammals to rustle past. This is a perch-and-drop hunter, and unlike the buoyant searching glide of the Barn Owl it often sits on a branch and waits for its prey to pass. It drops down, loops low, and catches its prey by both sight and sound. At the very last moment, feet extended to strike, it closes its eyes—partly because it is long-sighted and can only see a blur at very close range, but also for protection—it knows exactly where the prey is, and with its excellent hearing and eyesight it has already pinpointed its strike with perfection.

I said to Michael that he might want to think of protecting his pond from now on as Tawnies have small territories, per-haps only a square mile, depending on prey availability. They operate by perfectly memorising their patch, right down to the positioning of individual trees, so that they are less likely to collide with unexpected obstacles in the woods at night. In this way Tawnies can act swiftly and economically and never need to leave their home patch over the course of their entire life. The opportunistic Fish-stealer would probably shortly be back to snatch more juicy fare.

People used to assume that the huge, deep black eyes of the Tawny Owl could somehow magically see into the dark of night, and consequently pierce into the soul, but of course this is not the case. The owl has special adaptations for its powerful vision—we all know that owls have super-large eyes. To carry their extra weight they have become tubular and fixed, unlike ours which can move around in their sockets. Owls cannot swivel their eyes and so are restricted in their field of vision. This is why the owl needs to be able to rotate its head—so unnervingly flexibly—around 270 degrees. Extra vertebrae and blood vessels enable it to do this without cutting off the blood circulation to its head.

As the owl's retina needs some light to be able to transmit information to the optic nerve, so a greatly enlarged cornea and lens allow the maximum amount of light to fall on it. A very high density of rods in the retina makes its eyesight extra sensitive, around three to four times more powerful than a human's in low light, and well adapted to hunt at dusk and in the broken darkness of a forest. An added adaptation of the eye is that the retina and lens have been brought closer together as the eye evolved, making what the owl sees sharper and brighter in poor illumination. Experiments that were conducted to find how much light owls need to find their prey in dark woodland have shown that the most nocturnal European owls—the Tawny, Ural, and Long-eared Owls—can see their prey and approach it directly from 2 metres away in very low light. Other species such as *Homo sapiens*, and more crepuscular and daylight hunting owls, see nothing in the same level of light. But even the Tawny Owl cannot see in the complete dark, and in order to thrive it also needs to rely on its range of other skills, such as its hearing and its spatial memory of the particular shape and geography of its patch.

In towns, where there is usually copious artificial light to help it out, the Tawny can feed on anything small that moves, even the rats, earthworms, lizards, and beetles that are attracted to our gardens. In spring, it might take a few small nestling birds or weaker adult passerines as they roost. But despite the close proximity of these owls in our urban areas, like most people I had never seen one in my garden.

Strix aluco. She had been there, calmly staring at me, right through the glass, right in the eye. At the time I thought: this owl has been here before, many times, and she's seen into the lit room, and it's just that *I* haven't seen *her*. And I know it is a she, because in the night she'd intermittently broken our sleep with her screeched *kee-wick*s. We often hear the proverbial *too-wit too-woo* around town at night, but this human expression belies a misconception: it is an amalgam of both the female and the male owl's call. It is their conversation. The female's *kee-wick* is piercing but often less robust, less tuneful than the male's hoot, my book tells me. The male can *kee-wick* too, as an occasional aggressive response to intruders, and confusingly the female can sometimes hoot. This female owl had been calling close to the house, and all the while the soft male hoot could be heard, further away.

It strikes me that each time one of these rare visitations happens it opens the conversation a little more, embedding these creatures into our consciousness by dispelling myth and enfolding them into familiarity. So when we come across them again we remember they are not just an alien, disembodied voice. Paying attention to them like this might avoid the blandification that happens to so many "cute"-faced animals. As we cutify and commodify the natural world they risk becoming ornaments: a static picture on a screen, a shiny cup, egg cosy, or tote bag. Once we have encountered one, on the other hand, had contact, been brushed by the downdraught of its swoop or been awoken by that spine-shivering cry, or even attempted to feed or attract one, it becomes more solid, and a subtle but vital part of our being.

)

AT A FARM SHOP recently I noticed shoppers busily stacking their car boots with 10-kilo tubs of rodenticide. We love to have a cup of tea from those owl mugs you can buy, but at the same time some of us may be unwittingly, unconsciously causing real owls harm. Barn Owls probably suffer the most from ingesting rodenticide poisons because they live so closely beside us and particularly in agricultural areas, but what of the Tawny?

I contacted the Predatory Bird Monitoring Scheme (PBMS), an umbrella project that encompasses the Centre for Ecology and Hydrology's contaminant monitoring. It investigates just these sorts of questions and carries out long-term UK-wide testing to determine the current and emerging chemical threats to birds of prey. The PBMS have found that when poison is put out for rodents, it usually takes several days for the toxins to kill them, leaving them vulnerable to being predated while the poison is still active in their bodies. During this period, while the poisons remain concentrated in their livers, the predators that feed upon them are particularly likely to be exposed to toxic effects. The contaminants that pass up the food chain can often be measured in the dead birds that are subsequently found. The PBMS can determine how, and if, the birds have been affected by ingesting the toxins, and the monitoring they undertake can then be used to address conservation issues.

"Predators that feed upon rodents are particularly likely to be exposed to these compounds," the PBMS told me, and together with other studies, they have shown that there is widespread exposure, often as an accidental by-product of pest control, and that mortalities can and do occur as a result. The PBMS have monitored anticoagulant rodenticides in raptors such as Barn Owls, kestrels, and red kites, as well as Tawny Owls, and have presented long-term trend analysis for Barn Owls and kestrels. As an indicator or "sentinel" species, Barn Owls are still monitored each year.

Since 2006 more sensitive investigations—using "Liquid Chromatography–Mass Spectrometry"—have resulted in lower concentrations of these compounds being detected than was previously possible. So from 2006, the proportion of birds in which anticoagulant rodenticides have been detected has increased compared to previous years. In 2015 they were detected in 80–90 per cent of Barn Owls and around 68 per cent of kestrels; most of the red kites examined (91 per cent) had detectable liver concentrations. A quarter of the red kites analysed showed signs of haemorrhaging thought possibly to be associated with rodenticide poisoning.

The poisoning can even persist through the generations. The proportion of owls with detectable second-generation anticoagulant rodenticide residues—SGARs—was found to be two-fold higher in England than in either Scotland or Wales. SGARs have been increasingly used since the 1970s, as rodents began to develop resistance to products like warfarin. Tawnies are known to have declined in Britain since the 1970s, but whether that is directly due to rodenticide is considered less likely than with other raptors. Tawnies' health would likely be as affected by anticoagulant rodenticides and other poisons put out by humans, but their habitat and foraging are different from Barn Owls' and they may escape the worst concentrations of poisons. However, one concern is that, because this owl is more common and less cherished than the Barn Owl, less interest may be generated about how the Tawny tribe might be affected.

It would be a serious mistake to let our guard down—doing this got us into trouble before when the widespread poisoning of top predators like otters and peregrine falcons went unnoticed until it was almost too late. So the PBMS have carried out a quiet but authoritative study into SGARs in Tawnies. Their work is not always widely known about, but depends on members of the general public donating found carcasses. These projects are vital in monitoring the responsible use of toxins and their presence in the environment, and they depend on this citizen science; many people may not think to donate a dead bird, and might merely look at it and walk on. So if you find one, make a note where you found it (it might be useless to science without this information), pick it up, and send it to the Department for Environment, Food & Rural Affairs (DEFRA), who maintain a wildlife incident monitoring scheme, or the PBMS so they can add it to their collection of data.

STRIX ALUCO. I SAY it out loud, listening to the sonority of the Latin taxonomic name of this bird. *Strix. Aluco.* It sounds like the duet of calls that the owls make.

Over two hundred years ago Carl von Linné, or Linnaeus as he is known in his Latinised form, the Swedish naturalist, set about clarifying the categorisation and nomenclature of wildlife by classifying all living things with a system of names. Birds were given names consisting of two Latin words: a noun to classify the genus, or family; and an adjective to describe the species that was often drawn from the appearance, call, or nature of the bird itself. Linnaeus was drawing upon a long history of the coining of phrases and many thousands of years of naming. *Strix* might originate from Aristotle's ancient description in his pioneering natural history text, the *History of Animals*, from the fourth century BC. His Greek *strizo* means "to screech," and was later Latinised as *Strix* by Linnaeus to classify the group of owls that were thought to be a related branch on the evolutionary tree, so the name must originate from the screech sound made by the owls.

The name "screech owl" should be clarified at this point. Certain owls have always screeched, but neither Tawnies nor any of our European owls are related to the true Screech Owls. The Screech Owls are a different family, of the genus *Megascops*, native to the Americas, and there are twenty-eight species of them. They are all pictured in Heimo Mikkola's fascinating photographic guide, *Owls of the World*. The Western screech owl, for example, *Megascops kennicottii*, lives solely in the Western United States and is found as far north as southern Alaska, as far east as Texas, and as far south as Mexico. There are no true Screech Owls in Europe. This family of small owls with ear tufts often have light-coloured eyes, ranging from pale yellow to amber, although some, such as the Cinnamon Screech Owl, *Megascops petersoni*, that lives in Peru, has deep-brown eyes. Confusingly, many of the Screech Owls do not actually screech but utter staccato notes like *bookbookbook* or *bububububub* sounds; some even emit a high trill or make a sound like a cricket. Confusion has arisen over the name "screech owl" because both the Barn and Tawny do appear to screech, and are sometimes commonly misnamed or locally known as such, but they are not true Screech Owls and are taxonomically a different species altogether.

So perhaps *Strix* came from "screech," but there is more to the name than this. Embedded in it is an undercurrent of clues about how our ancestors may have perceived the owl as witch-like. *Strix* has a resonance that my books do not seem to connect: in Latin *striga* means "witch," in modern Italian *una strega*. In many cultures the Tawny is named after the eerie sounds of its call at night and these seem in some cases to be distinctly feminine: in Gaelic it is known as *cailleach-oidhche*, "the old woman of the night"; in France as *le chat huant*, "the hooting cat," as if shape-shifting was one of its abilities. It seems the name for the sound of the screech, its association with old women, and the fearful superstition that owls bring messages of doom are braided and inseparable: the demonised night-woman or the creature who might know more than we, and the frightening bird that inhabits the dark, all of whose presences are as disturbing and unsettling as magic. In ancient Greek mythology the god of the underworld, Hades himself, was represented by an owl familiar. In yet another battle between the seasons, Hades captured the daughter of Nature, plunging the world into winter as Nature mourned her missing child. The captive daughter Persephone knows that if she tastes any food she will be condemned to a life in the underworld. According to Roman poet Ovid, when Persephone was observed breaking the rules and eating a pomegranate seed, she turned the tale-teller, the orchard keeper, into an owl as punishment: "She threw into his face water from Phlegethon, and lo! a beak and feathers and enormous eyes! Reshaped, he wears great tawny wings, his head swells huge . . . a loathsome bird, ill omen for mankind, a skulking screech-owl, sorrow's harbinger. That telltale tongue of his no doubt deserved the punishment."

This antique tale is not the only example of shaming a person for transgression by turning them into an owl. In the *Mabinogion*, an ancient book of tales originating in pre-existing oral storytelling and Welsh mythology, and composed in the Middle Ages, it happens to a famously unfaithful wife. In the fourth branch of the *Mabinogi* stories the young man Lleu (the Welsh version of Lugh, the Celtic god of summer we met earlier) has been forbidden from ever having a human wife and so one is magically created for him out of the flowers of oak, broom, and meadowsweet. Named Blodeuwedd (pronounced "Blood-ay-weth"), or "flower-face," she is associated with spring. In some versions of the story, wherever she goes a trail of white flowers springs forth. But Blodeuwedd has a mind and life of her own, and she has a love affair with Lleu's rival Gronw. Together they plot to murder Lleu.

To compress this magical and complex story, in brief, the two lovers are thwarted when Lleu, having been run through with a spear, comes back to life later as an eagle, and as a punishment Blodeuwedd is transformed into an owl. She is told: "You will not dare to show your face ever again in the light of day, and that will be because of enmity between you and all other birds. It will be in their nature to harass you and despise you wherever they find you. And you will not lose your name—that will always be 'Blodeuwedd (Flowerface).'" The story additionally tells us that 'Blodeuwedd' means 'owl' in the language of today. And it is because of that there is hostility between birds and owls, and the owl is still known as Blodeuwedd."

It seems that the medieval Welsh stories met and twined with the Greek and Roman ones. One thing is for sure: the owl's unsettling appearance and nocturnal aspects passed into myth and our storytelling minds daubed this creature with mistrust, darkness, and shame.

Strix aluco. And what of *aluco?* The word sounds like a melancholy greeting, a yodel without hope of a reply, like the same hooting calls that I had heard. I search for the etymology, and the books reply that Theodorus Gaza, a Greek who in the Middle Ages translated Aristotle's work on natural history into Latin, translated Aristotle's Greek word for the owl, *eleos*, into Latin as *aluco*, from the old Italian word for Tawny Owl, *allocco*. Aristotle had chosen sensitively: Eleos was not a goddess, or even a minor deity, but something much more insubstantial. She was seen as an entity rather than a person, and she was shy and vulnerable, and chosen as an embodiment of pity, compassion, and mercy. People didn't like to spend time around Eleos, for fear of being infected with misery and sorrows. This sounds about right. At the altar of Eleos, supplicants would honour her by ritual undressing and the cutting of hair. Anyone wishing to be the ally of Athens should make libations to Eleos in this way. Aristotle must have settled upon the name after hearing that supplicating cry clawing its way out of the dark.

BENJI, NEWLY MOVED into his cabin at the bottom of the garden—to allow him more space and independence—had been party to a whole nightful of owl conversation. Thrilled, he burst in through the front door. "Mum! Which owl goes: *Ee-eeeikk! Eee-eeeikk!*? Did you hear it? *Eeeee-iiikkk! Eeeeeeee-ikkk!* All night!" His face was alive with delight, enthralled at the disturbance caused by the owls.

"I know! It was a Tawny. I just saw it on the balcony!"

"Wow."

We moved about the house infected with owlishness. When I sat down to read a little more Benji put his head around the door: "Eee-ikk! Eeee-iikkk!"and I hooted back: "Hu-hooooo!"

Benji's condition had stabilised a little, but for the family our veneer of confidence had been worn thin. When he was aged nine, we realised we'd been noticing years of bizarre and puzzling responses that suggested he might be wired differently from other people. We became suspicious that he might have Asperger syndrome. Fears and phobias, anxiety about family gatherings, meltdowns at parties and other noisy social situations had long made us think that Benji was autistic. The very worst had been a memorably unpleasant school disco where after some searching he was discovered curled foetal under a table. Being very literal, and often having countless other misunderstandings at school, he had eventually been diagnosed, and we finally knew for certain that our highly sensitive, intelligent boy had high-functioning ASD, or autistic spectrum disorder. Once, we took him to the optometrist, thinking his trouble with writing might be eyesight-related. His eyesight was fine, but the optometrist contacted me by phone later. He had something on his mind. "Have you thought that your son might have Asperger syndrome?" he helpfully asked. We had considered it, but Benji's condition was complex and presented him with many challenges. Highly sensitive and meticulous, on the outside he appeared entirely normal, and highly articulate, but this masked the fact that on the inside he lived in a world that was often baffling and overwhelming to him. This new response, this entire body shut-down, was the most puzzling of all. We had steered as stable and gentle a course through the years as we could, taking him out of mainstream education and sending him to a small, sympathetic school. But now I wondered whether nevertheless the strain of his education and many years of disorientating social interaction in a confusing, frightening world might be some of the factors affecting his seizure condition.

When one of our loved ones is threatened, many of us search for help and guidance. Beyond the experts, who admitted that much of the human brain remains mysterious, and who did not appear to be able to provide many answers, perhaps encountering the owl could not have been more propitious. Benji was thrilled with it. It brought him alive. Any sign like this would be gratefully received, even if it came in the form of an owl. Especially (since that was the subject of my research) if it came in the form of an owl. We wondered how we could tempt the owl back to our garden.

Then I remembered my friend Stephen.

"You'd be welcome to come and spend the evening looking at the wild Tawny Owl I've been training," he had warmly said once, a year or so before. "It's a male that is habituated to me. He comes to my bird table—I've trained him so that he flies in when I whistle. I feed him. I'll send you some pictures."

The images had swooped into my inbox the next day: tantalising shots of a handsome, obsidian-eyed, amber-and-rust-coloured raptor with flecked cream-and-chocolate plumage and hefty talons. He was perched on a bird table close beside Stephen's converted barn, his black-pebble eyes staring directly into the camera lens in the unsettling way that only an owl can. I had some burning questions. Could we try to feed our owl, to attract it back to the balcony? On the phone, Stephen suggested chopping up some day-old chicks bought from a pet centre, so I nipped out to get some. The young assistant showed me to the freezer where the unsavoury items were kept.

"They're mainly used for snake food," she told me. I took five to begin with, worrying about how my family would react to the new menu. Just as she closed the freezer, a medium-sized rodent plopped onto the floor with a small thud.

"Oh," I said. "A guinea pig." I used to keep pet guinea pigs, and in this moment my resolve began to wobble. The shop assistant stuffed the unfortunate animal back amongst the heap of corpses and led me to the till to pay for my horde.

Having had no luck with my Tawny feeding experiment, I called Stephen. There was a biting east wind but he was out monitoring. By this time Tawny and his mate were in high courting season, performing love duets each night. During courtship, from late winter and into February, the male Tawny will come to perch near the female and puff out his plumage, giving him an even more dumpy appearance than usual. He might sway from side to side, then up and down, and perhaps lift one wing and then the other. If this is not enough to tantalise the female, he might grunt softly, plumage tightly compressed, and even slide one foot towards her and back in a flirtatious game of owl-footsie. He might pursue her with screeches and groans. Where all this might not always be a successful strategy between humans, it can work with lady owls, and if she is charmed, the female will let the male know by fluffing and quivering her feathers.

I could hardly contain my excitement at the pictures Stephen sent me of the owls together. They were investigating the nest box he had put up; the pair were caught snooping about it, and then each owl went inside.

In April a new missive came: the female was inside the nest box more often than out. Was she sitting on eggs? At intervals of forty-eight hours, Tawnies can lay anywhere between one to six pure white, round eggs and the female incubates them alone for twenty-eight or twenty-nine days.

Stephen's Mrs. Tawny came out less and less frequently. When she left, it was very brief, as Stephen put it: just for "a pellet, a pee, and a poo." Between her economical exits, the male devotedly uttered a beautiful trilling warble, a kind of soft cradle song, as if promising to be there always and to bring her food. From now on she would be highly dependent on his provision for the successful incubation and rearing of their chicks. I wanted to witness this but could not get away, trapped at my desk marking my students' essays. For some reason, when I thought of the owls and their sweet domesticity,

I was reminded poignantly of my husband Rick bringing me cups of tea in the early days after childbirth while I nursed my own young. It was a vulnerable, totally dependent and rather desperate feeling, and the small acts of sustenance, the flying in with deliveries of vital food and drink, were heartful and encouraging in those helpless first few days and weeks of child-rearing. Now, taken up with teaching and nurturing my students, and looking after Benji, it still felt as if, owl-like and brooding, I needed that tea. So often too busy to stand and stare, so taken up with the humdrum, we need to escape the nest box for a while and get some fresh air. Mental health experts corroborate it: we need trees and grass and birds to keep us sane. But it isn't just that we need the grass and the crows and the wind in the trees, it is that we need that emotional identification with the wild. And the wild needs us to feel that compassion—it goes both ways. We will not fight to preserve what we do not love. And to keep our love alive, we need contact.

With perfect timing, Stephen reported hatching. He had been monitoring closely, and with the emergence of the female he could tell the young were food-begging. With increasingly tempting daily email updates entitled enticingly: "The unbelievable truth!!!!" and "You have to see this!!!!!!!" I couldn't stand it any more. As work was at last easing up I grabbed the phone and finally spoke to Stephen, made a plan with him, then bundled myself into a coat, chucked my wellies and my notebook into my car, and flew into the greenest of green folds of deep mid-Devon, my worry lines lifting as I went: finally, I could stand amongst the trees.

WITH MY BACK to an oak tree, eyes closed, breathing the moist air of the woods, the rough, cool presence of the earth seeped into me. Evening scents of mulch and moss fill my nose. Ankle-deep in the heady tang of wild garlic, I felt my stomach begin to let go of all the knots of stress.

"He'll be here in a few minutes, definitely by nine," Stephen promised. Ahead of me and all around was a small mixed woodland covering the steep rolling hillsides of rural Devon. *Dumnonii,* that's what the invading Romans called the tribes of Devon: deep valley dwellers. The name is just about spot on. The people here can be rightly proud of their deep and hidden valleys. And this particular "nether cleave" had a bigger draw than most.

"Just keep whistling," Stephen instructed with confidence. "He'll be here. I'm going to finish cooking supper." He disappeared back down to the house leaving me alone with the tree and the echoing soundtrack of birds: thrushes, blackbirds, and a raspy sky full of rooks, crows, and jackdaws. I stole a glance upward, though only for a second. I knew he'd arrive silently, and I could blink and miss him in the fading light.

Through the new leaves of the treetops to my right, rising in the deepening blue, the moon was already up. I hardly dared look: when he came there would be no warning. To my left, over the downward curve of the meadow, a bat had begun its flitting evening's hunt. I whistled again, trying to sound like Stephen, but knew that to the expert ear of the one I was summoning, it must have sounded woefully inadequate. You can't normally simply whistle and summon a wild owl, but somehow, with the reward of raw chicks, and a great deal of patience and repetition, Stephen had trained this Tawny Owl.

Then, low over the foliage, he came. A swooping shadow against many shadows. So low he looked unearthly, running suspended on a loop of air as if there was a cushion between his wings and the ground. His wings splayed, soundless from the velvety fringes on his primary feathers. The silent arrival must have freaked out our ancestors. The wings of all the other birds make a noise when they fly. Why not with this one? And as the Tawny Owl silently hunts, all the other birds go mad with alarm. What could be more eerie?

As Tawny reached the perch he landed with only the slightest scratch of talons. I thought I could hear the sound as he gripped the perch and folded his wings, but I could not be sure. He stood and stared back at me. That stare. I was transfixed: shorter by far and different in silhouette than Stephen's tall, wiry contours, I melded myself into the tree, trying to be bark-like, rooted. The Tawny was perched beside the bait but he didn't take it yet. Distracted, listening, his head turned this way and that, and then back to me. He fixed me with a stare, suspicious, and now I was sure that he recognised I was not the normal shape who nightly laid offerings on this table.

He was so alert, and yet aloof, twitching his face around and around, this way and that, to capture every sound the forest had to whisper. His eyes spookily appeared and disappeared as his head rotated a spine-tingling 270 degrees. I had time to see Tawny's individual markings: his softly flecked front and dark bib of rust-red plumage just beneath the facial disc. Then he picked up the diced bait and flicked his head up, eyes closed, and swallowed it down whole. Then the next morsel; swallow; then the next. He glanced at me, watching, between each beakful and the next. One more fleeting glance and he was off, as silent as he came. I stood for a few seconds, adrenaline fizzing through my limbs.

Back through the gathering dusk, my wellies clumping happily over the hill, through the gate, through a lit window, back to the human world, I got an owl's-eye view. There was Stephen, putting the finishing touches to dinner: I could smell good things to eat, but the evening was far from over.

Stephen had put camera traps around the nest box when he realised the owl might bring a mate here. In the last few weeks, the footage had confirmed successful breeding and Tawny regularly bringing food. I could hear her calling now, from the screens in the living room. But as we sat down at the little table to eat, there was more to come. In unobtrusive but perfect spots along the nearby stream, Stephen had put more camera traps to track another animal's progress. We sat at a small table in front of a row of five screens, showing an angle on the nest box, and also on parts of the stream: a bend, a rock, the bank, some roots. With much devotion and close observation, and the help of the surveillance, Stephen had worked out many of these creatures' habits.

Before we could have any more encounters, however, we had to eat. Stephen placed a plate of delicious food and some garlic bread in front of me but I could hardly look at it. This was the most exciting TV dinner I had ever had.

"Don't take your eyes off the live screen," Stephen instructed through a mouthful of home-made curry. "When she comes we'll have to stop eating and there will only be a few minutes to get down there."

My stomach was in knots. *When* she comes? She'll definitely be here?

"In a few minutes." This is what he had said about the owl, so I quickly managed my mouthfuls by feeling the food onto my fork and trying not to blink or take my eyes away from the screen. The food was delicious, I'm sure, if I could have tasted it.

The river's inhabitant was an old friend of mine: an otter.

I had spent four years tracking otters across the British Isles on my previous quest, and the thought of being reacquainted with another was tantalising. Stephen was out of the room fetching more garlic bread when it happened: a slim form appeared furtively around a bend in the river. "*There she is, there she is!"* I shrieked, spraying my mouthful of biryani in all directions. The otter's watery back appeared and then disappeared; she floated as if inflated with air, her face dipping beneath the surface, her tail a slip hardly breaking the flow of the stream.

Stephen pushed a head torch into my hands and knocking our poppadoms flying we ran down to a low bridge at the stream near the house.

Then, we waited.

"Are you going to be able to get up quickly from that position?" Stephen asked critically, eyeing my comfortable otter-watching lotus position.

"I'll need to get up?"

"Yes, we can follow her when she passes through. If you want."

After a few minutes, two eyes appeared on the water's surface, lit up by the beams of our head torches.

"Won't our lights disturb her?" I whispered when she dipped under the water.

Quietly untangling my legs I crept to the other side of the bridge. The otter's ears disappeared beneath the surface and she came up again, apparently quite used to the light. She was far too busy with the job of catching trout to take any notice of us. She had cubs to feed. (Stephen had noted when the dog otter visited her, when she disappeared to give birth, and that when she reappeared she was fishing much more urgently.) Just once, I noticed her lift her nose and test the scent on the air: something was different; did she sense that a new person was here? She threw us passing glances, but then she was back in the stream, herding terrified trout into the shallows. One shot out of the water in fear and beached itself on the pebbles. Instantly she was on it, champing it up head first—how could it be possible to eat up all those spiny bones, flesh, and fins so fast?—less than a minute and there was not a silvery scale left of it. And back she slid again, into the flow without so much as a wipe of the whiskers.

I dangled my face over the edge of the bridge. At this proximity, through the ripples I could see her water-smoothed pelt, her back legs working hard, her whiskers sweeping the pool. A 10-inch trout was holding still, petrified, in the shallows. She shot past him, her flattened corneas scanning, her ears folded into small triangles. She passed within a few centimetres of the trout's immobile body, sweeping her snout this way and that, but she couldn't see him in the dark, stirred-up water.

The trout shot under the bank, under our noses, and she powered after it, furiously ruckling everything to chase him out. Reeds and water dropwort flew in all directions; she surfaced, clearly almost out of breath with the effort, seized a mouthful of air, and was gone again, water roiling in wrinkles off her sinuous spine. I'd never seen so much strength and determination to kill; a blur beyond wolves and elk, beyond cheetah and gazelle, this was water turned into a frenzied muscle, into supple, gymnastic knots of water; water and otter and fleeting fish in a whirling vortex.

We followed Hammer Scar—named so because of the shape of the healed flesh wound on the tip of her nose—for a while longer. Otters often get scars on their snouts from fighting, and male otters can grab females by the nose to subdue them, so the scar may have been inflicted by her mate. Once she came out of the ditch and ran over my feet, glancing up at me, surprised but not alarmed. What amazed me is that we were able to witness this incredible night-time ritual, this dance of life and death in the tiniest and most unobtrusive of streams, because Stephen knew (almost) her every move, from the time she came out, to her exact route, to the time she went home to rest.

But not quite her every move: perhaps we had not been expecting the moment she leapt onto the pinnacle of a mossy tree stump and sprainted there, looking back through the beams of our head torches as if to say: *Ha! You didn't know I could do that.* (Stephen knew, of course, but I was enthralled.)

We trudged back, out of breath and imbued with otter.

Eventually I slid back out into the night for the hour-long journey home. The sky was full of stars. "Here—" Stephen pressed a cassette into my hand. "Listen to this on the drive." I floated through the miles of Devon with an old BBC recording from 1984, *Year of the Owl* narrated by Andrew Sachs. I drove through owl-scapes that filled the dark inside the car.

Back home, I slipped into the bedroom. The radio clock said half past one. I felt my way under the duvet and wondered how I could wrench any of it into words? Even so, some made it, articulating something Tawny, I hope, from somewhere out there in the deeper dark.

REGULAR NEWS BULLETINS came from Stephen. Apart from the fact that I forgot my wellies by the back door of his porch, Tawny's young could still be heard. Soon, they would appear. Stephen said we'd avoid the nest at this point: Tawnies can become very protective of their young and will not hesitate to strike if they feel threatened. Wildlife photographer Eric Hosking famously lost an eye when he got too close trying to get a good shot, and he told of it in his book *An Eye for a Bird*.

When would the young owlets fledge? At night, when Stephen went to feed Tawny, some of the bait was taken into the nest box. I would have so loved to know what was going on in the dark privacy of that nest. Then, to my joy, Stephen generously offered that I could house-sit while he made a trip to Northumberland to watch seabirds. Full of impatience, I spent days flitting in and out of a fantasy in which one of the owlets fell down and I would have to rescue it. I decided that when I was there I would spend as much time as possible in the woods, just in case a plummeting owlet needed putting back. As Tawny babies become more exploratory they frequently take a tumble, but they are such good climbers that they can often get back to safety. If you find one on the ground, it is usually best to leave it, especially as the watching parents know exactly where they are due to the constant calling. Even if you simply attempt to place it back on a branch out of harm's way, an angry parent owl would whomp you if they saw you approach or touch their young. And without a motorbike helmet to protect against those talons you'd risk certain blood loss.

Young Tawny Owls will normally fledge twenty-eight to thirty-seven days after hatching, and the ping of a new email shattered my owl-rescuing dreams: from Stephen, entitled "And you're not going to believe this" with eight exclamation marks. Hands sweating, I opened the mail. Filling the screen was a picture of the owlets taking flight! I'd missed it! A short film showed one, two, and three, as they sprang from the box and flew gracefully away. My delusion came crashing down. The owlets had fledged. I would not be an owl mummy, even for a moment.

"They haven't gone that far," Stephen assured me. "You'll be able to find them in the trees. They can move some distance from the nest, but you'll still be able to hear them." Tawny young remain "branching," perched in trees on the nest territory, for several weeks, venturing further and further as they practise their flying skills. Jenny and I packed the car with wild camping equipment. As well as looking after Stephen's house, we would sleep out beneath the trees where there would be hooting owlets. We could listen for them, and should see them, no problem, Stephen reassured me. Their patch in the wood was small and according to him they would be noisy enough to locate with ease. Jenny would revise for her General Certificate of Secondary Education (GCSEs) while I worked, and in between we would observe the wildlife, feed Tawny each night, and experience the excitement of the evening fly by.

At two minutes to ten, from her surveillance position at the five screens, Jenny cried out: Hammer Scar had appeared on screen two, and we piled into Stephen's four-by-four and hurtled down to the river. This time, she brought a cub with her, and we spent nearly an hour with the pair as mother fished and uttered whickering, whining cries as she summoned the cub to come to eat. They seemed so habituated to the light from our head torches that they repeatedly ran and swam through the shallows very close to our feet, and at one moment Hammer Scar swam on her back looking up at me, whistling all the while to her cub.

The next day, Stephen disappeared early to go on his birdwatching trip. His elusive and aptly named collie, Badger, who we were also looking after, lay at the far end of the living room, eyeing us suspiciously. "He's just socially awkward, Mum," Jenny explained as I attempted to buy his friendship with a cocktail sausage. "Just give him time." Later, whilst reading a book on the sofa, one hand trailing toward the carpet, I felt a snout lifting my arm just below the elbow. Badger was sitting beside me, a shy grin on his face, as if we were the oldest and best of friends, and he had only been pretending to be stand-offish for his own reasons. He even allowed me to remove a tick that I discovered whilst tousling his ears. I placed it dutifully in Stephen's tick container on the kitchen dresser.

A vet in his day job, Stephen had told me that the largest amount of cash he had ever been paid for his photographic work was for a macro close-up of a tick for a pharmaceutical company. Now he was following that up with a little research for the same firm. In a live experiment, he was breeding some ticks in an attempt to get a picture of the eggs hatching. An old ice-cream tub with some turf was crawling with six or eight of them, each at varying points in their life cycle. I was now used to the tick tub, but when Rick arrived on a visit it was another matter. "That is making me feel sick," Rick said over dinner, wondering what might be lurking in the grass. I shifted the tub and its experimental community to a more discreet spot, making sure to water the grass and checking none of the ticks could escape.

FINDING FLEDGED TAWNY OWLETS from below can be a challenge. Often hidden amongst spring and early summer foliage, perched high up amongst branches, they are watching us long before we see them. In the evening they emerge more conspicuously to call for food. There is only one sure way of finding them. By fixing ourselves to the spot, listening hard, and becoming as invisible as the owls themselves. You must stay still and wait, quiet as ivy, and listen. The waiting can be a long process, but stillness and patience are the needle and thread that stitch us into nature.

Young Tawny Owls have different phases of dispersal after the initial departure from the nest. First they find a perch nearby on which to "branch," simply to practise their moves, trying out new balancing and perching skills. At this point they do not venture far from the breeding site as they are still totally dependent on their parents for food. In Stephen's woods, amongst the hum and clatter of many other bird sounds, of wind and rain and leaf-rattle, the Tawny parents had guided the newly fledged juveniles to a suitable perch near the nest. From there the still-downy young were exploring, gangly-grey and unsure, never going far, and they called, during the evening and at night, to remind the food-providing parents (and us) of their locations. If they fell, they could easily get back to a safe branch by hooking into any available toe-holds of ivy, branches, and bark with their superbly adapted, needle-sharp talons.

The young's call is the giveaway. Sharp as a startled black-bird, high-pitched, elongated cheeps, and if you listen hard, soon they become recognisable and predictably repetitive. The juvenile Tawnies will stay in the vicinity where they hatched and remain dependent on their parents until the early autumn, by which time they are good flyers, and tuning up to be adults. Now they are more thoroughly independent, the parents may assist their move out of the territory amid much hooting and screeching. At this time of the year, there is a nightly cacoph-ony as adult Tawny Owls defend their territory from incoming youngsters trying to establish a new patch for themselves, and there will be a great deal of noise from dusk until late into the night as adults call out to repel the newcomers. Depending on the habitat and abundance of prey, a Tawny's territory may be quite limited. Ringing research shows that the average dis-tance travelled by adult Tawny Owls from where they hatched may only be between 1 and 4 kilometres. Where we live in the south the average dispersal is 1 to 2 kilometres, whereas in the north it is 4 to 5 kilometres. This may be due to climate, habitat, and/or density of prey species, but in any case, they are home-birds. Stephen's Tawny may never venture more than 1, 2, or 3 kilometres in any direction. Which may be why the bird can hear the whistle, and always responds with a fly-by each time Stephen puts out food beside the feeding station.

In June and July, Jenny became my owl-tracking part-ner. Her GCSEs were over and she was stress-free, about to enter the new world of the sixth form, and as yet still eager to accompany me. In between organising important social events with her equally footloose friends Erin, Hazel, and Kit, she came with me. "Why don't you bring them too?" I ventured naively. "Mum," came the exasperated reply, "my friends don't go outside."

So much of mothering, I was beginning to see, is about learning to keep quiet. Jenny was more protective of her privacy these days, and only sometimes linked arms with me when we were out in the woods together. But among the trees with the moss softening our footfall, the fluttering green light, and the potential sighting of owls, all that mother–daughter tension vanished. Sometimes, if the path was wide enough, I found her holding my hand as we walked along. I gained a glimpse of how our relationship was, and how it might be in years to come, when we would be free of the pitfalls and torments that are the minefield of mothering and adolescence.

"Listen!" we both said at once. "A young Tawny!"

The high-pitched begging call sounded a little raspy, like a knife being sharpened on a whetstone. "Ke-suipp, ke-suipp," it repeated. We gazed up into the branches, listening to the hoarse call and return of the young bird as it summoned its parents. Young Tawnies are well hidden to ground-dwelling human eyes. Their cryptic still-downy plumage keeps them safe from prying eyes, but their inexpert, persistent vocalisations give them away. Even then, the cries are piercing but hard for our mere human ears to triangulate, as an owl would, to locate its young. Another raptor, however, may find the repeating sound of the calls easily, and young owls do get caught in this way; buzzards, goshawks, sparrowhawks, and other owls in the vicinity could potentially overlap with them in the evening and have a go at making a meal of them.

Tangled in the undergrowth of old bluebells and wild garlic were the eaten remains of a dismembered woodpecker, recognisable only from one foot, the distinctively sharp bill, and the scalped skull where an edge of scarlet plumage still remained clinging along the forehead like a blood-red eyebrow. I removed the skull and popped it in a hanky to take home, some of the neck vertebrae still attached, planning to add it to my growing specimen collection.

"Mum, look!"

Jenny pointed at a shape flowing through the trees: the young Tawny had taken to the wing and was swooping low. Perhaps this was the only way we would see it, if it moved like this. We watched it settle into a new tree and soon it had blended in, but as we moved away, its face turned like a radar as if unable to tear its gaze away from us.

BACK ON OUR HOME patch Rick watched me as I bent down and carefully lifted a small feathered corpse from beneath a tree. I'd enticed him to accompany me on my favourite woodland walk, only to make a new find.

"Please. Not another one."

Our autumn walk on the edge of the moor had already taken a grisly turn. For me, it was gold dust. This Tawny was lying inert beneath a hawthorn beside a little Methodist chapel. It must have just dropped dead and fallen off its perch in the night. The corpse of familiar russet feathers was beautiful and intact.

"Do we have to take it?"

I examined the wings, the rust-striped primary feathers with their fine velvet fringes and softer-than-thistledown trailing edges. This was research. I must have it. I stared at the supersoft comb-like edges, called "fimbriate," meaning "fringe-like." These flutings, or fimbriae, act to silence flight by breaking down air turbulence as it flows over the wing, avoiding the gushing noise most birds create when they fly. The fimbriae create "micro-turbulences" instead, and these effectively muffle the sound of the owl's flight.

Having checked for maggots and blood, or anything else unexpectedly leaky, I placed the freshly dead owl on the dog blanket on the back seat of the car. In my reading I'd discovered that there are two types of Tawny Owl, each with different colour "phases." In the north of Britain, rather than being a warm russet colour, the Tawny often has greyish plumage: this is the grey phase. The name is confusing because it sounds as if the owl has phases and will change its colour, but this is not the case. Although Tawny plumage can vary, individual owls never change their colour. As Britain was separated from the rest of the European land mass around 8,000 to 8,500 years ago, it is possible that with our geographical isolation two distinct species have developed: *Strix aluco aluco,* and *Strix aluco sylvatica.* While the first species can be found further north in Britain, the southern russet-feathered Tawnies are probably from the latter subspecies, and as their name suggests, inhabit primarily woodlands. Much research and copious museum collections of their skins bear this out: there could be two types of Tawny Owl! My Tawny is probably a *sylvatica,* judging by its plumage, but I expect it is all subject to debate, as owl research still has some way to go.

"What'll you do with it this time?" Rick asked.

Back home, the Tawny went into my frozen mortuary before we sent it off anywhere—by this point we had bought a special freezer just for my specimens that now contained:

One dead chiffchaff (window strike)
One dead Barn Owl (found at a Barn Owl site)
One juvenile rat (brought in by cat, uneaten)
One field vole (roadkill)
One shrew (cat again)
Six day-old chicks (bought from pet shop as Tawny fodder)
One woodpecker (parts, found half-eaten in woods)

OUR FRIEND HANNAH eventually solved the conundrum of the growing collection of dead things. She bumped in through the door with a muscular box of dissection implements, powders, and strange pots of chemicals with Ali Douglas, her friend from Queensland, Australia. Ali works as senior preparator in taxidermy at the Queensland Museum. She didn't seem to mind Hannah's suggestion that she spend an evening of her holiday doing what she normally does at work, that is, skinning a dead owl. On the contrary, she was happy as anything to make an evening of it.

In the far corner of the room, lights glowed on our Christmas tree. An owl decoration glared wonkily out from the top where an angel should have been. "Let's do this. Then we can drink gin later," Ali suggested heartily. "Have you got tonic?"

We sat around my dining table. Hannah wanted to learn the art of taxidermy so, knowing I had some specimens, she had requested we skin one of my owls—and Ali reassured me that it wouldn't affect results at the research lab when I sent the owl's body off.

"They don't need the skin; they probably only need the livers to test for toxins," she said. "We can save all that for them."

I had thawed out the owl and set up a camera to record footage of our evening's work. Why, I wondered, would anyone want to reanimate a dead thing whose colours and life had faded and bring it back to an appearance of life? It seemed like a powerful metaphor suddenly, that during our era, when species are declining at such a rate that we have named the phenomenon the sixth great extinction, we would wish to fake a revival of this one creature. Is it that we are diminished without these wild things, and to know them, to understand them, we need to come face to face with their impermanence?

The video recorded the bird lying peacefully, still intact, then Rick moving through the room at speed with a rapid mumble about being outnumbered by three women, a dead thing, and a proliferation of sharp knives.

"I'm not usually squeamish," he said, closing the door behind him.

Ali often gets requests to teach how to dissect animals, or to help out with taxidermy work. "And it's always women. We have dozens of volunteers at the museum and they are almost always young women."

"Why is that?" The gender imbalance seemed bizarre.

"I don't know. It seems like some kind of fascination with dead things."

Is it that we might need to learn about death and loss before we can bring life into the world? Perhaps we're just less afraid to admit we're curious.

Hannah, absorbed in making sure we had everything we needed, concentrated first on lining up her scalpels. Ali got more equipment out of the box: rat tooth tweezers for removing flesh from hard-to-reach places, pliers and scissors, wire cutters and fine metal scoops designed specifically for scooping the brains out of birds' skulls. She had a selection of drill bits too, for working on the larger bones and for fixing specimens to wooden perches.

How did Ali get into taxidermy? I wondered. She told me that it might have come from her upbringing—her father was a great naturalist, and it might have been watching him doing a little taxidermy as a hobby when she was young, but later in life she found herself becoming more and more interested in working at the city museum, and started out learning as a volunteer. She had developed a fascination with animals as she grew up, but as an adult she moved into it from working on visual props and puppet-making for theatre. There she found a love for the skeletal nature of some forms of puppetry. Again, that bringing to life of lifeless creatures, that imaginative leap into sympathy for a dead thing, that fascination for the creaturely inside and underside of things, for how things work. But above all, taxidermy for Ali is about contact, conservation work, and education: "It's about teaching people about the animals. This is the only way many people can get up close and be able to look at them properly."

Is that what is behind this fixation humans have with cutting up animals and preserving them? A desire to get up close? In antiquity it was all about preservation, and at first taxidermy animals that had been brought back from far-flung places as skins and had never been seen in the flesh were set in misshapen wire frames. Inaccurate, conspicuously awkward-looking works soon became a scientific art, concerned with more than simply *taxis* (the Greek word for "arrangement") and *derma* (meaning "skin"). As humans found better and better ways of preserving the skins of their quarry, taxidermists learned their skill from the increased demand for tanning leather in the nineteenth century. At the same time, people became gripped with curiosity about the strange foreign creatures brought back by explorers such as Captain James Cook, who had shipped a kangaroo skin back to London from Australia as early as 1771. In 1798, when Captain John Hunter sent a pelt and sketch of a platypus, it was thought to be a hoax. To be convinced, people wanted to see what these creatures would look like in real life.

After a taxidermy competition in America in 1880 where specimens were judged on everyday lifelikeness and their realistic context, the appearance of these artifacts became less odd. Now a new scientific accuracy was required: Charles Darwin, for example, would not have been allowed to travel on HMS *Beagle* and collect his many samples had he not been proficient in this key naturalist's skill. The natural history museums of Paris and London drew increasing interest from the public—for the Great Exhibition of 1851 taxidermists from all over the world had gathered to present their now-popular form of art and natural history.

A century later, taxidermy had a new resurgence with a folk-art revival in the late twentieth century. Now it is in fashion again, and few towns are without their resident taxidermist. On some level does it still reinforce notions of human separateness, that we alone can somehow restore life after death? We arrange these animals as still lifes, aesthetic close-ups, lifelike creatures placed in supposedly charismatic poses. But a stuffed animal's conspicuously dead eyes sparkle with irony. The animal looks less glamorous than mortified. Trapped in our gaze, it is held in some kind of freakish netherworld.

ALI HOLDS THE SCALPEL like a quill pen, as if we are practising calligraphy. The owl looks asleep, eyes shut tight at an angle of 45 degrees, two diagonals aligned with its long bill. The facial disc is crumpled tight into a wince, making a perfectly symmetrical heart shape. Then I think that it's a frown, a protection of the tender little face, the ruff of the brow dipping defensively between the eyes. It's somehow soulful, even in death.

The intimacy of what Ali does takes me by surprise: to part the breast feathers and find a point where we can begin takes ultra-delicate fingertip searching amongst the dense breast feathers. And then she takes the scalpel and strokes the exposed skin with the tip of the blade, making the softest of scratches as the bird's front opens. There is no blood, only dark muscle. Her skill finds the sternum through the thin skin, and as Ali searches I'm painfully reminded of picking up one of my chickens when she is broody and feeling at my fingertips the sudden heat emanating from her silky-warm brood patch, the place where she warms new life from her clutch of eggs.

Taxidermy, Ali says, is making dead things look lifelike. Sometimes the collections in the museum have a label that hurts the heart: a "last-known example of . . ." and the loneliness of the creature comes to life all over again. In that moment I feel it is not just the animal's loneliness, but ours, too.

The sternum becomes visible as Ali makes the cut. The quietest of sounds, like cutting through tissue paper. Hannah gathers pinches of a white powder called borax. I can't place where I've heard of this but it sounds domestic, a chemical product housewives used during the 1950s? The borax goes into the skin in little sprinkles, to dry out the thin fatty layer underneath. Owls cannot afford to be fat, and here the modest layer of butter yellow is micro-thin. Even this meagre body fat shows that it was well fed; it did not die of starvation at least, as many inexperienced owls do in their first year before they have learned to be good hunters.

The drumsticks are broken so that they can slide out of the skin—I begin to feel more uncomfortable as this perfect owl is dismembered and effectively turned inside out.

"You're taking the skin off like a glove," Ali says. "The whole body will come out in one piece, more or less."

We're avoiding fossicking through entrails as this is not an autopsy, it's skinning. By not puncturing the chest or abdomen, we are left with what looks like a miniature chicken carcass, but the rich red colour of hung pheasants that I have seen in butchers' shops. And now we need to hang the bird upside down, to undress it from the tail up over the chest. The face scrunches even tighter as it is pulled like a snug-fitting jumper, and the expression "skintight" will never feel the same to me after this day.

The scalpel does its work, leading the hand to peel and prise the skin off by increments. Now the breast is exposed, meaty, and muscular for flight. The colour remains imprinted on my retina—indecent, purplish-red, rich as heartwood. The whole length of the neck snakes out from its skin, a rope of braided cartilage, invisible in life—when the owl is sitting, it doesn't look as though it has any neck at all, but brought out from underneath the feathers, it's S-shaped, sinuously attached to the skull.

It's a challenge to pull the skin over the skull and hoist it off. We look at the skinned cranium, and I notice its shape. Owls owe much of their popularity to their flat, humanoid faces, but without the covering of the feathered facial disc, the skull reveals something altogether different. The eyes are angled slightly apart, to give a wide field of view, and the overlap is small, so the owl must bob its head to maximise its binocular vision. The owl's bill is much longer than at first shows. Usually it is buried within the central ridge of feathers of the facial disc. Now I can see that the long bill allows for a wide gape—just the size to easily swallow down a plump vole and smoothly eject a pellet.

Owls have such large eye cavities! The empty eye sockets have their strange cartilaginous tubes, totally rigid, the sclerotic rings that are there to keep the huge eyes in but prevent them from moving. Now I can physically see how it cannot turn its eyes, and why having such a long and super-supple neck is paramount. Visibly, the owl has an extra-long neck, and compared to us it has additional cervical vertebrae—we have seven in our neck, the owl has fourteen—and it has recently been discovered that the spaces within each vertebra are enlarged for increased blood flow, which explains why it can turn its face in almost a complete circle without giving itself a fatal embolism.

With the owl's body in my hands, I question again what it is that drives us to do these things. Beyond the taxidermy, is it the ardour of science, fetish, or maybe simply the desire to find out something intimate, to tell the animal's story, and perhaps through that to see a new side of our own? This evening has been a kind of exploration of the owl as an unknown continent, we the explorers, discovering the bird's geography. I don't always want to think about the mania humans have for collecting trophies, the creation of artificial theatres of stuffed animals for our curiosity and entertainment, while so many species have been and still are being pushed to the edge. We manage, engineer, and mediate our experience of wild nature, and in doing so, do we diminish our experience of it? The stuffed specimens are at least preserved, the science is logged, and yet our curiosity, our need to know more, still drives us onward. To what? *Homo sapiens*, the wise human. Sometimes I wonder just how wise. So often the specimens we hold in our hands are all that we have left.

Athene noctua

LITTLE OWL

The owl of Minerva takes flight only when the shades of night are gathering.

—G. W. F. HEGEL, *Philosophy of Right*

THE HIGH MOORLAND WAS WOVEN WITH AUGUST colour, splashed with purple heather and coconut-scented gorse. Sunshine bounced off white cumulus clouds and warmed the backs of roadside-grazing wild ponies that distracted drivers and caused mini traffic jams. There was a stroking southerly breeze that seemed to whisper through the grasses warning of the end of the summer: "There will not be many more days like this. Make the most of it . . ." On the slopes and tors the soft air threw light and clarity in every direction, and from the top of Sharp Tor away from all the people and cars we stood with the breeze in our hair and took in all the contours of the moor. Amongst its carpet of green, mauve, and gold we saw meadow pipits and golden plovers, a great spotted woodpecker, wheatears, and best of all, the dark crossbow form of a hunting peregrine.

Wind-thrilled and footsore, we finally turned to head home, and as we dipped into the farmland on the fringe of the moor I saw it. Something odd that just caught my eye from the car window, tucked in close to a dry-stone wall. A little bump where there should have been no bump, a fence post that was slightly higher than it should have been. The post was topped with a roundness, a smooth shape that morphed into feathers, and two eyes now brightly peeking at us.

I pulled over and peered through the window. Jenny gasped.

"Mum, Mum, it's an owl! Oh, my God, it's a Little Owl, right there!"

The Little Owl glared with ferocious lemon-yellow eyes. We held our breath, delighted.

In her poem "Little Owl Who Lives in the Orchard," Mary Oliver suggests that the Little Owl's short beak is as sharp as a bottle opener, and that however beautiful, he always stares belittlingly right through you. This Little Owl bore out the poetry, scrutinising us with intimidating outrage. I am sure that nothing about us escaped its fierce gaze. It must have taken in the window with two pale, excited faces, the car trespassing on its front lawn. Its old-codger-style eyebrows knitted in vexation, static electricity bristled from its whole small being. We were transfixed.

Little Owls, I had read, appear to have something named "small-owl syndrome" and regularly punch above their weight. Even here where they are very rare, this one was trying to singe us with its stare. Not much bigger than a song thrush, they can't hurt people, but often take on birds that are larger than themselves, and frequently get mobbed because of this aggressive tendency. For this reason, they have an "occipital face," the trace of false eye-markings on the very back of their head. This is an evolutionary adaptation that mimics a "hard stare" to fool the mobsters that they are being watched. Perhaps (and I say perhaps because my owl quest was far from over) the most characterful of all the British owls, this small grey-brown owl with speckled, spotted, and streaked camouflage is the size of a scruffy tennis ball but with an endearing pear-shaped silhouette. What it lacks in size it makes up for in ferocity, with its furious glare and exaggerated white brows.

Then, our hearts leapt again. On the ground at the roots of the hawthorn there was a hissing sound, and some movement. Here was the reason for the compressed rage. Distinctive *shreee shreee* begging calls were emitting from the

ground, and the adult Little Owl flitted about anxiously trying to distract us. But we stayed quietly put. My binoculars
homed on a dark hollow—and a delight hidden between the
roots—a downy cache: two, no, *three* tiny grey owlish faces.
A Little Owl nest, on the ground! We stifled our squeals,
bundling them in our throats.

The gnarly bark had been disguising their hiding place
but now we could clearly see three faces: three Little Owlets, still softly plumped out in their juvenile plumage, flecked
with white, haloed with soft ash-grey around the edges. There
was something charming about the defiance of the adult as it
stretched up tall on its long legs, all outrage and threat.

Goblin-like, every Little Owl has its very own individual
facial pattern, and we could see it now, particularly around
the eyebrows. I'd read about it in my Little Owl book by
Andy Rouse, in which he notes that the quirky features give
the whole species an especially human quality. The barom-
eter of expressions can vary from surprise through intense
concentration to menace, and like most owls, they never
look pleased to see a human. My friend Paul Riddle, who has
been monitoring the Little Owls in his area of Leicestershire where it seems there is a concentration of them, has a
stunning array of owl photographs on his blog "Owls About
That Then." Paul claims they are by far the best owls because
of their wide range of eyebrow styles. There doesn't seem
to be any evolutionary reason for this variety but it does
make them seem as individual as people. I hadn't considered
before that any of the owl species might be the best, or even
become my favourite, but these Little Owls were suddenly
strong contenders.

"They're a lot easier to see than you'd think," Paul had told
me modestly. "It's just a matter of knowing where to look, and
being patient. Sometimes you can just do the 'kissing' call, the

kind you'd do to attract a cat, and they come to you to check you out. Then you can just snap them."

Although he made it sound easy, Paul had put in hours of tracking of these birds and had learned that the "kissing" call mimics a rodent in distress. Any predator might react and come along to see if there was an easy kill. You can do it to attract stoats, too. So that day I decided to try my first Little Owl kissing call. But the owls had got the measure of us, and the sentinel parent soon lost interest. Peering through the windscreen we could see it fluff out in a relaxed manner and begin to preen its primary feathers and breast. Shortly afterwards it gave a sharp call, then another, and the three young, visible only by their wispy little heads, tottered further out of their nest hole. Another adult flew in, slightly smaller than the first, so possibly the male, although it is very hard to tell—unlike other owl species there is limited sexual dimorphism in Little Owls—and presented them with a worm. At this point they suddenly grew tall and scuttled to pick it from his bill. One of the charms of Little Owls is how athletic they are when they run about. Now there were five owls in front of us, all within a few yards of the car window. Two siblings battled over the poor invertebrate in a tug of war until it was stretched like pink elastic. We watched aghast until finally one of them conceded and the winner swallowed the victim whole.

We left them to it, and drove home on the wings of *Athene noctua*, the ruffian with downy legs and sulphurous stare imprinted at the back of our eyes. I had been so enamoured of the ghostly glamour of the Barn Owl, and the unholy softness of the Tawny, that I truly hadn't thought anything could top them. This new owl affected me differently. It had sat in broad daylight and stared spikily back at us, person-like, challenging.

At home that evening I looked up Little Owls. This was Athene's owl, the emblem of an ancient Greek goddess revered enough for her image to have been printed as an owl on Athenian coins—proud and distinctive, and recognisably the Little Owl. But why was Athene associated with a Little Owl? John Lydus, a sixth-century scholar, claims it was because "she shared the nature of fire; and the owl, her sacred bird, stays awake all night to signify the human soul which is never lazy, always in movement by its very nature, which is immortal." This bird, it was believed, could see in the dark when others were blind and had the wisdom to remain hidden all day when it was persecuted. The Greeks saw wisdom, knowledge, and prudence in its behaviour and so connected it with Athene, the chaste goddess of wisdom.

This ancient Greek description of its character seemed to fit with what I had seen, both in my Little Owl encounter in the wild, and in captivity. Flitwick, the perky Little Owl in my local owl sanctuary, instinctively remains hidden for most of the time, although she has the space to fly free. But she is also feisty—she will perch contentedly on an index finger and wait with the utmost confidence to be fed. If you try to stroke her with the back of a finger, she pecks fiercely: this is not a creature to be petted—and stroking can remove valuable oils from the owl's plumage. She is to be respected, in spite of her small stature. In the wild, Little Owls understand the need for discretion but they will fight off predators such as buzzards and Barn Owls, giants in comparison. With these they will ferociously defend their young, battling to the death if need be. Sadly, they are often beaten and are frequently predated by these larger raptors.

Through my reading I discovered that the squat, cross-looking, flat-headed fellows that I had seen were not a native British species. Even though born here, and this owl-with-attitude has been present here for generations, it is still considered to be an import. Native to continental Europe,

Athene noctua is the most regularly seen owl in southern and eastern European countries, perhaps due to their diurnal and crepuscular activity patterns, but they are now a Species of European Conservation Concern. In Poland, for example, numbers have rapidly declined, possibly due to changing agricultural practices, and much research and conservation effort has been put into nest-box schemes to aid their preservation: in some Polish towns, nest boxes have significantly contributed to the Little Owl's breeding success.

The Little Owl thrives in warm, dry countries like Greece, and as it particularly likes to look out from tall vantage points (such as roofs, posts, and walls), the richly colonnaded Parthenon, the temple dedicated to Athene, with its tree-like columns, ledges, and many shady cavities, must have made a particularly attractive perch and drawn the owls in. Is this another cause of how Athene came to be associated with the Little Owl? The bottom of the truth is probably lost in time. Some mythographers believe that the owl-goddess association might come from even older origins than the Athenian story, from a Minoan palace goddess associated with birds, or even an old European bird-snake goddess.

Long after the ancient Greeks had faded from the scene, Little Owls continued to be attracted to the ruins of the Parthenon, and so it was that the Little Owl found itself linked with a more recent iconic historical character. In 1850 a young woman was visiting the Parthenon. A small flurry caught her attention, and when she turned, she saw an owlet falling from its nest amongst the rubble. It was too small to fly, and was immediately set upon by a band of merciless children who began persecuting it for fun. The young lady was outraged and chased away the youngsters. Battered and in shock, the dishevelled victim sat at her feet. She scooped it up in her hands and popped it protectively in her pocket. The Little

Owl, unaware of its good luck, had been rescued by Miss Florence Nightingale.

Florence took the owlet home with her, cared for it until it recovered, and brought it up. The pair became so attached to one another that they went everywhere together, and "Owlet Athena" travelled around contentedly as a captive owl, although her sharp beak was deployed to peck anyone who attempted to pet her. For five happy years Owlet Athena and Florence kept their companionship. Florence believed a pet could help people in their recovery, and Athena joined her mistress on house calls, often helping patients to forget their pain with her endearing antics. At home she perched on the mantelpiece between statuettes of Theseus and Mercury, and would fly to a plate of food to see what she could devour. On one occasion when Florence's sister entered the room wearing an unfamiliar cotton bonnet she flew at it, ripped it off, and attempted to shred it. The unfortunate headwear was never worn again. She entertained everyone by pouncing on flies and running around the room chasing imaginary mice, but the joy was not to last.

As is often the case with wild pets, Owlet Athena had a bad end. When war broke out in the Crimea, Florence was called upon to take her nursing skills abroad. Athena could not accompany her into a war zone, and she was left behind in Florence's attic, where Nightingale believed the owl would be cared for by visits from her family. It was hoped she would be able to feed herself on the large population of mice that lived in the eaves of the house. But Athena was too domesticated to hunt for herself and couldn't live merely on the insects in the room. Missing her companion and devastated by loneliness, she starved and died. Florence was heartbroken, and arranged for a taxidermist to embalm Athena for posterity. "Poor little beastie," Florence mourned. "It was odd how much I loved you."

A little book was written as a memorial about Athena by Florence's sister: *Florence Nightingale's Pet Owl Athena, A Sentimental History,* by Parthenope, Lady Verney. Nursing in the Crimea, Florence confessed to missing her pet and one evening she wrote home: "Athena came along the cliff quite to my feet, rose up on her tiptoes, bowed several times, made her long melancholy cry and fled away—like the shade of Ajax—I assure you my tears followed her."

Athena's body was preserved in a characteristic pose inside a glass case in the family home for many years until she was acquired by the Florence Nightingale Museum in London. Amongst the Nightingale collection, perched on her branch, the lifelike Little Athena's eyes still burn through the glass.

)

DESCRIBED AS "NATURALISED but not native," this owl is our smallest in Britain—it is only just over half the size of the others, at 23 to 25 centimetres long, and weighing as little as 150 to 170 grams on average—but it has a big story behind its arrival here. The Little Owl was introduced to Britain during the 1880s by bird collector and 4th Baron of Lilford, Thomas Powys. He brought the first pair of birds over from Holland himself, with the aim of adding some more variety to our avifauna. At that time, Britain was home only to Barn Owls, Tawnies, and Long and Short-eared Owls, with an occasional blow-in to the highlands of Scotland of a Snowy Owl. The Little Owl was welcomed at first and employed as a form of pest control, feeding as it does mainly on cockchafers and other beetles and small rodents. The first breeding pair were recorded in Rutland in 1891 and within fifty years the new species had spread far across mainland Britain, although it is a lowland species and even now it does not look as though there are any beyond the borders in Scotland, perhaps because of rough or wet weather, which is always a threat to the owl.

The arrival of a non-native species was for a time considered to be a harmless aesthetic "enhancement" of the environment, an interesting addition to our comparably dull range of owl species, but random introductions of this sort can be disastrous for native wildlife. North American mink have nearly wiped out the British water vole population; Japanese knotweed is busily overwhelming native riverside vegetation; and grey squirrels imported from America have brought with them a pox that has threatened the survival of our defenceless red squirrel. How would the Little Owl's presence affect our own precious species?

It turned out that the Little Owl was able to fit in well. It did not compete with other birds of prey, feeding mostly on invertebrates, of which there were plenty to go around, and so it slotted into the ecosystem without any discernible impact. Occasionally it fed on the same prey as Barn Owls and buzzards, but they in turn could predate it, if it got too big for its boots. However, at first gamekeepers, always on the alert for predators, were highly suspicious of its effect on game, and it was persecuted during the first part of the last century on estates where it was believed that it would damage valuable pheasants. In the 1930s the British Trust for Ornithology commissioned Alice Hibbert-Ware to carry out a Little Owl Food Inquiry and thoroughly examine Little Owl prey species. The persecution abated when in 1938 the findings were published and the Little Owl exonerated.

While it might have taken the Little Owls some time to settle down in England, they are natives on the Continent. And when I found myself holidaying to France that summer, they were there waiting for me. We were going to a village just outside Paris, attending a civil ceremony. Jenny was pleased with the knowledge that this was one up from joining the local Pride march, and we formed a trium-feminate of three generations: grandmother, mother, and daughter. We packed our bags according to what we each thought would suit a French gay wedding. It was all very exciting, but apart from the regimented Paris parks and gardens, we'd be far away from the wild. I fretted that there would be no owls at all.

I shouldn't have worried. As we exited customs and found our way to the train into the city a giant pair of eyes smacked into mine: a 3-metre-tall poster presented the face of an owl in vivid shades of blue and violet, its fierce eyes gazing out over us all. This owl was advertising insurance to the passing commuters, homeless, travellers, and tourists—just as we entered the escalators to descend into the underworld of the Métro.

Resurfacing into the Paris streets we left the guardianship of the violet owl behind and flowed into a cacophony of taxis, buses, and motorbikes. The late-summer sunshine bounced off lines of neatly coppiced city trees and beamed into our eyes. Scents of street food, crêpes, chips, and waffles hit our noses. Over the cathedral of Notre-Dame flocks of pigeons and jackdaws fluttered and bickered. Along the high walls of the mud-brown river Seine's carefully engineered banks, amongst the plane trees and trinket sellers, collections of art prints lined the pavements. My eyes lit on a magnificent nineteenth-century portrait of a pair of Tawny Owls. I paused to look. The natural mottling of the plumage, the greens and browns of the whole painting, made a harmonious picture, situated as it was amongst the fallen leaves, dusty greys, and shadows of the city's walkways. Beneath the owls, captured in their natural habitat of a rough, knotted oak, were three young, crouched in their nest and peering beadily out of their crook amongst the branches.

Perhaps it was that my peripheral vision was on the alert, or I'd been thoroughly sensitised to this creature, but I began to feel haunted. The owls wouldn't leave me alone. After the painting, my eye was drawn to the window display of a book-shop three doors up from our hotel: one side was entirely dec-orated with a collection of owl books for children. I nipped in and lovingly chose a colourful hardback, *Le Bonheur des Chou-ettes* (The Happiness of Owls), but left *Hibou* (Owl) and *Bébés Chouettes* (Owl Babies) for another time. The pleasant feath-ered faces of the owls stared out of their book covers, human-like, watching over the street and attracting customers. On the waxy cover of *Le Bonheur des Chouettes* two rotund owls nestled close to one another. Once we had checked in to our hotel room, I needed to find out more about the owls' secret to happiness and devoured the story. According to the charming tale, all the other birds wonder the same thing: What can it be that prevents the happy owl couple from bickering, as all the other animal couples do, after many years of marriage? The two owl lovers wisely explain: "We love to watch the turning seasons of nature: the gentle arrival of spring, the leafy sum-mer, the autumn rich in colours, and then the blanket of snow in winter when we can snuggle up together and keep each other warm." The other animals can't believe it, and return to their bickering.

What is it about owl stories? Perhaps due to the round, motherly shape, the appealing, large eyes, and engaging faces that owls have, they have been used to reassure children and to teach them with heartful and cheering storylines: "Ewayea! my Little Owlet! / Who is this, that lights the wigwam? / With his great eyes lights the wigwam? / Ewa-yea! my Little Owlet!" the wrinkled old Nokomis warmly sings, cradling the infant orphan Hiawatha in Longfellow's poem. Just when we are at our most tender and learning to be properly human, the creaturely kinship we have with owls becomes a kind of comforter and guide. I had many of these stories read to me as a child and got them all out of the loft to read to my own children when they were old enough. They loved them. A favourite for all of us was *The Owl Who Was Afraid of the Dark,* about a baby Barn Owl named Plop. This one, by the children's author Jill Tomlinson, was part of a series that encouraged children to get over fears and challenges: Plop is a fluffy little Barn Owl who is quite new to flying and has a fear of the dark. "I want to be a day bird," Plop declares, but his mother explains that he needs to go and find out about the dark in order to understand it and learn to be less afraid. "You are what you are," the mother Barn Owl explains. "And what I are is afraid of the dark," Plop argues. But of course, along with Plop we slowly learn about stepping through fear of the unknown and into possibility: and how exciting, necessary, wonderful, and beautiful the dark can be. This one was one of Benji's favourites. He listened to a cassette recording of it at bedtime repeatedly for months.

Why was the owl the best kind of animal character to help out? In *The Owl Who Was Afraid of the Dark,* apart from being nocturnal Plop is the best possible guide and companion: he looks and feels like an authentic person. He has two legs like us, and most of all, a flat, human-ish face. Owls' faces, more than any other birds', resemble ours. It is the flatness that makes them so familiar, and their especially large, round eyes that create attraction by their babyish, helpless beauty. They draw empathy from deep within our cerebral cortex, provoking our suggestible human emotions.

Then there is their gaze. Because an owl cannot move its eyes, it must turn its head to look directly at the object of its attention, so it appears to be deliberately meeting our gaze, and its look feels laden with importance. Above all, the owl's upright stance and its confident, superior poise appears human. It is like us, yet seems to be party to some secret intelligence. The apparently magical ability to see in the dark and to fly unafraid through the night, as well as its prodigious hunting skills, must have accumulated to make it seem magical, and eventually useful as a symbol of wisdom, and a wise teacher for our children's stories.

Animals have always been used to educate, from cave paintings to Aesop and La Fontaine: they have always been sequestered for storytelling and metaphor, perhaps precisely because they can't talk back. So we imaginatively put words in their beaks, snouts, and jaws, and have them explain the world to our smallest ones in a (mostly) unthreatening way. But isn't it strange that such an emblem of wildness as the untameable owl has come to seem so domesticated?

As well as our urge to follow, learn from, explain, and tame wild things, we have also attempted to tame our children with these stories. In Beatrix Potter's *Tale of Squirrel Nutkin*, the eponymous hero and his brother Twinkleberry sail on little rafts that they have constructed from twigs to Owl Island to gather nuts. Each day they respectfully ask permission from the resident owl, Old Brown, but the impertinent Squirrel Nutkin taunts him with teasing riddles. The owl eventually loses his temper and nearly skins the squirrel alive. Nutkin escapes, but loses his tail to the vicious Old Brown. The story warns what can happen if we break the rules and disrespect authority. At the same time, it is also an accurate natural history story with sensitively observed depictions of wild creatures and their characters—not once does it tiptoe around the violence and power of the owl.

It is a very different portrayal from the heart-warming illustrations of the owl couple in my newly bought children's book.

Back at the hotel that evening I open *Le Bonheur des Chouettes* again and savour the last page where the owls "se blottirent l'une contre l'autre, clignerent de leurs gros yeux ronds, en s'envolant dans leurs pensées empreintes de sagesse."

"THE OWLS BLOTTED [pressed] themselves together, blinked their big round eyes, and drifted off to sleep with thoughts imbued with wisdom." The patience and devotion that the two owls display, their acceptance of the seasons, their tender nurturing of their young, and their capacity for gentleness teach about the simple joys of family life. Both stories contend with a creature that in many ways is like us, but while one focuses on the need for love, the other focuses on the need for respect. Arguably, love cannot exist without admiration and respect, and I think on some level, for all our human stupidities, we truly admire and respect the owl. All through time, perhaps this is why owls have been employed to attract and educate human youngsters.

Waking the next morning I lie in my hotel bed rolling an owl dream around my head. A Little Owl had been sitting beside me, on the bedstead, clicking its beak and showing me its young, all three lined up beside it, fluffing out their feathers and chattering, as if trying to say something that I could not quite grasp. Perhaps I was beginning to feel a little paranoid, or perhaps something else was coming into focus: if humans and animals were once much more closely allied than we like to think about in our busy, technology-driven lives, perhaps the owls and I were simply re-establishing a better relationship. By paying attention to them properly, I was seeing their personality and resonance more clearly. That was why they were getting into my dreams. I was recognising that they had something to say. After all, unlike us they live in instinctive harmony with the planet—might we not have something to learn from them?

In his essay "The Ecology of Magic," American philosopher David Abram suggests that to ancestral humankind, wild creatures were purveyors of secrets, carriers of intelligence that we often needed: "It is these Others who can inform us of unseasonable changes in the weather, or warn us of imminent eruptions and earthquakes; who show us, when foraging, where we may find the ripest berries or the best route to follow back home." Perhaps paying close attention to them could bring us to tune into a different way of seeing our own world; what Abram describes as the "ability that an alien form of sentience has to echo one's own, to instill a reverberation in oneself that temporarily shatters habitual ways of seeing and feeling, and leaves one open to a world all alive, awake and aware."

I got up to a tummy-settling breakfast of fresh croissants. We had planned a day of sightseeing—but the owls still would not let me alone. As we headed on foot toward the Picasso museum and the Marais district via an astonishingly beautiful array of tree-lined avenues, we walked down rue Bonaparte. Owl sculptures and owl tapestries dotted the windows of the galleries that approached the École des Beaux-Arts. Jenny stopped in front of a shop named Le Chat Huant and demanded a translation—The Hooting Cat—a medieval French name for "owl" that probably derived from the fact that owls can look and sound a little like cats. When perched, the owl's silhouette and demeanour can appear feline, especially those owls with cat-like feather tufts that stand up like two pointed ears. This appearance is no accident: the owl evolved its ear tufts to resemble predatory mammals in order to protect itself and frighten off other predators and competitors, including other owls during threat displays. At night the owl's hooting can sound unsettlingly like the sound cats make during amorous encounters and territorial battles. This resemblance to cats has not escaped many peoples and cultures: a common local name for owls in Finland is *kissapöllö*, which means literally "cat-owl." In Costa Rica a common name for owl is *cara del gato* (cat-face).

The window of Le Chat Huant was bright with exquisitely painted fingernail-sized pottery owl totems. We resisted the shopping opportunity, crossed the river (passing the Tawny portrait once more), and headed for the Marais district. In the rue des Archives my attention was arrested by the Musée de la Chasse et de la Nature. I left Jenny and my mother Shirley, who both needed second breakfast, and with them seated happily in a café I paid my eight euros and entered one of the strangest interiors I have ever seen. Multiple wood-panelled rooms housed animal-themed exhibit after exhibit, from tapestries to stuffed wolves, boars, and bronze antlers growing out of the ceiling. The owl room, however, was guarded by the imposing face of a yellow-eyed Snowy Owl. Lined with deep billows of green silk, this dark installation was conceived as a homage to Diana, goddess protector of night and of hunting. The uncannily feathered ceiling had assembled six spooky, feather-surrounded owl heads. The effect was that the whole appeared to be swamping the onlooker from above, a giant amalgamated feathered body with huge owl faces staring down, their porcelain eyes shining, disturbing and semi-human.

Recently, patches of feathers had been mysteriously disappearing from the exhibit. Flemish artist Jan Fabre had to be called back to repair the naked patches. No human could have reached up to steal the feathers, the curator told me. In the end it was found to be *acariens des plumes*: feather mites! The mystery was solved. The installation had to be carefully repaired by the artist with feathers that were less prone to attack, and treated to make sure that there would be no repeat of the offending bald patches.

In the first room of the Picasso museum in rue de Thorigny it dawned on me that as well as women, goats, and bulls it turned out that Pablo Picasso had an intense attachment to owls. They were everywhere. In 1947 Michel Sima took a striking black-and-white picture of Picasso holding—guess what—his pet Little Owl. I used to live in France, and I visited these museums; how could I have forgotten all about this fascination? In the photo Picasso fondly holds his owl, named Ubu, cupped in one hand. He shows his pet to the camera as a proud owner, a look of tenderness around his brown eyes that renders his face rounded and owl-like.

The story goes that Ubu had been found after he had become injured at the Chateau Grimaldi museum. He had broken his leg but fortunately the practical Picasso knew exactly how to fix it with a splint. Following the owl's recuperation, he was kept in a cage in Picasso's kitchen, where he was well fed on house mice, and became a kind of muse for the artist. A great number of owl ceramics, pottery jugs, plates and vases, photographs, and paintings featuring the owl ensued. A pair of Little Owls decorated a brass vase; owls peeped out from corners of the gallery, guarded doorways, and watched over arches with a far from cute, slightly bleak, and often threatening air, as if they captured all the moods of the artist. And he captured theirs, entered into their owl world, portraying their myth, indifference, aloofness, their concern only with one thing: the capture and dispatch of prey. It strikes me that this might be one truth about Picasso's genius and his ideas, but also the truth about owls: their gaze lacks concern for the human world, always looking through or past us, and so we perceive them to be neutral, a canvas upon which we can impose our stories.

I went back to look at the photo of Ubu. In the Sima photograph of the artist, three monochrome forms, like inverted teardrops, created a harmonious trio. The central teardrop, the actual owl, held close to the man's large-eyed, owl-shaped face on the right, drew attention to the striking similarity of the eyes. Then there was the third: only just out of focus on the left was the self-portrait as an owl with its piercing vision loitering in the background. It was almost as if we were seeing into the artist's mind, the symbolic owl making manifest an inner and an outer wisdom, its sharp-eyed gaze staring out from beneath brows that were darkly precise and yet familiar. In another painting, *Le Hibou de la Mort*, 1952, Picasso even traced his own name, begun with a cryptic "P" hidden within the owl's wing.

THE DAY BEFORE the wedding we visited Christine and Marianne's house in their village outside Paris, and right inside the front door, on the sideboard, somebody had left the barred primary feather of an owl. I saw it as soon as I walked in. Immediately I picked it up to scrutinise it: *"Une chevéche,"* Christine told me. A Little Owl.

I stared at it, no longer astounded by the flood of coincidence. She saw the pair most nights, she told me, perched on the rooftop opposite in her street. That night in our hotel deep in the French countryside I vividly dreamt again of being alone in the house with a tame Little Owl. This time it perched in my kitchen, bathed in a bowl of water, and ravenously hungry, called repeatedly to be fed.

The next day was the wedding. Christine and Marianne stood side by side looking preened and immaculate. Around her dark brown curls I could see that Christine was trembling. I signed the witness papers as we watched our friends shyly acknowledge their love and commitment. Finally with this ceremony we were allowed to witness them, celebrate seeing them openly after all these years. We stood in a wide, appreciative semicircle of family and emotion. Christine's mother was not there, nor was one sister. But another sister was, coincidentally named Myriam, and afterwards she clasped me appreciatively. We all applauded while the Beatles rang out with "All You Need Is Love." I didn't want the moment to end. Suddenly knowing that we had gained a new family, waiting outside the village hall for the music and dancing to begin, I bent down to pick up another darkly barred primary feather.

I tucked it into the smooth card of my wedding invitation and slid it in my bag. Later, as we sleepily looked at the feather in our hotel after the festivities, I decided there was something special about it. It was deeper gold than the feathers of the Barn Owls at home, and darker brown, with a slate-grey tip. It could have been the continental species *Tyto alba guttata*, the Dark-breasted Barn Owl. There are plenty of them around, Christine told me later, her arm sweeping over the view of sun-kissed fields, drying sunflowers, apple orchards and small farms.

Tyto alba guttata is found in France but does not generally occur naturally in the UK. In fact, it has been found from southern Sweden (where now it is thought it might be extinct) through Denmark, the Netherlands, Germany, Poland, western Russia, Austria, Hungary, Switzerland, and Bulgaria. The birds are variable in appearance but classically *guttata* are generally the dark twin of our "common" or "white-breasted" *Tyto alba*. They have deep, richly buff underparts that can appear as a complete covering of gold rather than the white front, legs, and undertail coverts of *Tyto alba*. *Alba* sometimes has buff tints over the upper breast and sometimes even the lower, but the buff in *guttata* is encompassing and always extends over the feathered tarsi, or legs, and over the undertail coverts. *Guttata* is often clearly speckled on the breast, the speckles often extending all the way down the tummy. Any bird showing a contrast between dark breast and pale underbelly is not true *guttata*.

The face is different too: the buff colour is visible as a dark surround radiating in the facial disc of *guttata*, particularly around the eyes, giving it a strikingly shadowy, smudged purple-brown mascara look. Females may appear even darker here than males. A key feature of a classic *guttata* is the abundance of silvery grey marbling on the crown and back or "scapulars," and this can extend to the primary flight feathers which have clear grey tips, and their bold dark barring extends all the way across the feather on the outer primaries, a pattern which is not usually found in *Tyto alba*. However, the distinction between the two is not always clear: a 500-kilometre-wide transition area has been identified across Europe where *alba* and *guttata* interbreed, birthing young that are "intergrades" between the two, making identification challenging.

Would we ever see one of these lovely specimens in Britain? A female *guttata* did breed in East Anglia in 2008, and it is thought that vagrant *guttata* have been found in the parts of Britain closer to the Continent, mostly in East Anglia, but how many there might be is not confirmed. In any case, the warmer, drier climate here in France just south of Paris, coupled with the rich patchwork of farmsteads, meadows, orchards, and woodland edges, is an ideal habitat for many owls, most especially Barn Owls, but also Tawnies and Little Owls, far better than the rainswept, unpredictable, and intensively farmed conditions in south-west England. Christine tells me that she has seen Long-eared Owls here in the protected forest around the chateau, and Eagle Owls can sometimes turn up. As for the Barn Owls, it is the dark kind she often sees, she tells me, but whether it is mostly *guttata* or an intergrade around here, we cannot be sure. The feather, I check later, has a faint grey tip: I think it is *guttata*.

"CAN WE HAVE an owl?" Benji asked me again when we returned home and I showed him my pictures of Ubu, Picasso's owl. We went to visit Flitwick again, the rescued Little Owl that lives in the animal sanctuary nearby.

"I really don't think they make good pets."

Pete, who works at the sanctuary, showed us Lady Jane Grey, his Great Grey Owl. The difference in size between the two species was outrageous. The Great Grey is 70 centimetres tall, the Little Owl around 20 centimetres. Lady Jane blinked, somewhere deep in her gizzard a crush of bone and skull compressing. She could have squashed Flitwick like a ripe blackberry. Being ladylike doesn't mean anything in owldom. Flitwick looked at us with indifference. About the size of a songbird, she seemed to have no idea how tiny she was.

Benji spent a large amount of time stroking Flitwick with the back of his index finger. For him, the owl conceded and closed her eyes. Did she enjoy the contact? She could simply be reacting to the preening by protecting her eyes, fearful, or hoping for food. Her closed eyelids were soft and feathered.

"You should come to Owl Club," Pete encouraged. "There's usually an owl going."

I felt Benji's ears prick up.

"Owls are wild," I said as we walked home. "We can't have one."

But still, that inter-species contact with Flitwick had left him enthralled, as if the alien, aloof animal was showing him some acceptance. And even if she was just resigned, it still felt like a privilege, as if we'd been singled out for company by a creature that seems so perfect, so well evolved, so self-contained, that they are usually reluctant to allow us anything. Perhaps that's the wild-animal effect. They don't need us, they don't want us, so when they allow us to get close, consciously or unconsciously, it feels precious, exhilarating. It brings us into the present, into the perfect moment, time outside time when beings can just be. And owls are the most stunning example of this. Watch people's faces light up when they get close to one, captive or otherwise. The effect is entrancing.

A LITTLE OWL had been calling in the old apple orchard near my home. At least I thought it must be a Little Owl. We stopped one evening to listen, the dog looking up at us, curious. An eerie truncated hoot, deeper than that of a female Tawny Owl, was ringing around the apple trees, rising at the end of its note with a questioning, melancholy air. Tawny calls are so distinctive, usually the *kee-wick!* shriek of the female and the *hu-hooo* reply of the male. But this was clearly a different owl. "Keeooow," it said. "Keeooow." I tuned in my ears, acclimatised to the mournful phrase. It floated, repeating like a question thrown out into the dusk.

When I searched for a Little Owl expert, straight away Dr. Emily Joáchim, who had just completed her doctorate on Little Owls, popped up. Here was the Little Owl advocate behind the Twitter handle I had found: @UKLittleOwls. Emily began the UK Little Owl Project because Little Owls have declined by 65 per cent in the UK in just twenty-five years. There is so much we do not know about this declining species. To research and preserve it, Emily invites people to record their Little Owl sightings nationally as part of her project. The project is an inspired piece of joined-up thinking: the kind that brings together citizen science and academic research in order to rescue a species. Without the countrywide fund of information Emily was collecting we might never find out what it is that is causing this wonderful owl to vanish.

"The owls are disappearing and we don't know why," she tells me. "It could be climate change or something else—we don't yet know—but in all likelihood it could be for a number of different reasons such as habitat changes, increased insecticide use, and more competition for nest sites and food."

Emily has researched breeding biology since 2008 (Little Owls have a habit of nesting in unusual places, as I had discovered: rabbit burrows, piles of rubble, stone walls, derelict buildings). She has studied dispersal behaviour, diet, and feeding behaviour, and crucially has set up nest-box cameras, and recorded video footage. Year on year, working with other experts, including the photographer Andy Rouse, she is learning more about Little Owl ecology. By looking at long-term data sets, monitoring individual pairs, and linking their breeding productivity with habitat, she may soon know more than anyone about this small predator.

Little Owls in this country, it appears, are often attracted to equestrian centres and riding stables. The mixed grazing, mature trees, hedges, and horse dung all provide good habitat and feeding. Emily's study of Little Owls has been centred across south Wiltshire, for example in Tytherington just south of the Salisbury Plain, where a few pairs have been attracted to nest. Loss of mixed farmland with hedgerows, long and short grass, and a sharp decline in insects due to the use of pesticides are thought to have hastened the Little Owl's disappearance. But here, where there is a healthy mixture of grazing, hedges, and mature trees, as well as long fences with many posts and nearby heaps of fly-attracting dung (even though Emily tells me they have significantly declined in Wiltshire), I know I am more likely to see a Little Owl.

"We were down to ten breeding pairs in our boxes in 2017, from twenty-three pairs in 2000," Emily informs me with some concern. She has been tirelessly spreading the word about the mysterious decline of the Little Owl with her research work and her talks, as well as a particularly fabulous website, littleowlproject.uk, dedicated to Little Owl research and conservation in the UK. The sharing of information is always crucial with this kind of project, and needing to see a big picture, other experts and enthusiasts have joined together and compared their research findings. "With similar work in other counties, such as Little Owl nest-box projects run by Bob Danson in Lancashire, Alan Ball and Bob Sheppard in Lincolnshire, Vincent and Gary Cartwright in Oxfordshire, and Roy Leigh in Cheshire to name but a few, we regularly contact each other to share our Little Owl news and to do the best we can for them," Emily emphasises, showing how truly this work is a joint effort.

Her Little Owl Project website is peopled with Andy Rouse's exquisite images of this highly photogenic, defiant-looking bird. Catching on, local landowners have joined the crusade and put up hundreds of nest boxes. "You can't just put a nest box anywhere," Emily tells me. "Little Owls, like Barn Owls, are creatures of habit and extremely site-loyal. You have to put up a nest box where you know there is a Little Owl, otherwise it will be a waste of everybody's time."

And it's not always easy to know where the Little Owls are. There's an element of mystery about them due to their mainly nocturnal behaviour. But hearing a Little Owl (and verifying the call correctly) counts as a sighting, says Emily, and so I could register my sighting and the calling owl I heard on the database on her website. There appear to be far fewer Little Owls in the west of England now, and this needs to be investigated. My evidence would be useful, and this kind of sighting is often shared between county bird groups. It strikes me how apt it is that hearing an owl counts as much as seeing one, as owls themselves rely on their "earsight" for locating prey during their nocturnal forays. But how does this "earsight" work?

The owl's sense of hearing is prodigious due to astonishing adaptations within the structure of its ear. Part an owl's feathers and you'll see not the usual small round opening that most birds have but large half-moon-shaped vertical slits. These are very deep and the outer ear is wide enough to insert a fingertip into (not that you would want to). The slits are surrounded by the stiff feathers of the facial disc, and skin flaps or conchae can be erected at will to capture and funnel sound. The inner ear of the owl also makes a big difference: it is large enough to contain many more nerve cells than most birds. All this aural dexterity enables owls to scan parts of their surroundings in the same way that some mammals can move their external ears. This, combined with its asymmetrically placed ears, means the owl can locate and pinpoint the exact position of its prey even beneath thick snow or in total darkness. It isn't that the owl can see in the dark; it is that with a combination of knowledge of its surroundings, acute visual acuity in low light, and its extreme sensitivity to sound, the owl can bob its head and create a mental map to help it locate its prey. Earsight.

I COULDN'T BELIEVE, with people like Emily working to promote this small owl, that it would be allowed to vanish. "Every encounter with them is exciting," she enthused to me. "Their wonderful frowning expressions and quirky behaviour—especially the way they run about and hunt on foot like a little person—makes it a pleasure to observe them, whether it's watching them sunbathe on a warm summer afternoon, or quietly hunting at dusk."

In the interests of conservation science, Emily has monitored the entire breeding cycle of these owls, recording the most intimate scenes with nest cams. From mating to egg laying, hatching, and fledging, with all the thrills and spills in between.

"The owls begin to breed in mid to late April," Emily told me. "I'm always amazed at how brave and hardworking the parents are when rearing their young. The mother incubates the hatchlings almost continuously for their first five days. At this point they're covered in white down and their eyes are closed. They can't thermo-regulate so they rely on their mother to keep them warm, and huddle up together if she briefly leaves the nest site. The father owl does most of the hunting at this stage. He hunts mainly at dusk and during the night, and slows down at dawn. They are extremely devoted, with the male flying in and out of the box continually with prey items whilst the mother does most of the provisioning."

When I met Emily she was giving a talk to a group of enthusiasts, and she showed pictures and video footage of the nest boxes. Little Owls readily nest in these specially designed boxes, but each must be placed high enough and the nest opening must be small enough to prevent predators from entering. The females lay their clutches of nearly spherical white eggs on consecutive days; they can lay up to six or seven, although on average will lay only three or four. After hatching, in a few days we can see the juveniles begin to try to stand on their talons, but they remain very wobbly at this stage and can only walk a few steps. When juveniles are seven days old, their down changes from white to pale grey and they start to look like proper owlets. Their talons and tarsi (ankles) are continuing to develop and they are a bit steadier on their feet now. The mother has to hunt more to keep up with the juveniles' increasing food demand, and prey items might include moths, amphibians, worms, small mammals, and small birds such as sparrows and other finches. One birdwatcher who lived close to the seashore claimed they impacted on populations of little terns, and a farmer found a nest site covered in the legs of skylarks. Little Owls are also thought by some to benefit from all sorts of carrion, although generally this is not believed to be the case, but they will often take ground beetles—the floor of one Little Owl nest box that I inspected whilst working with the Barn Owl Trust contained exclusively many hundreds of beetle cases.

To demonstrate one of the threats to Little Owls, Emily showed the group a dramatic video. In it a camera showed the female in the nest with her four white eggs. A Barn Owl flew in and somehow squeezed itself along the narrow tunnel and through to the small nest box. The cornered mother Little Owl rose up and fought fiercely to defend her eggs, and the larger owl (which looked at least three times the size) retreated, causing a shiver of sympathy and relief amongst Emily's audience. But it got worse: just as it seemed they were safe, the Barn Owl returned a week later when the young had hatched. Again, the female Little Owl bravely defended her young from the attack of the much larger owl, but unfortunately this time he took one chick and injured another. Emily told the startled audience that two chicks survived to fledge, miraculously, a testament to the fortitude and sturdy parenting of this tiny owl.

Mark Avery, writer, environmentalist, and former conservation director for the THE ROYAL SOCIETY FOR THE PROTECTION OF BIRDS, has pointed out that because Little Owls are an introduced species they are not always popular with NGO charities, nor are they on the International Union for Conservation of Nature (IUCN) green, amber, or red lists that categorise the conservation status of species. If they were, Avery suggests in his blog entry "Little owls—would you miss them?," they would be amber listed (declining) and possibly heading for red (threatened). In response to his blog, other enthusiasts have contended that the Little Owl may be present but simply going unrecorded, and in places like South Leicestershire and the Huntingdonshire fens they may be locally more common than is thought. However, as Emily points out, overall, they have been assessed as in "rapid decline" by the British Trust for Ornithology (BTO): "So we do need a new survey. There may be hot spots, but we need more information!"

This may be the case, but as a farmland bird they will be as vulnerable to changes in farming practices and the use of pesticides and rodenticides and other chemical interventions as the next bird. One serious issue may be the loss of nest sites as mature trees die off and are not replaced. Equally, as with the Barn Owls, many nesting sites in old agricultural buildings are falling into disrepair and not being replaced with anything useful to owls. In order to give a helping hand, the Barn Owl Trust and Nicholas Watts at Vine House Farm in South Lincolnshire (of Vine House Farm Bird Foods, a two-time recipient of the Silver Lapwing award for farming and conservation), have pioneered the construction of "bird buildings." These are tall towers that are suitable for tree sparrows, bats, and other wildlife but have large enough nest holes for Barn Owls, Little Owls, stock doves, and kestrels. If these wildlife-friendly buildings would catch on, some of the threatened birds and wildlife struggling to survive in our farmland might stand more of a chance and even begin to thrive.

Part of the charm of this diminutive predator, I think, is that though it may be tiny, it has charisma. The poet Mary Oliver captured some of the reason why it is so charismatic when she wrote that it is not its stature but its powerful energy, a "surge" that puts us in touch with something visceral, and real.

)

I TELL BENJI that we have a special person coming to stay in our house.

"Is it an owl? It's an owl, isn't it!"

I have his complete attention. It is indeed an owl who is coming to stay with us. Until now, I have been wary of looking after captive birds. An owl is the essence of wildness. Domesticated, what is left? Is it ever OK to keep these animals for our own uses? Tame—or as tame as an owl can be—their ankles tethered with jesses, their musculature weakened, trained to perform for the pleasure of humans, to me they can appear as sad as the captive dolphins that at one time were kept in tanks and used to perform for entertainment. Taken out of their context, away from the woods and fields and wild places, away from their hiding places and their seasons, devoid of their nesting and territories, what was left? Isolated and ungainly, they seem freakish, sad. Benji knows this argument and we have been over it together. How could a tame bird be anything like those in the wild, and what use will studying one be to me, anyway? What would it tell me more than I already know about wild animals being kept in captivity?

Perhaps that was the whole point. It might tell me something. Even if it was simply to confirm my opinions. But Benji's excitement told me to open my mind; his childlike enthusiasm was teaching me to be curious in spite of my misgivings. And curiosity, after all, was what this quest was about.

The question mills around my head as we spend the morning cleaning and tidying together. We do this not because having a neat house will make any difference—nothing about the inside of our house will make any sense to the owl—but because in spite of myself I simply cannot sit still.

Our visitor is named Murray. He is a captive Burrowing Owl, and if that sounds as though it isn't a real species please think again. Murray (named after the British tennis champion) is *Athene cunicularia*, a species native to the Americas, and very closely resembles our European Little Owl. I asked my friend Mike Toms, owl expert from the BTO, to help me understand why this resemblance existed, and he patiently explained that following recent taxonomic work, the Burrowing Owl and the Little Owl, from opposite sides of the Atlantic Ocean, are now in the same genus—because *Athene cunicularia* and *Athene noctua* share a (relatively) recent common ancestor. Depending on which source you read there are now thought to be between four and seven species in this genus, and there may be even more. So they resemble one another because they are closely related, rather than because of convergent evolution (where two unrelated species end up looking similar because they are being shaped by the same evolutionary pressures, just in different places). Somewhere way back, continental drift separated the species, eventually producing several different *Athenes*. When this could have happened is known only to deep time, as far as I can see, as continental separation was happening between 200 and 100 million years ago.

I rush to my photographic bible, *Owls of the World* by Heimo Mikkola. Although owl taxonomy is even now still in flux, and new species are still being identified (the Northern Little Owl and the Grey-bellied Little Owl were only identified in 1988), it looks as though all the *Athenes* we currently know about are in there. There they are, staring crossly out of page after page: the Burrowing Owl, *Athene cunicularia*, from the Americas; *Athene noctua*, the Little Owl, from Eurasia ("There are possibly over ten subspecies within the *Athene noctua* genus alone!" Emily told me); the beautifully pale Lilith Owl, *Athene lilith*, found from southern Turkey and Cyprus to Israel, Sinai, and the Arabian peninsula; the Ethiopian Little Owl, *Athene spilogaster*, found only on the western coast of the Red Sea from eastern Sudan to northern Somalia; the Grey-bellied Little Owl, *Athene poikilis*, so far found only in the West Sichuan Province in China; the Northern Little Owl, *Athene plumipes*, from the Russian Altai to Mongolia and parts of China; and *Athene brama*, the Spotted Little Owl or "Spotted Owlet" in India and South East Asia whose earth-brown crown is so brightly spotted with speckles of white it looks as if it has been paint-flicked with a glittery toupee of tiny stars. Some of these have several subspecies, and as Mikkola points out, the entire group of *Athene* is still in need of further taxonomic study. Exciting PhD or postdoctoral research with global travel opportunities, anyone? I feel tempted, as I do each and every time I open this delight of a book, but someone somewhere is probably on it, as we speak.

Spread south to north all the way across the Americas, our Burrowing Owl normally inhabits the deserts, savannahs, pine scrubs, pampas, and plains from Tierra del Fuego and extreme south Argentina to a swathe of the western United States. There is even an isolated population in Florida. There are not any actual Burrowing Owls in Europe, nor anywhere else outside the Americas. Not in the wild, at least. We have only the Little Owl, and between the distant cousins lies a huge sweep of Atlantic Ocean. In its behaviour and characteristics, though, there appears to be a kind of memory of distant ancestry.

Unaware of any of this, Murray the Burrowing Owl was bred from captive parents in a special owl-breeding centre in Cheshire, England. As the taxonomic name suggests, *Athene cunicularia* is the most terrestrial of all the owl species, and like the Little Owl it often runs after ground-dwelling prey on its athletic little legs. But there is a key difference. The Burrowing

Owl doesn't make its nest on the ground amongst roots or tree stumps like the Little Owl; it nests *underground. Cunicularia* is derived from the Latin *cunicularius,* meaning "miner," or "burrower." This clever Little Owl is able to excavate all by itself, but for ease it usually sequesters spare chambers in the burrows of mammals such as prairie dogs and rabbits. In the US, faced with humans encroaching ever further into its territory, the Burrowing Owl has opted for the pragmatic approach and adapted to inhabit man-made areas: it can be found living on golf courses, in cemeteries, at airports, on pastureland and agricultural land, as well as moving in to nest in urban parks, on people's drives, and even in their gardens. Adaptable and resilient, it stands lookout on mounds of excavated earth and resembles our Little Owl almost perfectly, only a slightly more vigilant-looking, upright version. It stands up tall and straight, 19 to 25 centimetres tall, with a wingspan of 50 to 60 centimetres and a weight of around 140 grams (although females can be a good deal heavier than males, sometimes weighing up to 250 grams); its vital statistics are all similar to those of the Little Owl.

One look at its features and you can see why it has been grouped by taxonomists along with *Athene noctua.* But there are some subtle differences. The Burrowing Owl has slightly longer, lankier-looking, more sparsely feathered legs. Its upright stance perhaps evolved to look out for stealthy ground-dwelling threats such as the egg-gobbling, chick-swallowing rattlesnake; in a sandy environment it appears to behave the same way as the on-the-alert standing to attention of meerkats. The familiar small-owl stare is almost identical to that of our Little Owl, however, and it emanates from the same piercing lemon eyes set beneath a prominence of seriously frowning white brows, all evolved no doubt to threaten and deter ferocious terrestrial predators.

In the dark burrow of his travelling box aboard the Virgin train that right now was rushing south towards us, Murray's bright eyes would be softly closed in sleep. Nothing but the best for Murray: to minimise disturbance to passengers, and also to avoid the shock of any loud noise that might distress his sensitive ears, he always travels first class.

On the phone I ask his keeper, Anita Morris, whether chicken casserole will be OK for supper?

"That'd be lovely, we both eat chicken," she tells me.

I make some mental adjustments. Will Murray be flying about while we eat? He might perch on the back of a chair at the table. Benji is too thrilled for words.

Parts of a day-old chick lie in the dark alongside Murray in his box as offerings just in case he wakes up hungry. The box has been made especially for him on his commute, for Murray is a working owl. More specifically, a therapy owl. He works with Anita and goes to raise awareness about birds of prey, to help the sick, visit the isolated, and educate the young. Today he is travelling all the way from Widnes in Cheshire, watched over by Anita. I find myself feeling honoured that they are coming, and both Benji and I pace about and fidget restlessly as if a celebrity or film star is about to arrive.

But Murray *is* a celebrity. He has his own Twitter handle and regularly tweets as Murray the Owl. A book for children has been written about him entitled *Murray the Smallest Owl*. Anita sent me a copy. Without wanting to give away any spoilers, the aim of the story is to depict and help with the feelings a very small person might experience in a world of an awful lot of big, noisy, clever, capable people. In the story, Murray (played by himself, in delightful photographs) feels very small. He wonders how he can possibly be of any use when everybody else appears so big, strong, and capable. What can I say? We've all been there at some point in our lives. I remember some particularly scary maths lessons when I was about eleven years old. How I wish Murray had been there to sit on my shoulder and tell that terrified little girl that it was OK to say that I felt confused, and instead of feeling worthless, and enduring that gnawing sense of failure, to remind me that actually there were plenty of other things that I was good at.

"The book is designed to help build children's self-esteem," Murray's handler Anita explains. By identifying with little Murray and his moments of self-doubt, it helps young people towards self-awareness and self-confidence about their own talents and capabilities, however small they may feel. I think it's about compassion, and self-compassion. It seems to me that this kind of emotional intelligence is exactly what we need right now. In schools, on buses, in businesses; everywhere. Anita's work is tapping into something we all need. When I tried her book out on Jenny I noticed her eyes quietly well up in recognition. Another seventeen-year-old, Caroline, read it, and it had exactly the same effect. I think the book will be a hit. It seems to help us remember to be more human. I feel like suggesting there should be one for grownups, too.

Anita is a psychologist and director of Hack Back cic, an innovative social enterprise that helps improve the mental health and well-being of people of different abilities, ages, and backgrounds but, groundbreakingly, by using birds of prey. Having trained as a psychologist and with her research into emotional intelligence in business management, Anita became a life coach, but a coach with a difference. She and Murray work in schools, care homes, hospices, and secure mental health units. Together Anita and Murray work as ambassadors, their pioneering work raising awareness of the benefits of combining psychological therapies with birds of prey interaction. This area of psychology is new: golden eagles can be used in leadership and management training; falconry can help bring autistic young people out of themselves; and Anita uses owls to work on people's emotional understanding. Conquering one's fear, maintaining a positive regard for the creature, trying to earn its trust, not taking advantage of it, and learning to respect its animal otherness are all things that can help people's well-being, empathy, creativity, and happiness.

Our plan for now is simple: that Murray, Anita, and I will spend some time together in Plymouth collaborating with Eloise Malone, creative director at Effervescent, a social enterprise charity in the city, and a group of children. We will be working in the Radiant Gallery, a space that curates exhibitions with children, and I will watch what happens. I'm fascinated to see how Anita works with the children and how they will react to Murray: if they can learn something from their time with him, if they can benefit, and what the outcome might be.

Before we can do this, however, we have to get Anita and Murray's bedroom ready for their arrival, and above all make sure to firmly shut our very predatory cat Malinki in the kitchen.

Later, after we have all settled, enjoyed the chicken casserole, and had some wine, Murray is perched atop the back of a chair, and the forgotten door creaks open. Malinki saunters into the room, tail up, all innocent, and the teacup-sized Murray turns into a puffed-up flagon, all staring eyes and angry chirps. The cat freezes in surprise, and with both of them rigid as bristle brushes I pick her up and rush her back into the kitchen. Benji sits with us after supper and we talk. He dons the glove and holds Murray. As the conversation flows I notice out of the corner of my eye that Benji has his face very close to Murray. He is very gently scratching him on the cere of his bill and Murray has tipped his head to one side and closed his eyes.

"Goodness, I didn't know he liked that." Anita looks touched and thrilled all at once.

This isn't the first time I've noticed that Benji has a gift for finding a creature's friendly spot. He has a way with animals; if there's a frog to be rescued, a spider to be ousted, a stray chicken to be rescued from a high branch and placed back in the hen house, or a nervous horse to be beckoned, Benji is usually the one to step in.

Benji and Murray quickly develop a rapport, despite the fact that, in the account of his life with owls, *The House of Owls*, naturalist Tony Angell describes how the Burrowing Owl was the species he found to be least amenable to human company. Once one was rescued and brought to him, and he described it inside its unopened box as a "demented gnome," which in spite of being fed and looked after, turned into a wild dynamo and would never come to tolerate him. The Burrowing Owl, he concludes, is used to rugged desert life and shares territory with rattlesnakes, badgers, and coyotes; a human is just another untrustworthy creature. When the owl escaped it jammed itself in a dark nook behind the bookcase and refused to come out. Angell prised it out and built it an enclosure, but again the owl did what Burrowing Owls do and disappeared into the dark. When he needed to check its safety, Angell made the mistake of sinking his arm into the artificial cavity only to be met with a spine-prickling imitation of a rattlesnake, a sound so convincing that he instinctively whipped his arm back out, afraid to try again.

Just like the Little Owl in its natural habitat, the Burrowing Owl is in decline as agriculture and human settlements expand. Herbicides and pesticides are a threat in America in the same way as they are in Britain, destroying the bird's natural prey, building up at the top of the food chain, and weakening the owl's system. It all sounds very familiar. As with all the other owls, raising awareness through education could help, such as the placing of nest boxes where the owls can be protected but also observed by interested visitors. Watching birds is good for mental health, the research tells us: it reduces anxiety, stress, and depression and builds a well-being connection that might remain for life. Dr. Daniel Cox, who led a research study on the links between birds and human well-being, found that interacting with birds provides health benefits, particularly for urban dwellers. The research, published in the journal *Bioscience* in 2017, suggests that bird–human interactions are potentially of great value. And the value is for the birds as well as for humans: we'll truly work to protect and preserve something we recognise and have come to know and love.

ANITA GETS MURRAY out of his box in the city gallery where we are working with an assembled circle of children. There is a collective gasp. Such is the delight and amazement, it is as if we have thrown the windows open and snow is suddenly falling inside the room.

Murray stands in this enchanted globe of wonder and swivels his head around, checking out each and every one of us.

Outside, in the ordinary world beyond the tall windows, the odd bus or taxi rumbles past, pedestrians and shoppers shuffle up and down the street, but inside, here, there is magic. One moment there was a black travelling case, with mysterious holes for air to get in that you couldn't see through: the next minute the little door creaked open and like a celebrity, out scuttled Murray the Burrowing Owl.

Amidst our wonderment, all soft speckles and brown feathers and bright eyes, quite reptilian, he runs on his bony little legs, his talons tippety-tapping with his ankle-bracelet jesses trailing on the polished wooden floor. The children hold their breath in adoration.

The owl commands the space. The aura of awe holds our circle that is no longer an ordinary circle but an owl-circle.

Then, very quietly—they have been told that Murray's hearing is sensitive—they begin to fill the bubble of silence with murmurs. In soft little bursts, we speak of how small he is, how beautiful and perfect he is, and at the same time how fierce-looking. Those eyes! Nothing escapes them. And in the echoing space of the gallery every sound, every minute movement and rustle must crash into those feathered listening devices. We all want to reach out and touch, but we know from Anita that he may not want to be stroked, and we must respect that. There is a defiance in his stance, perhaps a remnant of the visceral wildness that Angell saw in his rescued Burrowing Owl when it hissed like a maddened rattlesnake at him.

Murray stands to attention, and we gaze. Perhaps in that moment we all recognise a connection with him: he too has come here from somewhere else; he is an outsider. He might be nervous. And so we must not frighten him. We must help him feel welcome, safe, and trusting.

Anita works with the children to bring them to an understanding of how we must be around Murray, how we must restrain our desire to pick him up: and so, taking turns, we are each allowed to wear the falconry glove that Murray has been trained to fly to. One by one each child is allowed contact with him. Faces light up, breath is held: each of us invites Murray to the glove. When he flies up there is pure delight, joy even, but also intense curiosity; a child face-to-face with an owl. The weight of him, his jittery, feathered presence so close.

What do we notice about Murray? He is very small and light; he might be nervous.

"Like me!" Lee suddenly declares, smiling. "He is like me!"

One by one the children have small epiphanies.

"He's not how I thought he would be," David says.

And Murray with his irascible, odd little personality, becomes a coach to help us feel something about ourselves.

"How can we help him to be relaxed?"

"We can speak to him nicely!"

"What can we say to Murray to help him to feel calm?" Anita asks.

"Good boy!"

"Well done, Murray, you're being brave."

"He can't understand what we're saying, but it makes us feel good to tell him," Anita says. "And he knows he'll get a reward."

"He can hear my heartbeat. He knows how I'm feeling," Jessica says.

"How can we get Murray to trust us?" Anita asks.

We play a game in which Murray has been trained to fetch a small cloth mouse and put it in a box. He gets a reward each time he does it right. When the children get too excited, Anita says: "We give the owl some time to recover when he's overwhelmed."

Murray goes back in his box for a little while. We are learning about empathy. And making connection. We are coming to terms with vulnerability. Ours, and the owl's. And the need for space, for kindness and understanding. Murray's and ours. It occurs to me that we are doing work that reconnects us, that draws us close against the bleak backdrop of the city and allows us to regain intimacy with ourselves, with one another. And together with this non-human friend, we are creating community.

After lunch Anita reads the children an owl story and for a while they loll on their cushions; listening, they go all dreamy, happy to absorb. The story is full of owl facts. The children are relaxed but attentive. Afterwards we quiz them on what they remember:

"Owls need to turn their heads right round, so they have extra vertebrae, and extra blood vessels to help their head swivel."

Everyone has been paying attention. "Not *all* the way round!"

"There's a horror film where a girl does that—her head spins around."

"And she throws up everywhere!"

"That's a horrid film called *The Exorcist*. You haven't seen it, have you?"

"No, but I heard about it."

Later, when Murray's shift is over and he is back in his box, it is home time. The delight and excitement are palpable. Suddenly the world is full of possibilities. The children go home ready for a new day when they will return and continue their work: they will begin to apply their new owl wisdom. Perhaps after all there is something to learn from a captive owl. He isn't living the life his species would in the wild, but he's been enriched in a different way, and has become an ambassador to help children learn empathy. Crossing the species border, the boundary line between ourselves and others, he has become a messenger to help us to think about equality and fairness. This little owl was teaching us consideration, to care for and respect community, and to be kind. In this, he's a little apostle of the future.

Asio otus

LONG-EARED OWL

"Long-eared Owls roost secretively in willow thickets"
RSPB diary

They hide their secrets
in willow baskets
that my grandmother has woven,
her fingers spindled,
like the twiggy legs of owls
under their brushed-fur feathers.

Orange-yellow eyes catch light
as they fall from the branches
into a long, slow arc of flight

oo—ooh—ooh they say
oo—ooh—ooh as their wings
beat deep and slow in the slow night.

—CAROLINE CARVER, "Secrets," from *Bone Fishing*

IF YOU ARE OUT IN THE WOODS ON A CALM SUMMER'S evening you might hear the soft *hoo* of the secretive Long-eared Owl. At Woodwalton Fen, a Cambridgeshire nature reserve where only two breeding records of Long-eared Owls existed, one spring several males had been heard calling. It was decided that there were perhaps not enough nesting sites for them. Long-eared Owls do not like to build their own nests, preferring to take over those of other birds—usually crows and magpies, but sparrowhawks and wood pigeons also find their nests taken over, and even squirrel dreys have been found occupied. Between 1981 and 1996 a study was conducted to attract more Long-eared Owl pairs to come and breed. Willow baskets, used successfully as artificial nests on the Continent, were provided for the lonely males. At Woodwalton they saved a bit of money by using fruit-pickers' baskets and dog baskets.

The ready-made nests were positioned where the males had been heard calling, and it did the trick. The owls took to the nests, but there was a problem. The new nesting pairs, their eggs and chicks, could not be easily observed due to the height of the baskets' rims. Extendable poles with mirrors attached were used, but these owls are especially sensitive when sitting on eggs, so could not be approached or even seen with binoculars to check how they were doing. A solution was found: new baskets were specially designed and at just 15 centimetres high, now the long ears of the nesting birds could be seen peeping over the basket rims (not real ears, of course, just their curvaceous, horn-like plumes that sprout upward to startle predators). This is what I love about ornithology: it is often a kind of make-do-and-mend operation, with some trial and error, but certainly with its heart in the right place.

The wicker-basket nests were regularly checked, and any unwanted grey squirrel lodgers with an eye for a cosy drey were evicted. Each year there were anything between three and twenty-three nest baskets available for the owls—inevitably, some nest trees fell down or baskets blew away. In the first year, nine nests were recorded as used, and over the fifteen years of the scheme, seventy-seven nests were used. About 50 per cent of the hatchlings that were recorded fledged, which probably counts as a success. But still, this shy owl is scarce in Britain, and very, very difficult to see.

Rock climbers have a rating system for the difficulty of an ascent: I think that if you do not know where the likely sites or roosts are, this system could also be a useful measure of owl watching. In climbing lore, depending on your skills and stamina, you might progress from a Moderate to a D for Difficult. The Long-eared Owl might just be the hardest owl to see in Britain, so I think we could deploy the more severe categories here, such as Extremely Difficult (ED). The north face of the Eiger in the Swiss Alps is ED2, for example. It was whilst searching for, and failing to find, the Long-eared Owl that I decided on this analogy.

The other owls might be placed at different points on the spectrum: Tawnies (Mod) draw attention to themselves by their conversational night-time hooting and their quiet roadside perching. Little Owls (Diff) like cats can sometimes be drawn from a hedge with a summoning "kiss," easy to produce especially if you own a cat. They both often live near to human habitations. Long-eared Owls (ED2), on the other hand, do not usually depend on human habitats—although as we've seen they can be tempted to inhabit artificial nesting sites, but even then, you might only see the tips of their ear tufts.

If you are very lucky you might catch a glimpse of this long-winged wraith as it emerges to hunt from deep within a copse of conifers, or you might witness it floating over the moors at dusk. If you know what to look for, you might notice the blunt, finely barred wing tips, the ochre-yellow tinge of the upper primary flight feathers, or see how its chocolate-and-cream patterning blends perfectly with the ground as it appears and disappears in the light and shadow of heath and moorland grasses. See how the pale belly is brown-streaked, the back finely speckled, the facial disc tinged with apricot, and how the long ear tufts can rise in alert as it alights on a post to perch. And those startling, jewel-like orange sapphire eyes as it turns to stare at you. All these would confirm its identification as the elusive Long-eared Owl. With its chameleon-like patterns in all shades of tree-bark brown, when motionless it can meld perfectly into any background of lichen-covered bark or dense foliage. Because it shares the woodland habitat of the Tawny and often feeds on the same prey, the two can come into conflict. The larger, bulkier Tawny is the Long-eared Owl's most effective competitor, and this might be why the Long-eared thrives more successfully in new-growth woodland such as thickly planted conifer plantations where the Tawny, who prefers to nest in the cavities of mature broad-leaved trees, is less common.

Being so elusive, this owl is often overlooked, and has not been as extensively studied as many other raptors. Consequently it is often under-recorded, but those who have looked into it, such as the Hawk and Owl Trust and the BTO, believe its numbers are declining, with between 2,000 and 3,500 pairs resident in summertime Britain. The European population is much larger, with somewhere between 250,000 and 400,000 pairs, so only 1 per cent of the population lives in Britain.

In autumn and winter, passage migrant owls can come from the Continent to feed in Britain, especially if food supplies (voles) have been in short supply. Some birds are known to come to the north-east coast of England from Scandinavia. The new arrivals can sometimes be seen flying in small groups and perching, tired and unwary, out in the open in broad daylight.

When the Long-eared Owl is perched, its face often has an angular, cat-like appearance. This is partly because when alert it usually has its tall ear tufts held erect, especially when it is threatened or alarmed. These ear tufts are nearly always visible, the exceptions being when the bird is in flight and they are laid flat, or when it is relaxed and the tufts gently subside. The owl can dramatically change its face shape to reach a tense, camouflage posture, and its jagged ear tufts, marbling, and texture can mimic the roughened surface of a Corsican pine. In flight its wings can seem to mimic all the colours in the mottled weave of winter bent grass, bleached fescue, and deer grass on the moor. When alarmed at its roost it can stiffen into a twig-like stance against the contours of a branch or tree trunk; at the approach of a perceived threat, it narrows its body and face and appears to solidify, relying on the blurring effects of its plumage to play tricks with the eye. Coupled with this, its silent, low, nervous flight often manifests as a shadow flitting across colours so close to its own it could be transparent. Its lack of vocalisations outside of breeding times make it almost impossible to locate by ear. Perhaps I could have waited for longer beside the communal winter roost in Norfolk, or searched harder for a random sighting over the edge of woodland on the quiet disused airfield in Dorset, or crept further into the dusk-misted pine woods of the Haldon Forest near my home in Devon. I could have visited Dave and Penny Green in East Sussex, who know more about Long-eared Owls in the south-east of England than almost anyone. But weary of stalking about on wet, cold, and fruitless winter nights, I no longer wanted to leave it to chance and followed a tip-off about an organised owl-viewing trip.

"Serbia?" Rick said.

I could see him mentally picturing armed police, gangs, and landmines.

I was sure all that was out of date. "It's OK," I said. "It's been safe to go there for decades. I won't be on my own. I'll be in a group."

Jenny steeled herself for a week or two of no lifts to school, and concerned that she would get cold and wet on her walk to school I bought her an extra-strong umbrella and some new gloves. Benji gazed at me with wholehearted approval, affectionately picturing many Long-eared Owls flying about my ears; his response turned out to be prophetic.

Having Benji at home with me while he recovered from his illness was turning out to be soothing for both of us. I could keep an eye on him, take him along with me, or rehearse my plans with him. I frequently ran my ideas past him about where I was going to look next, and he was always positive. Perhaps he was still secretly hoping I would come home with an owlet under my coat for him to care for—even though it was not breeding season, and despite the fact that even Murray hadn't changed my principles about keeping wild owls in captivity.

The diagnosis of non-epileptic seizure disorder, or NEAD, non-epileptic attack disorder, had left Benji adrift. One round of treatment had taken the form of some carefully structured counselling, but after it was over, we were none the wiser.

You could try anti-anxiety medication, or anti-depressants, the doctor suggested. But Benji did not seem depressed. Mentally he seemed OK, in spite of being disabled and out of work. Even though most of his friends had spread their wings and gone to college, he liked being at home, and had countered his isolation by developing a support network on social media. He joined a NEAD support group. He often chatted with his online gaming community, who regularly offered support and company, even contacting us by phone when Benji dipped out because he'd unexpectedly collapsed in a seizure. For now, it didn't feel right to drug him. We needed to find out more about what the triggers were for these collapses; we wanted to know what was at the bottom of it—more specifically, what was causing the seizures beyond what the doctors had labelled "psychological" and "stress-related" causes.

I wanted to take him with me to see the Long-eared Owls, but this trip was very ambitious, and potentially unsafe for him. For now, we erred on the side of caution, and Benji would stay at home with Rick.

As for finding the owls, I felt this time I was onto a winner. Tip-offs for birdwatchers sparkle as enticingly as nuggets in a gold pan, and this one was solid platinum. I knew it would be 100 per cent reliable because it came from People Who Knew: My birding friends, Ben Hoare at BBC *Wildlife Magazine*; ornithologist Mark Cocker, who had heard about it but not yet been to see; and above all, the Urban Birder, David Lindo. David was leading the expedition. Despite these solid credentials, the expedition was so unlikely sounding, the very last place I would have thought of to look. In previous years, Serbia had not had a good press, but David assured me that it was now quite safe to visit: the people were friendly and actively welcomed eco-tourism. David's contact on the ground, Milan, was trying to promote wildlife and birdwatching trips to help boost the ailing economy and raise the profile of Serbian wildlife. We'd be doing good, and owl sightings were guaranteed. And not just one sighting, which would have been magical, and would have been sufficient. No, this would be a multiple-sighting spectacular, a communal roost, at close range, in the wild. He would be taking me to see the largest-known gathering of Long-eared Owls in the world. We might see hundreds at once, and the website blurb confidently announced: "If you don't see an owl on this trip David will eat his binoculars . . . because it is officially the best place in the world to see Long-eared Owls."

Why the owls gather like this, I had yet to find out. Why would this normally solitary predator group come together in close proximity with a bunch of competitors? This trip was at the end of November; it would be just before the big freeze in Serbia. Were the owls gathering for warmth? Did communities form, with a pecking order or hierarchy, or were they arranged like penguins that pack together and regularly shuffle around so that each one gets a turn in the sheltered centre of the huddle? To find out, I would have to see this spectacular event for myself.

I looked on the website of Serbia.com and it told me that one year up to eight hundred owls had been reported gathering in a single town. I was almost too excited to sit still. David's website had close-up images of many owls seated together in their roosts. I pictured myself standing beneath owls arranged like bunches of fruit, like an owl-themed autumn festival. Although the trip was leaving in under a week and I was wary of the long journey, I knew it was one of those times you should just say yes. That space on the trip was me-shaped. But was Serbia really safe? I phoned my mum who is a veteran traveller to see what she thought. She always says exactly what she thinks and being my mum, I knew that she would object if she were worried for my safety.

"Look, just go," she said.

As soon as I was back at my desk, I clicked myself in, reserved my taxi, booked the train, sorted out the bus and plane tickets, and confirmed it excitedly to the family. I was going to the owl capital of the world, to their international headquarters, a town named Kikinda.

"This is my Kikinda town," quipped David on his website. We had seen him on the telly, and he had recently set up the Britain's Favourite Bird Referendum, in which we and many thousands of people voted. In one swoop, many young people had their first taste of the democratic process, and the robin had won its place as the UK's favourite bird. It was closely followed by the Barn Owl, which had my vote. (David had been hoping for the blackbird.) He would be my reliable, knowledgeable guide, along with his Serbian brother-in-birds, Milan Ružić, who happened to be president of the Bird Protection and Study Society of Serbia.

I went in search of a travel guide, but go into any branch of Waterstones and you will fail to find the word "Serbia" in any travel or nature section. The past resonances of ethnic clashes meant that it simply was not a popular tourist destination. The out-of-date tourist and travel advice I found online had not helped me; in fact quite the opposite—it fomented fear, mentioning landmines and police who may become aggressive and not appreciate cameras. One travel website mentioned the importance of avoiding large gatherings, and we were warned to not get mixed up in any demonstrations. Could groups of birders bristling with cameras, scopes, and binoculars be taken for a demonstration?

But by now, the trip was booked, and I felt reassured by the precedent of many other successful trips reported by David, not to mention my pressing need to see Long-eared Owls. The Air Serbia plane journey got off to a good start and my conversational British neighbour quizzed me about the binoculars and then looked bored when I excitedly laid out my plans. His smiling wife on the other hand turned out to be Serbian, interested, and full of questions. Where would I be starting my search? Did I know of the area of lakes in northern Serbia where many migrating cranes gather? I should be sure to taste the delicious speciality *riblja čorba*, a rich paprika-red fish soup. And there was much wildlife to be seen such as wildcats and Syrian woodpeckers. The husband endured our conversation, which was interrupted by a boisterous group of blokes conversing across the plane about hunting ducks and their different types of rifle. I hoped that they would not be heading to the same places as David had planned. My companion fell asleep and I eavesdropped on this hunting group. Serbia, I surreptitiously learned, is a very popular hunting destination. When the large containers marked "firearms" came through baggage reclaim, thanks to my eavesdropping I felt less alarmed than I might have done otherwise.

My next discovery was that Belgrade airport put Heathrow's Terminal Four to shame. It was full of more very friendly Serbs, was spotlessly clean, and had the most affordable sandwiches and refreshments I had seen in twenty years. David was visible from a distance hefting a large tripod and telescope. I picked up my bag and met with a motley group of enthusiasts, six of us in all: Wing Lok and Lee, who had come all the way from Hong Kong; Janet; and Nigel and Margaret, these last two bristling with anticipation and lenses of impressive girth. We were met by Milan, who greeted David affectionately and then took Janet and me by the arm to show us where we could exchange our sterling for Serbian dinar. ("No, not that much, you won't need so much here, things are very cheap!" he advised, noticing my £100 sterling.) Quite how cheap everything was repeatedly took me by surprise over the next few days of our adventure. Food cost next to nothing, drinks and clothing even less, and I procured a warm, fashionable, beautifully hand-knitted hat with owl ears and tassels in a craft shop for about 95 pence.

Our driver whisked us away in a comfortable minibus, through the dark to the hotel, Kaštel Ečka, an English-style stately home surrounded by tall pine trees and parkland. Inside its mid-nineteenth-century walls the rooms were plush and warm and, we were informed, had hosted guests such as the Austro-Hungarian prince Franz Ferdinand, composer and violinist Franz Liszt, and Serbian prince Aleksandar Karađorđević. Seated in a majestic ballroom, we were served a huge three-course meal, along with copious amounts of wine and choice beers. Serbia in 2015 could not have been more welcoming.

The next morning, well rested from our first night in the spacious bedrooms, we found our way out of our giant beds and fed on four-egg omelettes, steaming coffee, and heaps of savoury ham-and-cheese pastries. Then we were introduced to the rules of Owl Trip. There were only two rules: David's dictum, "Always look up," and Milan's rule, "Don't scare the owls." Having agreed to these, we boarded the Owl Mobile and set off.

In Britain, Long-eared Owls often inhabit rural places: heathland, forest, and so on. Miles from the nearest street lamp, unseen by human eyes, they hunt on windswept moors and roost in quiet patches of pine forest; they drift over swampy fens and quarter rough grassland; or they might even stop in abandoned military bases with empty-eyed windows that stare out over scruffy scrublands now rich and teeming with voles. Few people ever witness them, and even fewer still know what they require to survive; the Long-eared Owl is a very private kind of owl, and remains largely an enigma. Next to the charismatic beauty of the Barn Owl, and the noisy domesticity of the Tawny, the Long-eared Owl fades into obscurity and remains generally unknown and unsought. In Serbia, however, it is a different story.

Milan explained as we drove that in Central and Eastern Europe, particularly in Hungary and other Eastern European countries, owls, and a whole host of other wildlife, flourish in the remaining agriculturally undeveloped places.

Diversity of species, from invertebrates to large carnivores, vastly surpasses our Northern European count. From grass-hoppers to woodpeckers, shrikes, hares, and wildcats, these countries have stunningly rich fauna and flora. Brown bear. Lynx. Beaver. Wolf. Ural and Pygmy Owls, and a million more *orthoptera* (that's grasshopper and cricket species) than we could ever dream of. As we gazed out of the windows, Milan told us that all this wildness might be flourishing now, but the future was increasingly overshadowed by the threat of ever-intensifying agriculture.

We were driving through the flattest landscape I had ever seen. This was the Pannonian Plain. This vast low-lying area was once an inland sea: the Pannonian Sea. When the seas receded the remaining water created a natural, treeless, but salty wetland laced with saline lakes and marshes full of reeds and rich with wildlife. But now the area had been largely drained so that increasingly intensive farming could exploit the grasslands, and gradually mechanisation was encroaching.

Wintry mist hung in flat, muddy fields of sugar beet, and watery light caught on bare orchards and skeletal vines. The sky was low and grey, the horizon broken only by power sta-tions and lines of pylons stretching away endlessly across bare fields. The first question I had was why there were no trees in the Serbian countryside. "All of the trees have been cut down for firewood," Milan told us bluntly. "After the war and the sanctions people were very poor." They must have needed fuel. I looked at the road rolling out ahead, all these roads that used to be lined with trees, and I felt an ache for the lost shady avenues twining away into the distance. Now not one remained. But all around the towns and in amongst the houses and villages people had planted fast-growing conifer trees. These were for decoration, shelter, and fuel—and they were silver pine and spruce, the very kinds of trees favoured by Long-eared Owls. In the absence of other trees, they were prime roosting sites.

The owls came in from Eastern Europe and from Scandinavia, encouraged by the presence of other owls, thinking that this must be a safe place, protected from predators, and a good feeding ground. Year on year, they increased in numbers. The owls learned from one another that this was a good place to shelter. The many old-fashioned smallholding farms traditionally used grain and corn stores in open stacks which small mammals could easily enter; the rodents freely fattened themselves up and thus provided perfect foraging for owls. The sparse patches of conifers, the open grassland, and the protective scrub that surrounded the houses and homesteads all created reliable habitat and food supply for the swelling number of owls. Now it is thought that up to thirty thousand owls live in Serbia. In some villages, Milan told us, there are more owls than people. But Serbia, with its temperatures that plummet 30 degrees below freezing in winter, surely would not make a good stopover for wintering birds. Wasn't it too cold? It might in fact be climate chaos that is bringing them here, unexpected surges of milder weather allowing them to linger in this place. In years gone by this landlocked country would have been covered in snow and ice during the winter months, but now, for the last few years, it has been the same temperature as Britain and France.

All my preconceptions about this owl were changing. This did not look like the kind of wild landscape I had previously considered owls to favour. The austere grey horizon was broken by the occasional vertical of a gigantic chimney belching steam, and sparse clumps of spindly silver birch reflected weak winter light, their slender trunks brighter than the grim sky. Of course, owls were not concerned with aesthetics. This gaunt place suited them just fine. I wondered what it would be like in the snow when white ground would meet white sky and there would be little to distinguish land and cloud in the excoriating conditions of deep winter. The solid-frozen rivers, frost-cracked roads, freeze-dried plains, and snow-laden twigs of this desolate place would still provide shelter for hordes of down-insulated, feather-footed, iron-taloned predators. My friends Mark, Tim, and Matt would be visiting in January, in the full blast of cold, and later Mark spoke of its stark, crystalline beauty: the days were encrusted with sparkling white rime-frost that made the most ordinary things—the grass, the paths, the road, the twigs on the trees—completely magical and harshly beautiful.

In the winter months, as the number of small mammals in the fields diminishes and prey becomes harder to find, Milan continued, the owls come into town to roost. Here it is sheltered, warmer than the surrounding countryside, and there are plenty of rats to eat. The lime trees, white poplar, and above all the plentiful conifers are stuffed with roosting collared doves, blue tits, and many other small birds upon which the owls can easily prey. Even better, there are no buzzards or goshawks in town, and these are the predators feared by the owls; they are normally found in woodland, so it is much safer here than their normal habitat. The owls may only stay a few months, until the food runs out; in five months, Serbia.com reports, these owls may eat over half a million rodents. In the spring, they will disperse. Some might move north again to breed, perhaps returning to the Baltic states and Finland where other bird protection societies and groups like Milan's will capture and ring them, and slowly we will gain more information on the movements of this mysterious owl.

It seems that poverty and "behind the times" farming might be beneficial for the wildlife here. People simply cannot afford to invest in big machinery, so the traditional, wildlife-friendly methods of patchwork habitat remain: coniferous shelter belts, plenty of rough grass, free food for mice, and copious crevices for other rodents. Owl heaven. Additionally, unlike in Britain, where rodenticide is used routinely to destroy pests (and by sad coincidence, the owls who eat them), poisons are not used. I wondered, if the situation was the same in some areas of Britain where this kind of progress has intensified production, how many more owls we might have. Sadly, we define our owl species by their rarity, or often their absence. Here in Serbia, in these low-lying villages with their small houses painted green, pink, or sunflower, each with their hen runs, pine copses, and their sleepy, free-range dogs, there did seem to be more owls than people.

We stopped in one village and parked beside a school. The children were beginning to come out and walk home for their lunch. They wore pink, scarlet, and green puffer jackets and carried neat satchels on their backs. They glanced and grinned at us as Milan pointed up to flocks of sparrows and blue tits. "Willow warblers are common here," he told us, then pointed out a shrike, and, "Look! A pair of Syrian woodpeckers! All these are common in towns here. In spring, the dawn chorus is powerful. Try to imagine it," he suggested. "In the morning, all you can hear is the birds." Then, among some juniper trees inside a churchyard, Milan stopped and gestured for us to be quiet.

I see the ear tufts first, and as my eyes make sense of a narrow, bark-coloured owl, I see it peer down at us with bright orange eyes. At last! This is what we have come for, and it is the eyes which astound me. We are so close, standing beneath the trees and looking up. The owl is peaceful, and then, amazingly, I notice another, roosting against a branch, fluffed up and relaxed in sleep. I focus my binoculars on the first one to get a better view of its patterning. The breast-streaked pattern is for disguise when the birds are roosting, and the soft beige front is flecked with little chocolate vertical splashes, crossed like tiny pine-twig crucifixes. Its back is finely speckled and the colour of ashes, and in a neat vertical of pale splashes, the upper-wing coverts are dotted with white "braces," an adornment I have also seen on Tawnies. The feet are almost invisible, covered over by pale frills of breast down so soft it looks as if it has been brushed.

The owl's white facial disc and pale, vertical "eyebrows," its erect ear tufts and narrow, sleek, upright stance give it a startling appearance that looks almost affronted. But this is a face that also seems to have every confidence that it is pretty much invisible. And so the owl does not move; it narrows its bright irises to two glowing slivers and sits twig-like, in contrast to its dozing neighbour, which appears completely relaxed, its face drooping, eyes closed, feathers puffed and round as a ball. It looks as fat as butter, although this is an illusion; beneath that plumage it is no doubt as lean and svelte as its alert friend. Perhaps the more nervous owl is a newcomer; like many of them it might have flown here from a great distance, and might be more wary than its devil-may-care puffball friend. Gently curled around the rough skin of the branch I can just make out its two black talons. If its legs were visible, we would see that they are covered in creamy-coloured insulating down, specially evolved for the night-time cold. This owl may occupy a position somewhere between cute and ridiculous, but its death-by-stealth weaponry reveals a predator that is designed to execute without hesitation.

"How many do you think are in this tree?" Milan asks provocatively. "Six? Nine?" We try to count, squinting and staring. Eventually we give up.

"Twenty-seven," Milan declares. No! Twenty-eight . . . Twenty-nine! In one tree!" From our small group come several sharp intakes of breath. Disbelief, astonishment at just how invisible, how immobile these birds are in their roosts. The trees are not huge, but the junipers, with their evergreen blankets of aromatic needles and their copious, drooping boughs, create pockets of darkness and conceal their precious cargo beautifully. The trees rock ever so gently, cradling their silent dwellers.

Two, five, nine owls in each and every corner of the tree, some with a branch to themselves, others patiently sharing. "However many you think," Milan adds educationally, "double it!"

We gaze branchward. The owls gaze back. Some doze, some turn their faces away at our intrusion, but others embody a rainbow of expression: curious, alarmed, threatened, or irritated, the owls' facial ornamentation could be modified, giving each and every individual, according to its reaction, a different expression. The plumage varies too, depending on sex and age. Some ears are down, others erect: they can be folded at will and almost flattened, a little like those of a defensive cat; although this owl cannot snarl or hiss, but merely manifests a detached kind of stare. Inside the facial disc the colour is a soft rust, and on the females this is also reflected in the breast feathers which can be a richer, warmer colour than the males' pale beige. Every owl is different.

Children mill about us as we point and count as if possessed. For the locals, the owls have always been there, and are not often of interest. People used to take pot shots at them if they were bored, and laugh at the way in response to a gunshot a tree would suddenly blossom into a cloud of whirling owls. All that has stopped now, since Milan and his colleagues began their research and generated a campaign of owl PR. "Because it used to be a socialist country, everybody still believes what they hear on the TV," Milan tells us. "It's easy to get people to listen and to change what they do, because they are used to trusting the media and doing what they are told. So nobody harms the owls any more; they are even starting to be proud of them." People understand that the owls are protected, although some of them still cannot quite see why. There are just so many, it would be like visitors flocking to Devon to see the pied wagtails or the flocks of teal.

"In this village, that tree was the mothership," Milan explains. All around it, other, smaller, satellite trees had their own little bouquets perched nervously amongst the branches: "Those are the new owls. They are unsure, and although there is no pecking order—owls do not have a social structure as such—they come in and perch here before they feel confident enough to join others."

To understand any owl species, I have learned that you need to understand its habitat. Long-eared Owls are quite specialised in that they need dense arboreal cover and also rough, open grassland. This makes the Long-eared Owl a frontier species. It occupies the edges of these two very different habitats: conifers to hide from predators, and open hunting grounds full of small mammals. In Britain this combination of habitats may be quite limited, and could explain part of the reason why our Long-eared Owl numbers appear to be so low.

The woodland serves the owl because it contains old crows' nests, and although the Long-eared Owl can and does nest on the ground, they prefer to occupy pre-built homes. Often, Milan informs us, these platforms are not the most reliable. Corvids don't go in for aesthetics or design, and many of the Serbian Long-eared Owls' breeding attempts fail due to crumbling nests. So Milan and his friends at the Bird Protection and Study Society have set up a nest-box programme, providing warm, dry, and strong boxes so the owls can raise their young safely. This has increased breeding productivity by 1.5 chicks per brood, on average, Milan says proudly.

I am in the presence of someone who has studied these creatures for years, who knows more about the behaviour and ecology of these owls and also the other species in Serbia than perhaps anyone I will ever meet. If corvid nests in conifers are the only nests available, these will be selected, but if there are no conifers, and there are available nests in hawthorn or willow, they will be taken instead, Milan says. The denser the better, as during breeding, concealment from predators is paramount. This owl has evolved alongside many predators: goshawk, Ural Owl, and buzzard; as well as mammals such as lynx, pine marten, and wildcat. I am in awe of the knowledge Milan has about the whole interlinked ecology of which the owl is only a part. How many years has he been doing this? "For ever!" Milan laughs. "Since I was a small boy!" This is the study and work of a whole lifetime. I see it as science with passion, the kind of devotion that works with vulnerable species in a changing world. It is long-term, worth fighting for, and risks heartbreak. But isn't heartbreak often worth it, in the end?

We leave the smiling schoolchildren and the old church with its owl-lined branches weighed down by soft and uncountable silhouettes, and set course for Kikinda, only slightly better prepared for the safari to come.

Our excitement rises as we enter the town. At the end of October every year in Kikinda there is an owl festival. Townspeople are beginning to feel proud, and want to share the importance of this gathering of owls. As far as we know, it is the largest manifestation of this creature in one place in the world. During the festival's week-long celebration, school children are educated about the owls, make owl art, and sing owl songs. There is music and dancing. Owl poetry is created. Owl biscuits are baked. Owl posters go up. Owl stories are told. All in all, word has spread, and these owls are beginning to be cherished. Better still, groups of owl-aholics are visiting, bringing their long lenses, notebooks, and binoculars, boosting the local economy, appreciating the local food and culture.

As we arrive, with a big smile Milan dons an enviably silly hand-knitted owl hat. With a prominent bill and endearingly plaited orange, white, and grey tassels, it makes him look like a rugby player with Viking plaits. There will be an opportunity to buy one later, he promises, noting our admiration and desire for similar souvenir headwear. A huge sign with a picture of a friendly owl made up of biscuits and cakes welcomes us like a good omen. We pull up in a street of elegantly designed eighteenth-century houses painted saffron yellow and salmon pink.

"In Kikinda," Milan declares proudly as we pass the sign, "there is no mothership tree. Kikinda *is* the mothership."

We can hardly contain ourselves. There could be up to eight hundred owls in this one small town. Just the idea of the shadowy presence of all these owls is at once spooky and scintillating, as if we are walking onto the set of a horror film before filming has started.

As we leave the minibus and make our way to the town square I notice how friendly the local people are. They are used to the tree-pointing, owl-counting foreigners by now, and don't seem to mind this eccentric invasion. They appear to appreciate our presence, as it must bring in much-needed income to the ailing Serbian economy. Mostly there is a sense of ordinariness surrounding the presence of these creatures. People are used to them, and pass by no longer noticing the extraordinary thicket of eyes, claws, and feathers within the branches above their heads. There is a heartening sense of tolerance, even over the messy layers of pellets and wall-to-wall white splashes on park benches, pavements, and lawns. All this owl stuff appears to be viewed with resigned respect, good humour, and a spirit of generosity. Would the people of St. Ives, Bristol, Warrington, or Aberdeen ever regard urban starlings, or declining populations of urban-dwelling herring gulls, with the same spirit of kindness? A smiling man in a thick overcoat, holding hands with a small child, approaches and speaks to us in Serbian, then in broken English, taking my arm and pointing to a tree.

"In there, in there! More owl," he tells us enthusiastically, grabbing my hand. "And behind church!" His warmth seeps into me.

Obediently we all go to look, dispersing into the lawns and trees of the square, around the side of the lovely lemon-coloured church, and to the primary school where along the skyline and even at eye level just outside the chemistry labs, owls are perched, gathered in loose bundles of ten, twenty, fifty. We strain our necks, peering up, counting.

When in the town square I see one owl with something aluminium-coloured attached to its wing—this is one of the owls Milan has captured and ringed. He gets very excited; it is so close that we can read the number without binoculars. "Ao6! Yes! That one I ringed just last year!"

Does he ever run out of owls to ring?

"Sometimes. One year we got bored and ringed a whole load of blue tits. But they are vicious! The owls don't mind it, but the blue tits! They turn their heads right round like a vampire and rip you! They'll do anything to get blood. Sharp! Vicious! Blue tits are the worst."

Needing to give my own neck a rest, I wander away and find myself looking down, for a change, and notice I am standing amongst the largest, widest, deepest heap of owl pellets and white droppings that I have ever seen. I step forward, determined to collect one pellet and take it home. What exactly would the owls be eating, in the middle of winter, in this little-known southern European town close to the Hungarian and Romanian borders? What do they eat in the really cold years, when the rodents wear out?

"Fucking blue tits," Milan laughs, when I ask him. "When we ringed all the blue tits, a month later what did we find? All the rings! In the owl pellets. Every last one!"

Evidently, when small mammals run out, small birds are the next best thing.

I want to save and dissect a pellet, just one, from this huge pile, or perhaps two, and see for myself what they have been feeding on. No, first I would take a photograph of all the pellets with my small pocket camera. I had borrowed this ill-advised gadget from Rick, who used it to lend to his students in his job teaching in school. It was a pink flibbertigibbet of a thing, slim, and best of all, I thought, would fit easily into my coat pocket, like a spy camera. The Serbian police would not even notice it. I would swan through customs with it, and drift about innocently, whipping it out while nobody was looking. So I poised the camera to take a quick snap, not suspecting anything like the cataclysm it would cause.

Understandably, there is a law in Kikinda about not disturbing the owls. Deploying my mammal-tracking skills honed through years of otter-chasing, which involve mostly looking down, I had not, as David repeatedly advised, looked up. Amongst the high and low branches, staring down at me, the owls must have been round-eyed at my clumsy intrusion into their pine-needle kingdom.

Innocently, I point the camera. Perhaps, had they seen me, somebody in my group could have warned me. But they were busy looking up, deeply involved in counting more and more owls. They didn't see what was about to happen.

I am now close to the base of the pine tree, and hidden by a dense, sheltering canopy of deep green. In the midst of reassuringly calming, resin-scented needles, inside the tree's cocoon, it is dark and silent. My feet crisp subtly on the carpet of needles, the layers of fresh, glistening poo and the soft, crinkly piles of pellets. *Click* goes the shutter, quietly. A slight delay, and then . . . the flash.

The tree erupts. Silent winged things scatter in every direction, their quiet downdraught displacing the air, the branches, the twigs, the falling needles. I stumble out into the dusk to see my birdwatching group standing aghast. One hundred owls, all of them flying from their perches at once, swooping around, looping, confused, blinking, orange-eyed, and ghostly, up, down, around, and away and then gradually dissolving again into the nearby trees.

The next photo is an accidental one, a blurred field of grass, as I stumble within my own self-induced tornado of owls. It does not, however, capture the emotional maelstrom, and this is why I will never again carry a camera with me. Unless you are extremely experienced, cameras can get between you and the wildlife and spoil things. From now on, somebody more experienced with a lens can do the pictures.

I had committed the ultimate infringement. I had forgotten to switch off the flash. David, Margaret, Nigel, Janet,

Wing Lok, Lee, and Milan were stony-faced. The first rule of Owl Trip: do not scare the owls. My walk of shame brought me back to my friends in a swirl of disapproval.

When you look up into the branches of a tree in Kikinda, in November or December, you might see six or seven, maybe ten Long-eared Owls. But for every one that you can see, Milan tells us informatively (and too late for me), remember that there are ten more that you cannot see. And they are mostly watching you. This tree—he points at one—has the world record for holding 165 Long-eared Owls.

On the way back to our hotel, owl-fatigue begins to set in. We stop a final time. "I've got one more thing to show you," Milan says, enthusiasm swamping his otherwise sharp perceptions.

"Not more owls."

Milan is exasperated. "It isn't more owls."

It's a restaurant. Our stomachs all give gurgles of approval at the magnificent old windmill that has been converted into a strangely owl-shaped restaurant. We pile in, starving, slightly hysterical. We order beers. After draining a large one Milan leans over to me and confides: "If you really want to attract owls, what you do is make sparrow sounds, like this," and he purses his lips and uses his hands in such a way that the beaks of a hundred sparrows open and begin singing from somewhere, not quite at the table but somewhere above it, thrumming and twittering like a frenzied throng of finches. A few diners look bewildered, glancing upward as if looking for a flock of birds manifested somewhere inside the room, and then, seeing nothing, go back to their food.

"It sounds like panic, like there's a predator coming after them, and the noise of so many sparrows like this attracts the owls," Milan adds. After another beer, I catch myself beginning to suspect him of possessing mysterious powers.

With the success of the sparrow–predator impression, we encourage him to do his others. I want to hear the raven again. It sounds so guttural, gravelly and rasping and real, and, well, like a raven, it sends unnerving shivers down our spines. I close my eyes and see a raven gliding over a ravine. When we run out of birds, goaded by Wing Lok and Lee who have been showing their pictures of leopards, Milan does a jaguar. This is almost too much. Jaguars, it turns out, have a troublingly primal call that vibrates from the soles of the feet to the top of the scalp. Heat rises to my cheeks. This is the kind of sound that, although as jaguar-like as the bird sounds were bird-like, one might reserve for the privacy of the bedroom.

Later, I fall into my bed blurred by delicious Serbian dishes: turkey stew and many cakes, all washed down with a variety of beers and animal sounds delivered in a Serbian accent. The night's soundtrack has not entirely disappeared from my inner ears, when, lying back on my pillow, each time I close my eyes I see clusters of owls staring at me, ears erect, fiery eyes aglow. In the night I am woken repeatedly, fighting my duvet, confused by dreams infested with angry raptors and strange big cats.

The next morning I wake with puffy eyes. Janet is knocking ever so softly and politely on my door. "Miriam, are you OK?"

I slide out of bed, stick my head around the door, hair all over the place. Have I been talking in my sleep?

"It's eight o'clock—we're just about getting in the minibus," Janet whispers gently, noticing my state with barely concealed concern.

My limbs feel as though I haven't slept. I was up till midnight, then woke at 2:00 AM, 4:00 AM, and 6:00 AM, rigid before the accusing orange eyes of many Long-eared Owls.

The agreement had been that we would rise at six for a short owl walk around the grounds of the hotel, breakfast at seven, leave at eight to make the most of the short daylight hours. I had skipped all that, having been with my own owls the whole night.

Janet brings me a cup of tea and I struggle into my clothes. As we climb onto the bus, she pushes some pastries into my hand. I could kiss her. I do kiss her. She is a travel agent, from Bristol, and is used to this sort of thing.

As we drive through the treeless Pannonian Plain I discover that Janet has been all around the world on trips just like this one. A thoroughly experienced veteran of these group trips, she must be familiar with the "one who oversleeps." But there is more to Janet than that. She is, I also notice, exceedingly tactful and thoughtful about everybody else. The others are in couples, so thrown together by circumstance, she is happy to chat with me, and happy with silence. I notice that she does not talk about herself unless asked. I watch her looking out of the window. She has a guarded, reticent look about her as if she has had a loss, perhaps. Or maybe this is the best approach on a group tour. I do not ask, but, happy in our mutual passion for owls, we enjoy one another's quiet company.

"It's weird—I'm an early riser usually," I tell her later, attempting to alleviate the shame of having been the one who held up the group.

"Maybe my alarm woke you," she says, trying to remove any blame. "It did go off really early, and then maybe you went back to sleep."

But it isn't just me; there were other goings-on around the hotel that morning. As Wing Lok and Lee with their formidable lenses stealthily patrolled the grounds at the 6:00 AM rendezvous and owls flew about them, one had crashed loudly into the window of my room. It was unhurt, but as I passed I peered at the glass and found a light, ash-speckled feather, which I gathered up and slipped gently in between the pages of my notebook.

Later that day, outside another beautiful but crumbling church, Milan and I find more feathers, but this time, Milan says, they have been plucked. This is a predator incident. A kill. It could have been a goshawk. Unusual in the town, he adds, but it could be. Long-eared Owls do not have many predators, but if goshawks flew into town and happened upon a roost they would be a serious threat. There are not many leaves left on the trees at all, and any sharp-eyed predator would easily notice a bunch of owls nervously exposed on the branches of a lime or plane tree.

We cross the Danube, which is more muddy brown than blue. It swirls with grey cloud-reflections, like silty bathwater reflecting the open-skied expanses of this windswept land. With so few trees and a clear view from horizon to horizon, our eight pairs of eyes easily pick out any unusual birds, and we screech to a stop to view a great grey shrike, perched on a wire, watching over the field beyond. I gaze at the neat grey-and-white plumage of this striking bird with its creamy breast, stark black mask, cloud-grey back, and long tail. I have never seen the *Lanius excubitor*, the so-called butcher bird, which lies in wait for beetles, small mammals, and even birds, then skewers them and stores them in its grisly larder. As we look, a huge brown hare leaps out of the undergrowth and gallops away.

"God, it's the size of a cocker spaniel!" Nigel says. Milan explains that hares are very big here in Serbia. There are good grasslands for them, but the grasslands are threatened. Each year more are ploughed up illegally.

Thankfully, today we see more trees. I notice them mostly clinging to the sides of the rivers: white poplars, black poplars, alder; and in the fields, bare peach orchards and walnut trees. The endless sugar-beet fields are broken up by small farmsteads, each with a strip of woodland, but all these tiny havens are dying out, Milan says, in favour of the large-scale exploitation we know about in the rest of Europe. It's coming our way, he tells us sadly, and it won't be good for the wildlife. Many of the tiny smallholdings we can see are people's weekend houses, where in summer they go to tend vegetables and cut wood. The loss of these homesteads is not good for the wildlife, including the owls.

For now, poverty and lack of development also mean that many people still use old bicycles and horses and carts for transport in rural areas. In the villages crowds of old men and women bustle about with their shopping baskets, to and fro on their bikes. In one where we stop at a bakery for lunch, a farmer dressed in overalls sees us admiring how many potatoes he has fitted into his car. They are balanced on the roof, stacked three sacks high, and in the boot, he shows us, as well as filling every seat inside. The car is so weighed down it looks as if he might scrape the underneath or get stuck on a bump in the road, but his worn hands and leathery skin show that he must have had years of practice. We have no Serbian, and he no English—in fact, Serbian may not even be the language he is speaking, as this area is populated by a rich mixture of Hungarian-speaking and Balkan peoples, and in some villages three or even six languages may be spoken.

This land is the European bridge to and from Asia Minor and the Middle East—it is used to comings and goings, to cohabitation and tolerance. Language barriers aside, this farmer wants to speak with us as we wait outside the bakery, and when we come out laden with pastries for lunch he demonstrates how hard he has been working all day, miming this way and that way, backwards and forwards to the market, up and down these tree-lined roads, through the town, with his battered old East European car. We laugh together as he clowns himself bright-eyed and tearful, and we take pictures of his miraculous car, the car of a thousand potatoes, and we shake hands affectionately before he drives away to sell his teetering freight of root vegetables. We may not speak the same language, but laughter has no borders.

Political, social, and economic fortunes may have ebbed and flowed over this place, but the wildlife endures, rubbing alongside the people. Milan tells us that it is estimated that every year a couple of thousand hectares are illegally ploughed up, but the bird life demonstrates a kind of fluid resilience, even a permanence, which is not immediately obvious. The migrant birds, like migrant people, continue to flow through this place. The borders open, the borders close, but the birds know nothing of these artificial delineations. The bustle of human activity might benefit many animal and bird species, like the storks for instance, whose nests we can see on tall chimneys and towers, and the Long-eared Owls, who come for the urban trees, and the cranes that overwinter on the many lakes and fields of grass. But sometimes we may also drive out other species, which are then lost, like the great bustard, in a constant flux of tide and fortune.

As it gets dark and our powers of sight vanish, the land is re-cloaked in moonlight. Unable to see clearly, we have to use our ears. "Listen," Milan says, "listen." He tells us the Long-eared Owls have seven or eight different calls: they have a deep call, which means "well fed," and a breathy hooting territorial call, as well as low, soft hoots to communicate between pairs, and barking calls to use when alarmed. The male uses wing claps, and females sometimes also use this device when nesting, as well as distraction squeals, bill claps, and hisses. But now, at this time of year, the owls hardly call at all, so we will hear very little. Outside the breeding season there is no need to vocalise much, but they do have one sound, Milan promises. It is a kind of soft bickering, as if they are discussing between themselves. Usually if another owl lands to perch too close they do it. Beside the spruces, where an uncountable number of owl shapes are perched, we close our eyes and pay attention to the quiet conversations. From the branches, and all around, a soft, whickery "chitter" is drifting. Slowly we tune into the purr of their night-song, the music of owls waking and sleeping, as they speak to one another of space, closeness, and distance. What is it in these gentle voices? Clustered on their perches, they seem to speak of softening boundaries, of tolerance and acceptance of others perhaps.

Finally, when it is too dark to see anything more, our hearts light and our fingers and toes numb, we troop back to the echoing castle café for a hot drink.

As we sit at the table, our hands clasped around cups of steaming black tea, Milan explains his theory. "We've been able to convince people to protect these birds. We've said: Don't shoot them, they're protected, and people stopped. Boys used to shoot them for fun, now they get told off: they don't do it." Lulled by the vapour from the tea and the warm room, I let Milan's Serbian lilt wash over me. The Slavic accent sounds a little Russian, but complex and very pleasant, and in these tones he explains his theory of success for Long-eared Owls, which turns out to be a simple mathematical equation and chimes with the sensible use of the Barn Owl as pest control that I had heard about before.

"If every year one pair of Long-eared Owls eats 2 kilos of rodents, it will save the grain the mice would eat, saving or providing enough extra income to buy two more cattle. You could increase your milk yield by eight thousand euros per year, no tax or VAT! So! Put up a nest box."

When you say it like that, it's a no-brainer. Farmers should love and cherish owls. Perhaps many already do. My experience at home in England with the Barn Owls I studied was that many farmers were astonishingly fond of their owls. They were protective of them, possessive, even. Sometimes, they resisted our offers of ringing—not because they were being difficult, but because they didn't want anyone disturbing their beautiful owls.

On our way back to the minibus, Milan reassures me about the owl-pellet photo incident: "Now, if you really want to scare owls, you stand at the bottom of the tree, peer up, get eye contact with them, and make little scratching sounds, like a predator—a cat or a marten. That really scares them. They hate that." He laughs. I feel better. "We always put a ladder against the tree when we want to check a nest box or ring the chicks, and they don't suspect a thing as there's no scratching." In this area of Serbia, named Vojvodina, it is the grasslands that are the special habitat, and the local hunting societies (there is one in every village) have bought land to protect it from the threat of encroachment by increasingly intensive agricultural exploitation. Interesting, I muse, that those very hunters that I disapproved of on the plane out here might actually be partly helping to preserve some of this land for nature. Perhaps this aspect of the economy, although seemingly destructive, is in fact contributing to the conservation of wildlife. The moral landscape of conservation is not always as black-and-white as it might seem.

The next day we see what this duality means: at Slano Kopovo, a combined hunting and nature reserve where reed beds and lakes have been bought and protected, thousands of common cranes echo around us, their voices flooding the watery light of the sky like nothing I have ever heard. Some moments the sky is black with them; they flock from horizon to horizon as they converge at dusk on the shallow lake to roost.

We stop at a cabin converted to receive visitors, and I collect walnuts from the ground to eat for lunch. Wildcats stalk about in the grass here, in this place that at this time of year looks like no more than miles and miles of flat fields.

The Pannonian Plain has an amazing history, Milan explains. In centuries gone by it used to be a vast sea, then reed beds, then the grasslands that we now see remaining in patches and slivers, habitat for huddles of cranes, lapwings, and hen harriers. How long would all these wild birds still be able to come here if Serbia were in the EU, with its area-payment subsidies that support the development of monocultures, I wonder? It needs protecting! The cranes have come here en route from Scandinavia, and stop at this patchwork of low-intensive grassland and arable farming as a vitally important site to roost and replenish themselves before continuing their journey over Bosnia and Croatia, Turkey, and finally to Israel.

We gaze out over miles of subtly misted light that lies soft over the plain and try to imagine it as it once was, just water, reeds, and birds, without its chimneys and farmsteads. Ringing data tells us, Milan says, that the Swedish cranes go all the way to Spain, whereas the Finnish cranes head high across the Balkans, all flying in their vast, echoing, honking, trumpeting formations. Swamping the sky with their sweeping echelons, they bring a bleating music that has not changed for thousands if not millions of years. Aldo Leopold in his *Marshland Elegy* described the migrating crane as a trumpet in the orchestra of evolution, and a symbol of our untameable past:

> They live and have their being—these cranes—not
> in the constricted present, but in the wider reaches
> of evolutionary time. Their annual return is the
> ticking of the geological clock. Upon the place
> of their return they confer a peculiar distinction.
> Amid the endless mediocrity of the commonplace,
> a crane marsh holds a paleontological patent of
> nobility, won in the march of aeons, and revocable
> only by shotgun.

I wonder what the future holds for places like this. Resounding in our ears, they are a reminder of wild Europe, the laid-down layers of moss, peat, and water, and the unending reedy marsh. Protected by the hunters that own these lakes, for now they are a sign of hope.

Asio flammeus

SHORT-EARED OWL

At the beginning of time,
The owl was brought out of bog oak.
Over the water-blur of marsh and moor
In ruffled curves, eyes interrogating
The owl flits, god of the reeds.

—KENNETH STEVEN, "Owl"

DUSK IS FALLING FAST. MILAN HAS BROUGHT US TO a castle where he knows migrating Short-eared Owls congregate. The sunset colours the crumbling buildings and tips everything with scarlet as if the rust-red of the autumnal sphagnum and bog myrtle from the wide, wet tundra has reached us here. Milan tries out his distressed-mouse call. First nothing happens, and then from the uppermost branches of a clump of pines a gold-backed shadow swoops. Another follows swiftly after, from the exact same pine. Now we watch their long, pale wings, less uniform and subtly brighter than the Long-eared's wings. The Shorties have a clear, black carpal patch that shows up starkly against the pale plumage, like a small crescent visible on the "wrist" of the underwing. Milan shows us how the wings seem to be marginally longer than those of the Long-eared Owl, but the flight is similar: rapid wingbeats and then glides. They flit and whirl skittishly around when they see us, their pale faces turning and switching back and forth, confused.

"They are freaked out," Milan says, observing them closely. This is the most intense I've seen him. "They're disorientated; look how they're flying. They've just come all the way from the tundra, maybe a thousand miles, and they may not have seen people and towns before." Many Short-eared Owls migrate south in the winter and these two may have journeyed from as far away as Scandinavia and the Russian tundra. This is a bird that comes here to feed and shelter in the winter, and although it is not so obviously communal as the Long-eared Owl, it can be seen in parties at this time, quartering grassland and gathering to hunt and roost in small groups. These two must be following others, perhaps on a set migration route, as we spot one more high in a tree, then another. They're one of the few owls that can be seen in daylight in Europe and we're getting a treat here as we can look up and see them from below, dispersed in the pines. They seem anxious, uncertain. "The most important thing to remember," Milan says, "is to keep our distance, and not peer up and get eye contact with the owls while they are perched in their roosts. If you do that, they think you're planning to pounce, get startled, and take to the wing."

As we watch, Margaret slips away to see if she can frame one in her long lens. She is stealthy, and the only one of us who has not yet startled the owls, or had to endure a walk of shame. I observe Margaret as she quietly sets up a photo. This is an experienced photographer. She's so quiet, in her stealth-soft clothes. She wears a fleece that doesn't rustle, and soft camo trousers—and she is as unobtrusive and twig-slim as the owls themselves. It is very hard to get a good shot of these shy birds when what little light there is falls behind them in their pine-needle world. They are either in silhouette, or covered by branches. Later, Margaret sends me some of her shots, and I see her generosity as well, especially since I lost heart and took no more pictures after the Kikinda debacle. There we all are, looking up, as we have been trained to do by David and Milan. Observing the owls we have each developed our own tracking stance, as if the key to getting close to these creatures is not simply wanting to get a perfect image, but knowing that it is not about us, it is about respect, reverence even.

Just before the light disappears I catch one in my binoculars, perched on the high branch of a silver spruce. Its shadowy black eye-mask looks like strange goth make-up and is a stunning contrast to the pale, bulbous-looking face and vibrant yellow eyes. The owl is clearly bewildered by our presence. What must we look like to this tribe of the tundra? We, the strange wingless creatures creeping about like beetles amongst the echoing architecture of this building with its crenellations, smoothly plastered cliff-scapes, and confusing arches. Feeling my clumsy humanness I take a step back, wanting to let go of my curiosity, to disappear and cease this endless observation, this persistent chasing.

"It's so rare to see a Short-eared Owl on the edge of a village like this," Milan calls softly from beneath his binoculars, renewing my gaze. "Look at the way they fly—you can tell it is a Short-eared Owl by the way it flies around and around like that—it doesn't want to leave, it wants to go back to its same branch. They have to be economical, save energy. Once they find a perch they like, they stick to it, and return to the familiar spot."

I think how exhausted the Short-eared Owls must be. Perhaps for some of them this is their first winter migrating to a strange place. They may have flown here from the Arctic tundra to avoid starvation, to find voles and to shelter here in the milder climate of 10 degrees Celsius. What will they do when the really cold weather hits in January? I'll be interested to find out if the Short-eared Owls in Britain behave in the same way, but meanwhile Milan's close observations continue.

"But look at the way it flies when it is startled," he says, encouraging us to recognise the birds' special movement, or "jizz" as birdwatchers term it. In ornithology the word "jizz" is commonly used to describe an individual bird's shape, posture, habitual movements, and flying style. Experienced enthusiasts and experts can reliably identify a bird's jizz in this way with just a glance, in conjunction with habitat and location.

The etymology of this interesting word is obscure, but some believe it has been compressed from a Second World War acronym GISS, that was used for the identification of the general impression of size and shape of an aircraft. Now, sadly, the word has to be used with more care and can cause misunderstandings amongst people who are not familiar with birding jargon, as it can also mean something less pure than the flight and movement of a bird.

The owl circles on long, black-tipped wings, around and around, as if conflicted, wanting to go back, but too nervous. Surely this is how any newcomer would behave, unsure, awkward, not speaking the local language, jittery and slightly dazed by the newness of the surroundings, but clinging to whatever small thing is familiar. The world must be reduced to its essentials to migrants. Ground, sky, tree; water, food, shelter.

IF IT ISN'T the ears of this owl that turn out to be its most striking feature, it's the eyes that have it. Linnaeus spotted the dazzling yellow gaze and black mascara mask that marks out *Asio flammeus*, the flame-eyed owl, and named it accordingly. Many owls have yellow eyes, and this usually marks them out as daylight hunters. The amber- and orange-eyed owls might often hunt more in the low light at dusk and dawn, and the brown-eyed owls hunt almost exclusively at night. It isn't just the eyes that make the Short-eared Owl flame-like though— there's something about the way the light works to catch and brighten its plumage as well. The so-called short ears of this owl are again not true ears but neat tufts of feathers that the owl uses for communication and display. Even more confusingly, these small tufts are usually invisible, so at a distance, or in poor light, or in flight the owl could be mistaken for a Long-eared Owl (whose tufts vanish in the same way in flight) or even a Barn Owl. Its true ears are the hidden asymmetrical ears, embedded deep in the feathers behind the facial disc, just like all the other owls we've met on this journey. When perched and on the alert the owl periodically raises its tufts like small Beelzebub horns. They can protrude subtly from just behind the apex of the facial disc when the owl is startled or vigilant, and they can show to varying degrees when the bird feels threatened.

Milan has watched these birds so closely, tuned into their behaviour, observed them arriving, and watched what they do, even down to the way they fly and how different that is from the Long-eared's flight. He tells of how the "Shortie" has a more wavering hunting flight than the Long-eared, and although it is heavier built, its wingbeats are shallower, the wings more pointed, and during glides it sometimes holds them in a V-shape. I'm in awe of his forensic eye for detail.

In flight this owl's wings do appear slenderer than the Long-eared's, with a white trailing edge, and they are distinctly barred on the primaries, ending in those distinguishing black tips. It has a streaked upper breast and neck but a pale belly as opposed to the entirely streaked front of its Long-eared cousin.

Author Henry Tegner recounts the experiences and observations of a Northumbrian farm labourer, known as "The Molecatcher," who describes a windswept winter sighting of the arrival of the "horned owl." Whilst gathering sea coal that had washed in from the coal seams on the Northumberland coast, over the grey tumbled waters he noticed a large number of herring gulls circling and diving. It was a concentrated attack on a large bird flying just above the tips of the waves. When it reached the dunes it continued over the Molecatcher's head and plunged to earth in a clump of bracken. In its course overhead the Molecatcher had recognised the bird as a "horned owl," but as it landed, a goldcrest flew up. The Molecatcher mused that this tiny winter migrant to our shores had hitched a lift on the owl all the way from Scandinavia. Was this an example of "avian-assisted transportation"? Both birds naturally manage the migration from Scandinavia in moderate numbers each winter and are likely to be following the migration routes and air currents of the East Atlantic flyway. But would a tiny bird stow away on a dangerous predator? The flight of this owl when journeying is powerful and direct, and it has slow, steady wingbeats; you can see how a human might assume this to be a reassuring lift for a small bird.

BACK AT HOME, the winter winds grew big, swooping in from the west and north and tearing at trees and roofs. The Met Office had declared that any winter storm with the power to damage should now be named. The effect was supposed to be that people would take heed and sensibly prepare. So the fearful elemental power now shaking our house and battering the windows until they seemed convex had a name, and something about it had a character: this was Storm Gertrude.

In early December we had endured Storm Desmond, one of the most destructive storms to hit the north-west of England, and Storm Eva had caused more devastation over Christmas; Storm Frank had then delivered a new bout of misery to the south-west for New Year, cancelling most people's parties, flooding roads, and pulverising travel plans. Each with a personality all its own, winds were not winds any longer, they were malevolent entities. None of us in the south-west, from Penzance to Plymouth, would forget Storm Frank, whose monstrous waves had begun by battering Galway, Kilkenny, Cork, and Wexford. Then all across Britain, from west to east, from Dumfries and Galloway to Peebles and Hawick, homes lost power. In Cornwall and Devon horrendous waves crashed high over cliffs, floods rose, traffic was disrupted, and seaside walls, houses, cafés, and shops were smashed. Extensive flooding and power loss had spread from the coast of Ireland to the heart of Britain within a few short hours. And so with the next bout of lowering cloud in the sky and a swirl of violent weather systems on the forecast, we hunkered down and expected more doom-laden news. Then Storm Gertrude hit.

Rainwater flooded through our leaky bedroom windows. It kept us awake until the small hours. Rick ran back and forth with a tub to catch at least a portion, but most of it did what water does, and by morning the carpet was ruined. We had mopped up as best we could, and I thought of getting out again. Trips to the windswept high moors had become a winter regularity to look for what might have blown in on the breast of all the fresh winds. I had flown back from Belgrade in Serbia with a clearer picture emblazoned on my memory of the graceful flight, the long wings, and the stark form of the Short-eared Owl's face and the light fluttering glides it performed. I wanted to see it on local moorland, and I knew it would be there. This owl is quite diurnal in its hunting so can be seen if you can get to the moors or the coastal marshes, dunes, and reedy places where it likes to perch and hunt. Their perch is more slanting than many owls', but when in flight their sheer grace and agility are astounding. They swoop low, swerve and lift, clearly showing their bright plumage, white underwings, and smouldering eyes.

In the south-west, this owl is a winter nomad, forced to travel vast distances to seek its favourite prey, the vole. Ringed birds from Britain have been found as far away as Russia, the Mediterranean, and North Africa. Once an owl has arrived in Britain and it has fed and is in good shape it will turn and glide out west and north, over moor, mountain, and sea to reach safe spring and summer breeding grounds, often on far-flung islands in the west, like Skomer Island, Skokholm, and the Outer Hebrides. I had heard that some migrated to Devon in very small numbers. This was to be my biggest owl challenge yet. I knew it was a rarity here, but a regular rarity. Perhaps there could be one, two, six, or even sixteen. I hoped my search would be worth it.

I was convinced that if I looked hard enough, waited long enough, searched widely enough, winter would eventually yield at least one near where I lived. With a close eye on my birding friends on Twitter, I waited for news, and made periodic trips up onto the moors. Spring was just around the corner; any Shorties that were here would soon be making their way north to their breeding grounds. I consulted friends in the BTO who had volunteers studying them with the use of surveys in Scotland. It appeared that this species is one of the most difficult to count, and much of the survey work is carried out by enthusiastic and very dedicated members of the public. Was it so difficult, I wondered, partly because of the owl's ground-nesting habit, where nests could not always be found, and chicks could not be counted so easily as they were not confined to an artificial nest-box site? The bird's nomadic demeanour, extremely camouflaged plumage, and crepuscular dawn and dusk habits would surely not help. Coupled with this, all the reports admitted that individuals that do not nest successfully can easily go unnoticed and this could skew what we know about numbers in the UK. Consequently, one estimate ranged between 780 and 2,700 breeding pairs, a confusingly broad range! More conservative estimates put the owl's numbers at the lower end, but in reality we just cannot be sure and more survey work is required. So these numbers are amongst the most unreliable for any raptor or owl. Coupled with concerns about declines in the last two decades, I was beginning to feel despondent about ever seeing one on Dartmoor.

One way to locate owls is by their calls, and the Shorty's is quite soft; since it is diurnal and can rely on finding other owls of its kind by sight, unlike the noisy and sometimes complex calls of woodland owls, it can afford to have a simpler repertoire and softer call. The male's territorial call is a low *boo-boo-boo-boo* that owl expert Heimo Mikkola describes as resembling "the distant, slow puffing of an old steam train." The female may respond, Mikkola says, with "a low, ugly, harsh *'ree-yow'* or *'keee-yow'* call. Other calls are a soft grunted *'whu'* followed by hissing like a leaky tap." In spring, male Short-eared Owls begin their dramatic displays in which they may wing-clap in flight, but I knew that since they are not thought to breed on Dartmoor I would not see that this far south.

By the beginning of March, when much of the country was still battening down the hatches instead of enjoying the start of spring, I had almost given up searching. In South Devon, a wintery backlash was building, and this was bad news for breeding birds of any sort. Snow and ice were forecast and bitter cold and gales threatened to keep us all in an unusual bubble of arctic conditions. However, I remained hopeful, as this could mean good news for me: cold weather coming in from Scandinavia can often herald an influx of Short-eared Owls as they arrive to avoid the worst weather, seeking refuge in the milder climate.

Further north, a migrating Short-eared Owl was found injured, hit by a car near Lincoln, and was taken to be reha-bilitated in a rescue centre. Its outrage at being held captive was evident on its face when it appeared on TV, and I con-sidered getting on the train to go and see it close-to. Then I heard that two owls had been found dead on the moors in County Durham. This pair had been discovered by a member of the public out for a walk. Bizarrely, the two corpses had been pushed into a pothole near Selset Reservoir not far from Middleton-in-Teesdale. A quick search informed me that the reservoir is part of an Area of Outstanding Natural Beauty in the North Pennines, and is perfect Shortie territory—surrounded with open heather moors, as well as the peatlands, hay meadows, dales, woods, and upland rivers of the moorland, this area of the Pennines appears to be just the right kind of breeding habitat for Short-eared Owls, with an abundance of rough grassland and their main prey: voles.

The moorland reservoir is in an area specially known and loved for its tranquillity, wildlife, and night-time dark skies. Why then would a person wish to destroy and hide not one but two of these iconic moorland owls? Had they been destroyed to protect game birds? A post-mortem confirmed that they had been shot. The shooting occurred at breeding time, so the owls were possibly a pair, possibly nesting or about to breed. Other birds in the area include both red and black grouse, and the presence of strips of burned moorland—a method used to improve the conditions for raising grouse as it provokes fresh new shoots upon which the game birds can feed—revealed that a grouse moor was nearby. Could it have been that these owls, seen from a distance, were taken for the gamekeeper's bête noire, the hen harrier? Had they been deliberately and mistakenly culled to protect game for shooting? Unfortunately for the owl, female hen harriers' plumage closely resembles that of the owls, with a circular face, tail barring, and similar size. Without proper identification, the low, moor-washed jizz of a Short-eared Owl on the wing, often hunting in broad daylight as it does, and tending to hover momentarily over its prey, could be mistaken for the flight of a hen harrier. Even though all these birds are fully protected under the Wildlife and Countryside Act 1981, and the criminal activity of killing one could result in six months' imprisonment or unlimited fines, this is not always enough to deter somebody from setting their crosshairs on these rare birds. An untrained eye could easily have confused them and on impulse pulled the trigger.

The police appealed for information about the crime at the time, and investigators at the RSPB in the area reminded people of the rarity and conservation importance of the Short-eared Owls, as well as the fact that their prey is mostly small mammals rather than other birds. However, in spite of education efforts and laws and press releases by those who wish to protect wildlife, no perpetrator was discovered and no action taken. Months later, the story was forgotten, and nearby, driven grouse shooting (big business in areas like this) continued. There is no single bird in the whole of Britain that is closer to being rendered extinct than the hen harrier, perhaps due to the human habit of big-business shooting, and it is tragic that Short-eared Owls are sometimes caught up in the crossfire.

On further investigation I found a study from the University of Leeds that looked into the shared, threatened habitat of the hen harrier and the Short-eared Owl. The EMBER Project found that the impact of heather burning on moorland estates can alter the hydrology of peatland so that it can dry out and release heavy metals into nearby rivers and CO_2 into the atmosphere. These peaty uplands are not just the preserve of raptors, they are carbon sinks, effectively the Amazon of the UK.

The shooting estates respond that they are helping to preserve the rare black grouse on their moorlands, and more tangled and complex ethical questions are raised. How can we prioritise which species and which habitats to preserve and which to cull? Who decides which is more important, and where do we draw the boundaries? Such fraught conversations rage on about the contested habits and beleaguered species of Britain, and meanwhile some of them may quietly vanish.

ONE FINAL COLD AFTERNOON I ventured high on to Rippon Tor, a prominent outcrop on the southern moor. This windy spot gives a wide view from Dartmoor, sweeping down over my part of Devon and stretching all the way to the mouth of the glittery Teign estuary. Near the hilltop I sat in the lee of the granite tor and listened to the swish of the grass amongst the boulders and looked out across the fields as they fell away toward the sea. The sky was lit with an uncanny low grey layer of cloud with light seeping in rays beneath, washing the land with a watery paleness. I sat for a long while in a breeze sharpened with flecks of ice. In the air was the edge of a scent of snow.

A flicker caught my eye. Finally, after all this time, out of the gold of the grass came a pair of long wings, laden with all the browns and ochres of the moor, the darkness of bramble and old deadwood and winter bracken, the sepia and gold of the grasses. As it shimmered past I turned to see it hover a little, its wings in a V-shape, the pale circle of its face pointing downward. Aiming into the flax-blond grasses and the tangle of lichens and wizened furze it dropped vertically and vanished. I felt that was it, but when it came up again I was sure: this time I didn't need the binoculars. *Asio flammeus*, the flame-eyed owl. It couldn't have been more than twenty yards away. The owl lifted without moving its wings as some invisible draught blew it closer to me. Oblivious to my presence it hovered again and turned, revealing pale underwings with clear black wing tips and halfway down, a dark tattoo of a crescent moon: the carpal patch, close enough almost to touch. A Short-eared Owl!

My stomach knotted itself into a bundle. The owl lifted a little higher, drifted downhill slightly, and dropped by increments as it fixed its prey, long legs dangling and at the ready. A slant of light brightened the soft clotted cream of the leading edges of its wings, the beaten gold of the primaries, and the white trailing tips as the bird circled around, buoyant, and quartered back, still searching, now veering uphill towards me.

What happened next was so startling I could hardly believe it was real. In my cross-legged sitting position, surrounded by grass and rocks, I must have looked like a part of the landscape, for the owl came closer, fixing its haunting yellow eyes upon me until it was so close I could pick out the individual black masking around its eyes. And still it came. And then, it stretched out its legs, as if to land on me. All at once I could see the beige covering over its legs and feet, so soft I might not have minded, but for the deathly-sharp black claws that now splayed and reached right out towards my head. It was then that I flinched, letting out a yelp. The cry was a warning, partly from my own surprise and panic at this owl's mistake, but mainly to put it off course. To my amazement, the owl yelped back just as I ducked to avoid being scalped by those outstretched talons. In its error it had taken me in my brown camouflage gear and post-like stance for nothing more than a tussocky perch. It quickly swerved off, still yelping, its voice high with offence and alarm.

Veering with a light and less-than-dignified wobble in its flight, but still staying low to the ground, its feathery hues blended eerily into the glow of the hillside. Off it went, and I never saw it again. I don't know which of us was more shocked. I sat dry-mouthed, heart thumping, owl-dazzled from the follicles on my scalp to the tips of my toenails.

IF A SHORT-EARED OWL were to take flight from the boggy tundra in the centre of north Dartmoor, from the grassy whispering place where many rivers rise amongst the sphagnum and sundews, the only sounds it would hear would be the voices of curlew and plover, the rustle and whisper of the moor grasses.

The owl would muscle over the updraughts rising off the exposed granite ridge of High Willhays, the highest point of the moor: 621 metres above sea level. The thermals here would lift the owl and sweep it over the fields of north Devon, and over the Severn estuary, skirting the conurbations and cities, perhaps stooping to feed on voles in the edgelands, and then on over the moorlands and the Black Mountains that rise to the Brecon Beacons. The owl would find good hunting over the Welsh Marshes, and if it veered in a more westerly direction it would hear winds filled with the turbulent voices of seabirds over the coastal cliffs. Reaching the outlying islands that skirt the Welsh coast, it might be tempted in spring by a rich supply of young and fledgling seabirds.

Heading back inland it might skirt west around Wrexham or veer north, to skim the marshes that lie before the Mawddach estuary and the grassy Llŷn peninsula, matching its journey with the arrival of the ospreys as they travel back to their nesting grounds here. It would find good feeding in the vast areas of moor-covered upland, dry heath, and blanket bogs around the Berwyn mountain range; or heading east it would find good habitat in the Peak District, and still further east, the wide expanses of the windy Lincolnshire Wolds, then the long northering spine of the Pennines.

But some of the best places to see Shorties, I had heard, were further north still. These northern haunts may harbour the owls that have come down across the North Sea from northern Scandinavia, and are some of the best breeding grounds, rich with wild land stretching across the Highlands.

TO REACH THESE the owls must confront challenging sea passages, but they are fearless flyers, and easily capable of crossing the North Sea as they voyage to the British Isles. They can be found anywhere in coastal areas from eastern

Scotland and Northumberland all the way to the Outer Hebrides. My friend Esther reported them on the dunes around Aberdeen, and it was on the Northumbrian dunes that I had my first encounter with an arriving owl. In the Northern Isles my friend and author of the photographic blog "Owls About That Then," Paul Riddle, photographed some of his best shots of Shorties in some of their most spectacular breeding places in the Outer Hebrides.

I think, in my not very extensive experience, that the best attributes of all birdwatchers are patience and tenacity. On his trip to North Uist, Paul told me, "a lot of time" was spent waiting and watching (and this could mean days rather than hours, or the mere minutes that most of us flibbertigibbets are prepared to put in). The positioning of oneself is vital: if I have learned one thing from successful nature watchers, it is about putting ourselves in the animal's path. This means not just setting down anywhere, but selecting a well-researched, likely spot, one where a sense of the bird's needs comes into play. The skill is in thinking like an owl, knowing where it will perch and rest. And when an owl is not feeding it will be resting.

Paul told me how he put himself in these places; viewpoints where he could park his car by the road, set up his long lens before a wide swathe of woolly moorland and wait within view of a few fence posts and some distant conifer plantations. The winds would whisper, blowing mist in and away; mizzle would come and go; the car clock would turn; and Paul would wait, and watch for the owls as they might or might not sweep in to feed. Given that they only hunt and feed for a tiny proportion of the day, Paul must indeed have had a long wait.

North Uist hosts a vast plethora of feeding for Short-eared Owls, but you have to be hardy about the weather and also about the extensive, sullen bogscapes. It lies between Harris and Benbecula, just a short sail south of the better-known

Isle of Lewis. Like the other Hebridean isles it is a maze of low-lying and quite fragile wetland habitats, a "drowned landscape" of peat bogs and lochans, as well as a string of rare dunes of dazzling white sand and long flat beaches at its edges. How I longed to go there, hearing Paul's descriptions. How many of us store up these longings, sometimes for years, a packed-away desire to go somewhere, see something, stored in a cupboard in the mind? And then one day the door bursts open and we just have to get there. My time will come, and I am counting on that, perhaps next year.

Strong winds and westerly showers had blown in from the Atlantic for the entire three days of Paul's trip with his friend Adey, and the pair were nearly thoroughly disheartened when, on their final day, the sky cleared and before catching the three o'clock ferry they were able to drive slowly down a bare, unfenced lane called Committee Road. Watching and scanning, Paul parked in a likely spot. Although there are miles of crystal seas and white shell-sand beaches to look at, he headed here, to where much of the land is flat, boggy, and on first glance empty-looking. But for an owl, a naturalist, or a lover of the northern isles who adores the subtle intricacy and low-level beauty of these rich places, the opposite is true: "There was activity everywhere!" Paul exclaimed. "It was utterly amazing what a difference a mild upturn in the weather made." It is not easy wielding a 500-millimetre lens out of a car window trying to obtain flight shots, but Paul got some close-ups as the owl, making the most of the fair weather and concentrating on hunting, ignored the car and the lens and got on with the important business. When it had fed, it returned close by and perched on a fence post, and the resulting images were stunning. Having seen them, I planned to take Jenny there after her exams were over. Jenny had other ideas; she insisted on staying a little further south. Her plan was to spend a week exploring the Isle of Mull together, and going to stay on Iona, an island, we'd decided, everybody should go to at least once in their life.

That day on North Uist Paul saw not one but seven Short-eared Owls, proving what a fabulously rich habitat the isles can be for the species. The resulting pictures, now on his website, are entrancing. I think also that he has a very patient family who kindly release him to go on his birding forays. It pays off: the images capture all the colours of light on the peat bog in the plumage of the birds. We can see the brightness of the primaries in flight, and in one, the owl is perched, looking directly into the camera lens, its tiny facial feather tufts raised, along with the black eye-mask giving its stark, flaming eyes a look possessed by pure wildness.

JUNE CAME UPON US, the exams were over, and it was time for my trip north with Jenny. I knew she might not tolerate me on many more of these forays, at least for a few years, and so wanted to make the most of her company. We packed our bags as lightly as possible, including wet-weather gear as well as swimwear, and boarded the Caledonian Sleeper in the balmy but thick city air of Euston station.

As we lay tucked into our bunks I read about the chilling Scottish folklore surrounding owls. The word *cailleach* in Gaelic means "old woman" or "hag," but *cailleach-oidhche* means "owl." It seems that the owl in Celtic culture was often associated with the crone—the *cailleach* literally means "the veiled one." This was a magical old woman who possessed the elemental powers of nature and was able to conjure storms. The owl-crone embodied both wisdom and evil: a potent combination. Shakespeare tapped into such folk mythology in his Scottish play, *Macbeth*. "The howlet's wing" is plopped into the brew that the witches prepare on the stormy night at the start of the play to help to bring doom and destruction upon everyone. The scenes in the play when King Duncan is murdered are imbued with owl imagery. When Macbeth goes to murder him, Lady Macbeth excitedly imagines she hears a death messenger in the form of an owl:

> Hark! Peace!
> It was the owl that shriek'd, the fatal bellman,
> Which gives the stern'st good-night. He is about it.
> (II.ii.2–4)

The owl's threatening nature features immediately after the murder as well, when it is heard shrieking all night long:

> . . . the obscure bird
> Clamour'd the livelong night.
> (II.iii.60–61)

The same morning other unnatural things have been happening:

> A falcon, towering in her pride of place,
> Was by a mousing owl hawk'd at and kill'd.
> (II.iv.11–13)

Here the normally nocturnal owl is shown to be turning the natural, God-given order of things upside down. The owl, an untameable bird of night and death, had come out in the day and murdered a falcon (representing the king) in broad daylight.

In spite of the chilling reading, we slept deeply, rocked by the rhythm of the train. At 6:00 AM we awoke to a drizzly Glasgow dawn. Passing the monument to Sir Walter Scott, I felt sure the great Scottish bard would have something to pass on about owls as he was a great gatherer of traditional tales and song, fascinated with medieval romance, ballads, and ancient poetry, and was something of a cultural anthropologist of his time. Thanks to the 4G on Jenny's iPhone I quickly found what I was looking for. In his "Ancient Gaelic Melody," with a characteristic bouncing rhythm Scott demonstrates the aeons of darkness and superstition that have pursued the owl across borders and through time. In these two verses we encounter the hag and the owl bookending the poem together in one spell-like breath:

> Birds of omen dark and foul,
> Night-crow, raven, bat, and owl,
> Leave the sick man to his dream—
> All night long he heard you scream.
> Haste to cave and ruin'd tower,
> Ivy tod, or dingled bower,
> There to wink and mop, for, hark!
> In the mid air sings the lark.

> . . .

> Wild thoughts, that, sinful, dark, and deep,
> O'erpower the passive mind in sleep,
> Pass from the slumberer's soul away,
> Like night-mists from the brow of day:
> Foul hag, whose blasted visage grim
> Smothers the pulse, unnerves the limb,
> Spur thy dark palfrey, and begone!
> Thou darest not face the godlike sun.

On the grim dawn's train ride north and west to Oban it was easy to see from where some of the dark imagery might have sprung. The mountains never struggled free of the gloaming mist for the whole journey, and reading the poetry of Scott beneath that glowering sky we strained to see the mountain peaks in the mist, but soon the enticing islands drew us out of any reveries. On our short but spectacular ferry crossing, the season remembered itself, warmth broke through, and we shrugged off every hint of the "foul hag." We arrived on the Isle of Mull in spectacular sunshine, and hauled ourselves onto the waiting bus to Fionnphort. A long hour and a half of travel through moist mountains in all the shades of heather, bracken, and pine across undulating Mull (that I knew was perfect Short-eared Owl territory) and we caught our first glimpse of the little low heaven of our tiny island.

The next morning, we awoke in the St. Columba Hotel Iona to a persistent and strange sound. Far from tiny wavelets lapping at the white sand beach and thrushes chanting in the hedges, this was not the soundtrack we had been expecting. At first we thought it was someone fixing a fence with a ratchet screwdriver. We gobbled our breakfast, straining to see what it could be that was making the peculiarly annoying noise. I pocketed us a muffin each (succulent home-made domes of cranberry and white chocolate, I doubted they would last until elevenses) and we scurried out to walk the road that leads along past the abbey toward the north of the island. The ratchet screwdrivers continued. We searched the swaying meadow grass for a person with a toolbox but there was none, just a soft breeze sighing over the meadowsweet, yellow rattle, and wild carrot. And there it was again, persistent as ever: "Crex-crex-crex." Then I remembered. Corncrakes! Jenny looked at me sideways. Disbelief gave way to delight as we tried to spot these shy but noisy little birds by sneaking up: we could hear them, practically at our feet, but they seemed supernaturally able to cloak themselves in the grass.

The Hebridean islands harbour a rare population of this tantalisingly elusive crake, famous for being impossible to see. Twenty years ago there were none but now, due to the careful efforts of a handful of local crofters, the population is being restored. About fifty males arrive from Mozambique in April each year, travelling all the way to the south-western tip of the Isle of Mull, and across a final stretch to this low-lying, Atlantic-facing speck of an island-off-an-island-off-an-island. All week, night and day, our ears were rasped by the strange soundtrack of corncrakes, their calls carried on the wind and the waves. And all our time there, we searched and searched for a sighting that was never to be. One night of a full moon, a violent thunderstorm shook the isle, and from the moment that the first lightning flashed across the sound, the corncrakes raised the alarm, craking louder in response to the competition from the sky. Nobody got any sleep.

There are many local names for the crake. Its summer call was once commonplace in damp meadows and lush grassland all over the British Isles. The names attest to its lost habitats, a bird that in the 1880s could even be heard in London's Tooting and Streatham Common. Half the size of a grey partridge and far slimmer, this discreet bird was known as the grass quail in Cheshire, the corn scrack in Aberdeen, the daker in Surrey, and the hay crake in Yorkshire. The females sit so tightly and secretively on their eggs that they cannot be seen, and in the last century scythers were often upset to discover they had accidentally cut a brave bird from its nest. Poet John Clare captured it perfectly in "The Landrail":

> We hear it in the weeding time
> When knee deep waves the corn.
> We hear it in the summer's prime
> Through meadows night and morn:

. . .

> Tis like a fancy everywhere
> A sort of living doubt;
> We know tis something but it ne'er
> Will blab the secret out.

But now, all over Britain, after decades of mechanised mowing, the territorial grating rasps have fallen silent. Here in the islands, where the fields are too small for large machinery, and more sympathetic mowing has lingered, the corncrake has held on and re-established itself. The crake has snuck here to safety, to the rocky, remote places, where roads and buildings are sparse and where it can nest peacefully as no haymaking or silage-cutting take place until later in the year when the birds have bred.

We searched as the Hebridean winds rattled the sanctuaries of blue-green iris leaves. We watched and waited. The corncrakes' persistent, monotone bursts repeated as if a sprite was trailing a fingernail along a comb. We searched, but never saw one. These undisturbed grasslands host the mysterious "croaker of the corn" until September when they cease croaking and quietly return to their wintering grounds in southern Africa.

We ventured down across the low-lying *machair*—Gaelic for "fertile, grassy plain"—an exposed, wind-blown dune pasture that forms a graceful sandy border between land and sea. These wind-scoured expanses are sculpted and chiselled by the wind, and are dependent on marram grass to hold the ground solid. Particular to the edges of the Western Isles, this delicate coastal habitat is one of the rarest in Europe, its fine, snowy sands hurled inland by regular Atlantic gales.

The calcium-rich soil with its fine layer of white shell-sand and low-growing herb-rich cover of cropped grass has been produced by traditional crofting practices: the devotion of centuries of small-scale farming; the laying down of seaweed generation after generation, and the grazing of sheep. The constant erosion by weather, the scouring winds and rains from not just the west but all points of the compass, means that the land is under onslaught for much of the year. But this was June, it was warm, and the delicately nibbled velvety carpet (evidently trimmed by rabbits as well as sheep) invited bare feet. We walked without our shoes, gazing at the scattered colours of daisy, red clover, buttercup, eyebright, and harebell. Larks soared up from the wind-rippled marram grass, the lamenting voices of oystercatchers filled the air, and at last it was possible to forget everything.

Great yellow bumblebees and rare belted beauty moths thrive here, and in winter golden plover shelter among the dunes. Out to sea, we saw shelducks and great northern divers. Further round the coast, at the wonderfully named Bay at the Back of the Ocean, the eiders breed in spring, and their saucy 'Oooo! Oooo!' calls sound like Frankie Howerd peeping through a keyhole. When finally we clambered down to the sand, the smooth sweep of beach was so white it hurt the eyes. We sat in the shade of rocks and found clear five-toed otter prints trailing the eyes out into the tideline.

Further out to sea, gannets furled their sharp wings and sliced down into the indigo blue. Beyond that three peaks rose out of the Atlantic: the Paps of Jura, a jagged island on the horizon that appeared like a huge loneliness in the mist. George Orwell exiled himself to this windy, mountainous wilderness—where deer outnumber people—to complete his bleakest of bleak novels, *Nineteen Eighty-Four*.

The journey to get to this spectacular place—rugged, sometimes harsh, always beautiful—usually involves some kind of act of devotion. Here, on this blizzard-bright island, mother and daughter together, I felt that soon Jenny would be off to the company of her friends, in a different world that marched towards other things. But for now, our differences forgotten, our bare toes plunged in the sudden swish of cold salt water, and the wind mussing our hair, my heart felt ready to brim over.

"THEY CALL THEM 'Brown Yogles' in Shetland," Rory told us, scanning the moorland from the driver's window of his jeep. "Very difficult to see! I've see them there, though, flying in from the sea . . ."

Our week was nearly over, but I had felt sure there would be Short-eared Owls on Mull, and had posted a few tweet messages and then some phone calls. At Craignure we'd met with Rory, a local birding friend of a friend. Surprised that it was not sea eagles or otters that we wanted, he promised us he could find some owls and drove us back into the hills towards Bunessan.

"Bingo. Found one," Rory signalled from beneath his binoculars.

"Where?" Jenny said, looking at the exact spot Rory had indicated, a few yards along a fence by the road. The owl was so camouflaged, as if it were a piece of the fence it was sitting on, that, like the corncrake, it seemed to be shrouded in a cloak of invisibility. Jenny and I struggled to locate it.

"They hunt along the sides of the road in the long grass," Rory said. "I've seen six or seven at a time. But you need to know what you're looking for. They fly low, and really don't show up well."

Very softly he set up his telescope, and adjusted the height so we could see. It was as easy as that. Magnified in the lens we saw every detail of that owl's face. It was staring directly at us, ear tufts on the alert. We could see the startling eyes set within the deep black of its mask, so close that I felt goose pimples shoot up my arms and all the hairs stand up on the back of my neck. All those months looking and searching for a bird that seemed to be defined by its absence, and Rory had found one for me in minutes. Perhaps they were just more visible when they were in their breeding grounds?

"They always nest on the ground," Rory told us. "Just in a scrape. You have to know what you're looking for. There may be a nest nearby, or even several, as they can nest communally, but you wouldn't know it. They tuck them away and blend them into the grass so well. Did you know that when she's on eggs, the female has to squeeze her eyes nearly closed so that she doesn't show up with those bright yellow peepers? They'd show up on the moor like headlights to other birds! It's true of all the owls that have yellow or orange eyes, actually—they have to do everything they can to blend in when they're sitting on eggs. But even if they sit too long on the fence, or even on a tussock, the gulls come and mob them, and the crows can come and take the eggs, if they're not careful."

Jenny said nothing for a moment as she adjusted the scope for herself, and then she gasped. The clarity of the owl's spooky face magnified in the lens gave us both the shivers. The bright facial disc was starkly white-rimmed and almost heart-shaped, the white brows dipping down between the eyes, just like the Barn Owl. I had not remembered this from my previous sighting all the way down south on Dartmoor; the owl had approached me so quickly and then veered away. This time, having it magnified like this, I was able to learn something more, and as the owl swivelled its face, reacting to every tiny sound, we admired the dark flecks on the neck and creamy breast, the way the wings were allowed to droop slightly, as if it were ready to take off at any minute. And when it did fly off I saw, or rather heard, its display flight; as the sun flashed like brass on those long, slender primary flight feathers and it clapped its wings together the sound echoed sharply back to us; the brightness of it rang out, as if those wings had been mined from deep out of the moor, their surface forged from metal.

My quest to track down the Short-eared Owl had taken me from Serbia, to my home on Dartmoor, and onto a remote Scottish isle. And so it was, with this final sighting, I had completed a migration of sorts, and seen every species of owl in the UK.

Or had I?

Bubo bubo

EURASIAN EAGLE OWL

I come with messages
from the darkest place. An infant coughing blood
in the village, a woman on the bed of the Ruhuhu river,
her eye sockets hollow, a fist printing a boy's face.
I trouble the shadows with my mourning song:
hoot-hoo-hoo-buhuhu-hoo. They shot my love
with a wooden arrow and nailed his white chest
to the doorframe to drive me away.

—LIZ BERRY, "Owl"

JUST ONE GLANCE AT THIS OWL DASHES ANY THOUGHTS of cuteness into the flames of Hades. It is possibly the largest owl in the world; if not by wingspan (the fearsome Blakiston's fish owl is the other contender for the size prize), it might win by a few grams in weight. With prominent ear tufts, shocking orange eyes topped with vivid eyelids, a brown-streaked front and bright white throat patch, fully feathered legs and boxing-glove feet, this big guy is armed with truly intimidating weaponry. Its jugular-crushing talons and flesh-ripping bill appear to be forged from cast iron and sharpened to scimitar points. How can it be, then, that this menacing owl is increasingly popular as a pet in Britain?

This heavyweight ranges between 1,500 to 4,600 grams (the females are often up to a kilo heavier than the males). You wouldn't usually want to approach it without the protection of a riot visor or a motorcycle helmet at the very least. But surely one would never attack or injure a human? This is exactly what happens when owls such as these are kept in captivity and not handled with extreme caution.

The Eagle Owl, it has to be said, is not native to the UK. But once, many thousands of years ago, it was. It is believed to have disappeared from the skies of Britain ten thousand years ago, around the end of the last period of glaciation. The latest record of a native bird being found in Britain was from some subfossil bones that were discovered in Ossom's cave in Derbyshire, where Mesolithic human hunters may potentially have used the owl for food. The bone found was a ten-thousand-year-old tarsometatarsus, the bone that forms the lower leg in birds. In mammals the metatarsus bone is actually in the upper foot, and more horizontal, giving an interesting view into skeletal evolution: in a mammal the bone is in the foot, and in the owl it is elongated as if the upper half of it has extended and become positioned vertically. We will never know for sure what these humans were doing with it, but the bone marks the last-known record of this species in Britain. No later presence has been proven since. Until recently.

A secret (if tiny) feral population, possibly escapees or unofficially released from captivity, are known to be breeding quietly and successfully in the wild in the UK. With some splash publicity from the BBC *One Show* and *Springwatch* in 2016, very carefully filmed so as not to disclose the exact location, most people were surprised to hear about these owls. They may be big but they are shy, very camouflaged and wisely keep a low profile. Most of us would not even know they were there.

Occasionally, however, a flamboyant individual can cause more of a stir. When some startling news broke that a "giant owl" had swooped down on the head of a bald man in Exeter city centre in the spring of 2016, the local *South West* news presenters Ian and Kylie announced it with well-honed smiles. Nobody took much notice. But the story caught the attention of my owl-radar. It was the beginning of April and many people took the story for a Fool's Day spoof. A Twitter profile for the bird appeared and owl jokes proliferated. Meanwhile, more and more people reported being bruised and scratched by a mystery owl swooping down from the city sky. Victims claimed to be startled at first by a "booming hoot," then a downdraught from massive wings; those not alert enough to duck were "whomped" and worse, scratched by a set of outstretched talons.

The local rags and news stations finally cottoned on that it was a real owl, and that it was not going away. They began to spread the story of the outsize owl mysteriously on the loose in Exeter and people started to get nervous. The comedy-bald-man angle faded as other innocent passers-by, people with a thick head of hair or wearing a hat, were randomly assaulted by the terrifying bird roaming Exeter city centre and its suburbs at night. On the local news people were warned not to approach the owl. Some less scrupulous national papers joined in, and further fomented fears: could this threatening King Kong of an owl be large enough to be "dog-eating" and "cat-snatching"? The more trustworthy local news went to the experts, and the Devon Wildlife Trust concluded that this was most likely to be an escaped captive-bred owl, not a wild specimen, and unlikely to snatch larger pets. On further investigation it was decided that this was *Bubo bubo*, the Eurasian Eagle Owl.

In Britain the Eagle Owl appears in two forms: members of the harmless, secretive feral community, known to be in existence since at least 1996, and the captive ones. These last, when mishandled, are far more dangerous than the wild specimens. And as far as we know, the captive owls vastly outnumber the wild population. Since the friendly letter-delivering owls appeared in the Harry Potter films, they have become more popular in falconry displays and even fashionable as pets. Owl clubs have become more popular and widespread, and you actually can buy an owl and all the required equipment online. If my local owl club is anything to go by, there may be upwards of one hundred in captivity just in the south-west of England. Could the Exeter Eagle Owl have been a hungry escapee on the rampage or was it possible that it was wild?

Some believe the Eagle Owl never truly vanished from our isles. Some believe it has been here all along, visiting from Scandinavia or continental Europe and breeding in very small numbers. Was this a native bird that had just been keeping a low profile all along, hiding in dense forest and desolate moorland? There are old words for it in Cornish, Gaelic, Manx, and Welsh, suggesting it might have been a rare but more recent and familiar part of our avifauna. Experts maintain that the science shows the Eagle Owl died out in Britain when rising sea levels following the last period of glaciation meant that there was no longer a land bridge to the Continent. According to this school of thought, there is little or no chance that this sedentary bird, which normally sticks to a relatively small territory of around 14 square kilometres, would risk leaving its home on the Continent and fly far over water to the British Isles. In fact, this owl is not found on many islands at all. The sea is too great a barrier, so no Eagle Owls have been recorded in Corsica, the Balearic Islands, Sicily, or the Greek islands either.

However, *Bubo bubo* appeared in the British Ornithologists' Union (BOU) lists as a scarce or occasional visitor until 1996, at which point it was removed. Opponents to the *Bubo bubo*-as-native theory are convinced that these owls could not or would not cope well with a daunting sea crossing; the bulky size of the Eagle Owl would require far too much energy to fly for so long without landing, and any adventurous or foolhardy vagrants would probably run out of steam and ditch in the sea. So it could be considered highly unlikely that any wild specimens would arrive naturally.

In 1996, following reported sightings and accounts of Eagle Owls in the wild, the BOU compiled an extensive dossier looking into its status. They found seventy-nine reports of Eagle Owls living in Britain since 1684, but there was some mystery surrounding the birds' origin. It has never been clear whether the owls were being introduced by humans during the seventeenth century, when recordings of sightings begin,

and subsequent owls found since then have also been introductions. Expert conservation organisations such as the RSPB
and the BTO have suggested that this is the case. More recently,
many hundreds were registered as pets between 1994 and 2007,
and of the 440 registered birds in the UK nearly a third have
been reported as escaped and "not recovered."

In 2016 the RSPB recognised the presence of a small number
of Eagle Owls living wild in Britain, but reiterated that their
origin was difficult to prove, and that "there is no evidence
that birds other than from released stock have bred in Britain
in recent times." To be considered native, the bird must have
been endemic or indigenous for several generations, without
being reintroduced, so it must be more than simply born in the
wild here after a captive release has bred successfully. Indeed,
if this happened, and the population spread, it could possibly
be considered "invasive."

What fascinated me, as I began my research into this formidable raptor, is how little people know about it. The Eagle
Owl occurs naturally in continental Europe and across Asia.
In Scandinavia, where it is shy and frequently persecuted, it
is on the decline, but until the emergence of the Exeter owl
it had not been present—or appeared not to have been present—in Britain within living memory. Could it have travelled
unaided across the Channel or the North Sea? Other owls do
make this journey, as we have seen, but none so big and heavy,
as far as we know.

Part of me longed for the Exeter renegade to be a wild
owl. I wanted to believe in this magnificent wild creature's
resilience and "survivability." For me, this might be a story
about the resourcefulness of a species, a sign of hope, that in
spite of natural challenges such as dangerous sea crossings
and human threats this animal could possibly make it here.
It is living in the wild in many places all over Europe, often

adapting to live close to towns and even within cities, but it inhabits a strange grey area; it is a huge predator that is rarely seen. Of course there are the owl sanctuaries that allow us to come close to the creature and to learn about it. But here they seem to be presented as fascinating marionettes, performing on cue in flight displays once a week, as if they were semi-domestic creatures. But they are predators, one feather-breadth away from a proud, savage, and well-lived existence, dignified, living a life for which they evolved. Keeping an independent and powerful creature on display, what would happen to our experience of the wild?

On the other hand, our wonder when allowed close to owls can create miraculous responses. In 2014 an Eagle Owl helped Polly Weston recover when her sister had died aged twenty-two, and in the shock and grief of her loss she had not been able to leave the house ever since. But shortly before she died, Polly's sister had won a falconry experience in the New Forest. Polly decided to go along in her loved one's place and perhaps learn how to fly the birds. There was an array of beautiful animals, Polly reported, and the Eagle Owl was so strikingly heavy and so cold, she said: "the weight of the bird was the first thing that brought me back down to earth again." Somehow, the visceral contact with this owl had brought her back to herself, and had helped with the grieving process. Other stories of humans being helped toward recovery by birds of prey abound. There must be something about this privileged contact that lifts the veil of separation between ourselves and other species, and helps to heal us, and bring out our sense of connectedness.

On the other hand, not all the stories are good, especially for the owls. Falconers have tried to train owls to add a touch of drama to wedding ceremonies. To create a fashionable Harry Potter-esque flourish, owls are hired to silently and romantically float in with the wedding rings at the appointed moment. Unfortunately, being owls, they often have other ideas, and delay proceedings by going to perch in the rafters for a nap, or even flying confusedly into the large stained-glass windows, inflicting irreparable damage on themselves and necessitating expensive repairs to the church.

It is not rocket science to assume that in captivity these owls might make noisesome, vocal, and antisocial night-hooting arias. Their copious aromatic and messy excretions and extremely specialised needs mean that they make exceptionally demanding pets. When they reach adolescence and move into sexual maturity, these owls can begin to behave very differently from the sedentary, biddable owlets they once were. Barred from their natural behaviour, they become noisy and can lash out. Eagle Owls may score high on charisma, but zero for cuddliness, and people soon realise what a challenge they are to keep. These nocturnal trouble-makers can frequently become aggressive, or decide to shirk their jesses and fly off on their own. They can become lost easily, especially if their aviary is not secured with double doors or they are not ringed or fitted with a tracking device. Sometimes they are recovered by their owners, who should (but do not always) know how to keep a valuable raptor safely. But it is not always easy to locate, attract, and trap an escaped owl. Many of these pet failures are held captive in sanctuaries, or worse—in the case of Eagle Owls, they might even be illegally released into the wild where they cannot necessarily feed themselves or survive. They might cause trouble for local wildlife, and for humans, as in the case of the Eagle Owl in Exeter. Perhaps more serious is that they may affect the local fauna, predating whatever they can and potentially upsetting the balance of ecosystems.

My friend the Eagle Owl owner and psychologist Anita, who works with captive owls and lives on the Wirral, had an interesting contribution to the Exeter mystery. She had heard from her local police that Eagle Owls have been taken up by drug dealers in some areas in and around Liverpool, and are used instead of threatening dogs. Since an aggressive owl probably is the avian equivalent of a pit-bull, this would seem like a handy accessory to have in a situation in which you need to intimidate people. Had an irresponsible owner in a less than salubrious career found his or her threat-pet too challenging to care for and simply abandoned it in or near Exeter?

The *Exeter Echo* published the story of a plucky young boy who had been able to get close enough to snap a photo of the errant raptor. No harm befell the young photographer; he had a good head of hair and was small enough to be unthreatening, so had not been a target for the Notorious Swoop. The picture showed the outlaw owl glaring out of the upper branches of a city conifer, ear tufts erect, its white throat patch clearly visible. When the owl uttered its hoot, the throat patch puffed out, the boy said. Was it displaying, calling for a mate, or its lost owner? The subtleties of its behaviour were beyond most people: "I'm trying to revise for my exams but: 'hoot hoot hoot' #exetereagleowl" tweeted one harassed university student.

Research shows that in the breeding season the male Eagle Owl can hoot on average six hundred times per night. And it is loud. The owl has a big pair of lungs, possibly to carry its voice through forests or amongst cliffs, and its booming two-tone hoot can be audible from 1.5 kilometres away, and even, exceptionally, up to 4 kilometres. In a town at night, you would not miss it, even if your duvet was wrapped around your ears. This owl, in its wisdom, had picked a rooftop roost on a street full of university digs. Students are notorious for being up all night, studying, writing essays, socialising, and the like, so they were able to present a running commentary on the owl's doings. Pictures of the owl were taken through attic bedroom windows and garrets as it peered menacingly in through the glass, pointed ear tufts silhouetted like horns against the neon-lit night sky. Having chosen its roost on an attractive rooftop cliff-scape around the back of the Odeon cinema, it continued its siege.

Nightly, the tweets flooded in from unsettled and distracted students unable to revise for their exams, often accompanied by vivid, panicked photographs. The owl did not appear to be ringed, or wearing any sign of captivity, and it continued to pounce on people who ventured into its territory at night. People with hats, bald men, and anyone distinguishable by bright head parts could fall prey to its ferocious whims: often it struck from behind, worryingly, as if it was attempting to sever the neck vertebrae, as it would with its normal prey. A tall, willowy postgraduate student of mine, Rebecca, who has long blond hair, reported being genuinely whomped whilst returning home from late shifts at work. She only avoided injury by ducking at the very last minute as the threatening hoot rang about her ears.

The owl remained unclaimed by any former owner—but perhaps there was no one out there to claim it. Had it come here of its own accord? Some, watching other raptor migrations (the Short-eared Owl from Norway and Sweden; the occasional Snowy Owl from the Arctic), believed it could have made a sea crossing. My ornithologist friend Emma thought perhaps it could indeed have flown the distance from France, or even braved the North Sea searching for a mate or new territory. Wanderers often happen. In the summer of 2015, a rare lammergeier, or bearded vulture, was seen crossing the sky over Plymouth. Later it was reported heading on over to south Wales. This was an extreme and powerful example, but rare vagrant birds have been seen drifting over Dartmoor in this way.

The Eurasian Eagle Owl's European distribution ranges from the taiga forests of Scandinavia to southern Spain. In their natural habitats of cliffs, rugged gorges, and forests they occupy the same territory all year round and for their whole lives, never ranging far—making it extremely unlikely that the Exeter owl was a wild one that had wandered here.

After a while, the Eagle Owl of Exeter story vanished from the news, and from the Oxford Road student digs by the football stadium; the owl had vanished from the roof of the Odeon cinema. It left something of a cavity, a shadow settled into the memory, a question mark, a bird that disappeared. Perhaps it moved on. Perhaps this is how it should be. And maybe we'll never know.

DEPENDING ON WHO you speak to, the Eagle Owl in Britain could either be considered a menace or a majestic raptor making an epic comeback. In 1993 a nest was found in the Derbyshire Peak District and the presence of a pair of breeding Eagle Owls was discussed on national television by BBC's *Natural World*. There was a mixture of excitement and consternation in response. Conflicts arose. What effect would these powerful birds have on the fragile ecosystem, particularly on populations of other birds of prey? Top predators frequently do not tolerate other top predators, and this was the habitat of the rare hen harrier (with perilously few pairs left) as well as Tawny, Long-eared, and Short-eared Owls. Anything crepuscular or nocturnal sharing the Eagle Owl's nesting territory and night-time hunting would be in danger. To address this, a risk assessment was carried out, concluding that an increasing population of Eagle Owls might indeed pose a threat to species of conservation concern like the hen harrier. The RSPB, however, pointed out that Eagle Owls are not the reason for the absence of hen harriers across large parts of the UK's uplands, and that this is probably due to persistent persecution by gamekeepers on moorland shooting estates.

The World Owl Trust, in the owls' defence, suggested that they were a natural part of the ecosystem that had once been hunted to extinction and that they should be protected. Renowned owl expert Heimo Mikkola also agrees that these owls died out in Britain due to extermination by humans, after which the land bridge to the Continent disappeared, and the birds never recolonised. But due to concern over the protection of other raptors like the endangered hen harrier, the owls were cautiously watched. In the ten years from 1996 to 2006, monitoring showed that they had produced around twenty-three chicks.

In the Forest of Bowland in Lancashire, the breeding pair had hit the headlines when they began—unusually for this species that normally prefers to avoid humans—to attack dog walkers when they took a path that passed close to the nest site. Following the 2006 BBC television documentary, somebody took the law into their own hands: the female was shot. There was uproar at this news from the wildlife-loving public but the anonymous perpetrator was never found. Clearly the appearance of a large predator on a small, densely populated island raises some hackles, and the contentious desire of some to have a wild predator at large is not shared by all.

Meanwhile, in November 2016 at an extremely hush-hush moorland location in the north of England, BBC television pictures were shown of three healthy-looking Eagle Owlets, alive and well on the nest; the parents were arriving with plenty of prey in the form of rabbits, and the small family of owls was thriving.

Debates rumble on about the Eagle Owl's right to reside, and meanwhile the birds themselves quietly continue to breed. By this time the three wild chicks that were filmed in the secret location will have fledged. With careful monitoring it has been found that the owls here sometimes lay up to three eggs per year and many of these young have successfully flown. But some years at the Forest of Bowland, nest monitors have found that the eggs are abandoned; the owls are highly sensitive to disturbance and will desert the nest if it is interfered with during incubation; even worse, it looks as if on some occasions their eggs might have been stolen.

The story of the Eagle Owls raises wider questions about the ecology of the relationship of humans to the wild: How do we adapt to manage the limited fauna that is left, in a crowded country purged of its large predators? Advocates of rewilding say that we are poorer without these creatures in the wild, but the role of these vanished predators is complex: Should they remain confined to the imagination, to picture books, to wildlife documentaries, to fiction, and to zoos, or should we welcome them back into our shared natural space, as a matter of principle?

For me, the curious incident of the night-time Exeter Eagle Owl was a case in point of humans failing in their duty. At these moments, the most damage can occur. Wretched creature. If it had escaped, why had it not been claimed? These birds are valuable, but also vulnerable. It is their vulnerability that hurts the heart. If the owl had been deliberately released as pest control, to hunt the local seagulls, widely seen as a noisy, messy aggravation, why was it then not claimed when it had done its job? The owl was reduced to a misfit, pathetically confused, either mistakenly hunting, looking for a mate during the breeding season, or chasing people away from city streets, a battle it could never win.

The story, received with glee in the media, rapidly lurched into slapstick. Things were even sillier on social media. In laughing at this bird, we betrayed our lack of respect. For me, a wild Eagle Owl flying over the city had something post-apocalyptic about it. The scale of human indifference, where other species are marginalised and mistreated, slid into perspective. In a man-made world, these predators are still possible; they can hunt and feed themselves effectively amongst the parks and the concrete, the rat-infested cliff-scapes of a city dominated by humans. Perhaps the Eagle Owl could thrive alongside us if it weren't for the power lines, the stray electricity, the prey that could so easily be poisoned or disappear beneath concrete, the drug dealers, the aggressive gulls, the airguns ...

At an encounter like that of the Exeter Eagle Owl, far from seeing it as comic our ancestors might have slipped quickly into a different sort of thinking than we do now, a thinking where far more serious things were at play: for them supernatural powers might have been at work. They would have paid more attention to these random events of nature than we do now, rendering them poignant with gravitas and meaning. Animals were messengers and mirrors to ancient humans. What would the appearance of a powerful bird like this represent? We may have respected its powers of sight and flight and skills of hunting, and may have been fearful of it too. It is likely that its appearance would have been closely observed, used to tell a story, to fill in something about life that we were unsure or uncertain about; to comfort, predict, or to warn, whether it was to teach about the present or the future. Birds gave us signs, told us something with their behaviour, and nothing about it was seen as random. When they took off something had happened, as if they were communicating something, as if we were joined in a network of understanding.

Our own species evolved alongside these predators, and so our brains were honed to pay attention to them. Without this alertness, humans would have faltered. Migrant animals and birds would have come from the north to escape bad weather and famine, to avoid the harshest winter weather fronts that may have been following on behind them. Along with changes in the landscape, their arrival would have reminded us to store up our food and prepare ourselves. Owls may have carried these meanings for our ancestors, and as such they became vessels of belief, about storms and ill omen, which have faded but not altogether disappeared. They remain still in our folk memory, the hag, the ghoul, or the demon, in the seasonal rites we once observed more widely, in literature and story that resist change.

Even now it is attractive (if you're not a sheep farmer) to imagine that there might still be beasts out there. Many people believe that in the wilds of Dartmoor and Bodmin Moor, and in other parts of the British countryside, secret predators still prowl. It is as if we need the idea of the beast to satisfy something locked away, some forgotten, buried thought deep in our psyche; the human self that evolved to listen out for, and to fight off, wild beasts if need be. Long ago we eliminated the bears and wolves that threatened us and competed with us for prey, and where once we told tales of beasts around our campfires, now we, the powerful ones, can gaze at them in zoos, and re-create them in books and stories. As soon as we could, we wrote our beasts down in stories such as Homer's *Odyssey*, where creatures such as Scylla and Charybdis dwell, and in *Beowulf* as Grendel and his mother. Now we have contained our beasts in story, song, and more recently in literature and horror film. But we still need something a little scary out there in the wild. And often it is the spooky owl that carries that legacy of things that might come out of the dark to get us. Things that might devour us, possess us, or carry off our children.

Perhaps more than most owls that I have seen, the Eagle Owl seems the most aloof from humans. It resists our interference, and adapts to our doings only if it has to. Several aspects of the Eagle Owl's biology tend towards this. First, it is designed for stealth and camouflage: the brown-and-buff mottling of its plumage and its habit of staying immobile for long periods in its tree or cliff habitat keep it well out of sight and out of our reach so it can live alongside us and keep a low profile. And being crepuscular or nocturnal, it is very, very difficult to spot in low light, especially if you are not paying attention. Second, if seen it presents a sizeable target, and being a top predator, is a threat to humans. And yet the fact that it could be shot or eaten by us makes us a distinct threat to it. It is therefore better for both species if we stay separate: and now that we have our own highly effective weaponry (cars, guns, poisons, electrical wires), contact or even conflict usually ends badly for the owl.

AFTER AN UNSUCCESSFUL TRIP with Benji to try and spot the Exeter Eagle Owl, I was more determined than ever to see one of these magnificent birds in the wild. My next lead, Vincenzo Penteriani from Andalusia, southern Spain, confidently said he could take me to see his patch in the mountains where the Eagle Owl thrives. This was at the southern limits of the owl's range in Europe. But by the time I was free to take up his tantalising offer he would have moved on to a summer of researching bears. "You'll have to go and see my friends in Helsinki," Vincenzo told me. Helsinki? My mind did a small flip, swooping from the warm, dry southern edge of the Eagle Owl's range close to the Rock of Gibraltar where it bordered with the Mediterranean, to the outer reaches of Scandinavia and the cold northern limits of *Bubo bubo*'s snowy wilderness habitat.

Vincenzo told me about the great guys based at his old research area in Finland, in Helsinki and further north: Jari

Valkama who was now director of the bird monitoring team at the Finnish Museum of Natural History in Helsinki, and Jere Toivola, a brilliant young bird ringer who would, he promised, take me to see owls in the wild in Finland. This was the opposite to what I had originally visualised in sunny Spain, but it was beginning to sound good. This region of the Eagle Owl's range encompasses the Finnish taiga forests stretching endlessly up towards Lapland and dwindling into the tundra of the Arctic Circle. More than that, the north harboured the most mysterious owls in Europe, the few remaining species that I had not yet seen: the Hawk Owl, the Great Grey, the Ural Owl and even possibly the Snowy. This new trip might put these within reach.

Immediately, challenges presented themselves. I didn't speak Finnish and, as my dad warned me knowledgeably on the phone, "Finnish people are a bit funny." When had he ever been to Finland? Why do we make these sweeping generalisations about whole nations? But my father insisted. "No, it's well known! There's this saying about them: when a Finn stops looking at his own shoes and starts looking at yours, you know he likes you."

I wasn't going to let something like shyness put me off, and consulted my cousin Maggie who lives in Helsinki and actually lives with a real live Finn. "It's true," she said. "They are very quiet. And they think we talk too much," she told me on the phone. "Just remember—don't worry about silences." I prepared myself mentally. I would allow for silences, and I would try to be a better listener. It would do me good. In an email Jere, the young bird ringer, assured me (in very good English) that he had been ringing (or helping to ring) Eagle Owls since he was tiny, observing the breeding cycle of this ferocious owl from a young age in the arms of his owl-obsessed dad. He would find me some, no problem.

What I know now, and didn't know when I bought my ticket, was that Jere was not a traditional looking-at-your-shoes Finn. He was a friendly and enthusiastic guerrilla owl finder; I would later watch him scale down a dizzying glacier-smoothed granite cliff, without harness or helmet, scrambling nimbly down to narrow nest ledges, elfin as Legolas in *Lord of the Rings*, and then expect me to follow after. He could retrieve a brace of struggling, hostile juvenile Eagle Owls and place rings on them. More than that, he could dangle them from one hand, whilst climbing back and being dived on by the furious parents. This was to be extreme owling. Coupled with Jari's experience and expertise (not to mention generosity), Jari and Jere together, as well as Jyri my helpful host, were a dream Finnish owl team. All that remained was to pack my bag with midge hood, water bottle, and insect repellent.

FROM THE START of June there is a window of two to three weeks when Eagle Owls move from the most sensitive phase of their nesting cycle—incubating eggs and raising tiny chicks—to when the chicks begin to fledge and might be a little harder to see, Jere told me. This trip was always going to be a challenge, I reflected on the plane at take-off. At home, Jenny was sitting her AS-level exams, and Benji was settling into his new job at a bakery in town. It seemed as though they both needed me; but then again, perhaps they would be better off without me. Benji was in his second week as a baker, his first job in the eighteen long months of his illness. With a supportive boss named Jonathan, who liked him very much, he was enjoying the challenge of a quiet café at the start of the summer season. But the day before I was due to leave I had a call. Benji had left for work on foot as usual, but minutes later:

"Mum, I'm in the park. Can you come and get me?" His voice was weak. Stressed in the bright sun and hot weather, he had collapsed on the way to work.

I grabbed a blanket, jumped in the car, and drove the two blocks to the park. Benji was slumped on a swing, the nearest support he could find, partially collapsed, and the one dog-walking passer-by had not noticed that anything was amiss. Why would you? A grown man, twitching and listing—you might conclude only one of two or three things: mental health, drugs, or alcohol. The sad truth is that people feel suspicious and give these a wide berth. Summoning my reserves of calm I hurried up to him, hoping I could head off the seizure.

"OK, Benji, do you think you can walk to the car? Lean on me."

I wriggled his limp arm over my shoulder and supported him as best I could (almost twice my weight, I realise now, weighed on my nine-stone frame) into the passenger seat.

We made it to the step of the house and Benji staggered in and collapsed in the hall. What would have happened if this had been a different day, and I had already been in Finland? I couldn't think like that. I gentled a pillow under his head so he was comfortable, wiped the sweat from his face, made sure no circulation was cut off anywhere, wrapped him in a light blanket, and left him to recover in the breeze on the hall carpet while I went to make a cup of hot, sweet tea for both of us and think of some jokes to relax him and cheer him up.

Laughter always helped Benji. One time we had all gone to see the comedian Bill Bailey perform. It was his latest comedy routine, Qualmpeddler, and an owl had been promised in the blurb. Partway through the second half, there had still not been any owls, and it was me who was having qualms. When Bill came to the finale of his set I was on the edge of my seat:

Where were the promised owls? Were they just a red herring or were they going to be live on set as the dramatic finale?

Then Bill described going to a restaurant with his family in Beijing and being offered all kinds of interesting live animals to eat. He listed them, one by one. The comedic tension rose, but my heart began to sink. The very bad feeling rising from my stomach took a turn for the worse as the final item was revealed exaggeratedly on a giant screen; standing tall, wings vampirically folded, tangerine eyes burning, its horn-like ears rigid with satanic fury. An Eagle Owl.

I like to think I would have done the same as Bill did that day. Quietly he paid for the Eagle Owl and explained that he wanted to take it away alive. The audience were enthralled at the awkwardness of this scenario. In any country this might be a terrible faux pas; how would the restaurateur react? On the other hand, a wild creature's life was at stake. To the audience's delight, Bill explained that the perplexed restaurant owner obligingly went to fetch a giant roll of Sellotape. He firmly fixed the hooked bill, the powerful wings, and sharp talons (I don't know how one might do this without serious injury to oneself or to the owl), and gave Bill the bird, trussed like an explosive papoose. Bill demonstrated its eyes, popping with rage. (The image of a sellotaped owl was almost too much for the now-hysterical audience.) With a final protective layer of cardboard box around it (with breathing holes), the Bailey family trooped out of town and into the forest.

There, without ceremony, they opened the package and cut the tape. On his iPhone Bill filmed the owl's next move. For a moment it paused to take stock of its situation. Then its feathers puffed out and it shook its aviation gear to life. The 2-metre wings opened and the bird tensed, then sprang, rising freely against a moonlit Beijing sky. The audience whooped as in one final image, the magnificent wingspan dominated the night and the owl was free.

The entire auditorium of Plymouth Pavilions, seating four thousand, witnessing this extraordinary tale, was overcome. Cheers, shouts, and applause beat against my eardrums. I wanted to enjoy it, truly, but amongst the braying wall of laughter I sat motionless. A chasm was deepening somewhere inside me. I hung my wet face and my throat ached.

I AM LEARNING about the kindness of people. Right now it was the generosity of Finnish people. Take Jari Valkama for instance. Never having met me, he not only offered to meet me off the plane, and host me during my visit, but came to stay in the same hotel. He planned that we would have a meal in the hotel and talk owls, then he would take me to see the owl vaults in the museum the next day. But my Norwegian budget flight was delayed six hours when the handbrake of the aircraft became jammed before we even set out for the runway. I didn't know planes even had handbrakes. I texted Jari with apologies. No problem, he promised kindly, he would wait for me at our agreed destination at the Hotel Helka and we'd have breakfast instead.

The midsummer light had been streaming in through my Helsinki hotel window for the few hours that I had been lying there, sleeplessly staring out at the concrete and glass of the rumbling city. I was more than ready for the sumptuous buffet waiting downstairs. Finnish people, it turned out, love warm porridge sweetened with freshly gathered assorted berries. Very tall and very blond Jari in his plaid shirt and black jeans assured me, thoughtfully chewing through the Finnish silences, that in Finland children are brought up on porridge and berries.

We walked a block through the stately concrete, tree-free parts of this utilitarian city to Jari's workplace, the Natural

History Museum. The temperature in Helsinki was a delight: the midsummer sun (that had dipped lightly toward the horizon somewhere around the hours of midnight and 1:30 to 2:00 AM) was blazing now; people in the street were smiling and relaxed. Everybody seemed to be wearing a summer dress or shorts and sandals. I donned my sunglasses to cover my puffy eyes.

"I keep telling Vincenzo that Finnish Eagle Owls are bigger than Spanish ones," Jari told me, gaily shedding his initial shy veneer as we sat in his book- and stuffed-owl-lined office on the top floor of the Natural History Museum. It is true: the further north you go in the Eagle Owl's European range, the larger the owls; due to the harsh climatic conditions here in Finland, the birds need to be bigger and more robust than their Spanish cousins to survive the long winters. In fact, Jari explained, the nominate species *Bubo bubo* occurs from here as far south as the Pyrenees, and further south we have the subspecies *Bubo bubo hispanus* which is smaller, paler, and greyer, and which Vincenzo studies at his home near Seville in Andalusia. Apart from that, there are up to ten other subspecies in and near to Europe: the nominate race, *Bubo bubo bubo*, is found from Scandinavia and northern Russia to the Pyrenees and the Mediterranean, but other subspecies of differing colourations and size also occur. There is *Bubo bubo hispanus*, Vincenzo's Spanish variety; in north-west Russia we have *Bubo bubo ruthenspaler*, which is greyer and whiter; and a much larger version of that, the magnificent *Bubo bubo sibiricus*, a glowingly pale race that is distinctly larger than the nominate *Bubo bubo*. In this last subspecies, a large female can be almost twice the size of a small male.

There are other subspecies winging their way across Asia Minor, and some hybridised forms that have interbred exist in southern Iraq, Syria, Lebanon, and Israel. The desert Eagle

Owls of Egypt and North Africa present perplexing problems in terms of borderline cases between species and subspecies in the desert and semi-desert races. These can be distinct in terms of colouration and characteristics (some also have different patterns of featheration on their feet and toes), but all have been found breeding in areas that join and overlap, and debates continue as more research is still to be done to join up the dots.

With Jari's information a massive spectrum of Eagle Owls spreads its wings in my mind, a buff-brown rainbow from chocolate to silver, all with slightly differing colouration, size, and characteristics. One thing unites the species, however: in Finland, as in much of Europe and the rest of the world, throughout history the Eagle Owl has been persecuted by humans.

Hunting and deliberate elimination may be the reason it vanished from the British Isles, although we can only speculate about this as the changing climate may also have been a factor. More than any other owl, the Eagle Owl continues to be persecuted by farmers who feel their livestock might be threatened, and by game hunters, and in some areas of Scandinavia it has declined with worrying rapidity in recent years. There are other important factors to consider in terms of contemporary threats, Jari told me: accidental (or deliberate) poisoning; collision with traffic on roads; entanglement and death on power lines and tall fencing placed unfortunately close to its flight paths. Basically, this owl is so big that it cannot easily dodge hazards or swerve.

While we talked, Jari quizzed me about my arrangements with Jere. Appearing unsatisfied, he graciously made a call to check on Jere to make sure he knew when and where to pick me up. Once the arrangements were all set and Jari was happy that Jere would indeed be there to meet me, we carried on our discussion. I couldn't wait to see these creatures in their natural habitat in the forest, and Jari assured me that Jere knew where all the nests were and that we were guaranteed to find some fledglings.

"In Finland the Eagle Owl nests on the ground, and I've argued with the word ornithologists use in English to describe the young owls you'll be seeing with Jere tomorrow," Jari told me. "When do we stop calling them nestlings, and begin to call them fledglings, for instance? The juvenile Eagle Owl can leave the nest at four to five weeks, they can walk away from the nest, but they don't start to fly until nine or ten weeks . . . what do we call them at that in-between stage? They're vulnerable for a whole month on the ground before they can fly. They can and do wander, and if their nest is easily accessible——and it often is——they can get predated by a whole range of things. Raccoon dogs are the worst."

Jari told me how between 1928 and 1967 the Russians released eight thousand of these bushy, badger-like forest-dwellers in a bid to extend the population for hunting. The resourceful raccoon dog has been so successful that it has now reached the borders of France. The helpless owl chicks give themselves away at dusk and into the night as they call continuously to their parents. The many nocturnal predators like fox, lynx, wolf, and bear are not hard of hearing, but increasingly it seems to be the raccoon dogs that can locate them most easily by following the calls.

This was news to me: I hadn't thought that the owls would nest so frequently on the ground; in France, possibly because they need to avoid a denser population of people and roads, I knew they perched on cliffs, tucked in high amongst protect-ing ledges and rocks; and in other countries they roosted right up in the trees. I had never heard of these raccoon dogs. They sounded like the owl's worst nightmare. Despite its name, this alien species has spread from Russian fur farms and is not a raccoon but a canid, a primitive member of the dog family. It is native to China, Japan (where they are known as *tanuki* and in folklore can change shape), and across Siberia. Worst of all for the owls, *Nyctereutes procyonoides*—the Latin name means "night wanderer"—has an expert sense of smell and superb hearing. Armed with terrier-like hunting skills, this deadly forager has spread so rapidly and successfully in Finland that it has reached "capacity." The short-legged predator gets up at dusk and trots around all night, just when the owls are active, nose to the ground, in search of anything at all to eat. That includes frogs, snakes, mice, voles, insects, and molluscs as well as ground-nesting birds. With the unselfconscious nesting habit of the owl in Finland, it sounded as though the young owls did not stand a chance.

That evening in my hotel room I was reading Jari's research, and learned that in some areas of the taiga forest the owl has diminished by up to 60 per cent. The overall population is declining year on year in Finland, and could be around just 1,200 to 1,400 currently. Mining and hydroelectric schemes can interfere with their territory. In the south, increased road traffic means increased likelihood of collisions. Jari's paper on large raptors highlighted to what extent these birds are vulnerable. Big enough to be noticed and shot or poisoned, particularly to protect game, they are still seen in many places as competitors by humans. His research suggested just how interlinked our history is—so as well as the raccoon dogs, the owls have us to contend with—and showed how existing surveys suggest that raptors increase alongside game bird numbers. But not enough studies have been done to prove that raptors could be a limiting factor, so some caution, and much more research, is needed before we point the finger or lay blame. More than this, Jari's paper pointed out, there are vast differences in the complexity of predator–prey relationships in different countries, varying considerably from northern Europe to the south, where communities are far more complex. Where habitat loss has forced game birds and raptors into increasingly small and fragmented habitats, land use, biodiversity, and sustainable development need to be understood before any conclusions can be drawn or "management plans" created.

When all is said and done, the knee-jerk reaction to eliminate predators remains, and perhaps it will always linger. Due to the age-old competition for prey between man and fellow predator, it still bubbles uncomfortably beneath the surface of our hard human skulls. Before the 1980s (when the Eagle Owl gained full protection in Finland), every second Eagle Owl corpse that was found had been shot. Now the persecution has lessened, but the Eagle Owls have also become less shy of people. Recently and increasingly they have put themselves in danger by inhabiting areas ever closer to increasing human populations. One of the main causes of death now appears to be electrocution by power lines. Later, I read that three out of five Eagle Owl corpses recovered, whose deaths can be reliably identified, die by electrocution on power lines or on roads. And it is not just the Eagle Owls that suffer in this way: Ural Owls and White-tailed Eagles often suffer the same fate. How intermingled our lives have become with this bird that was once considered an iconic species of the wilderness!

After electrocution, the next highest death toll is from collisions with vehicles. One paper of Jari's shows a rash of fatalities around areas of denser human population, and these owls are often killed at dusk and dawn, times when their hunting coincides with rush hour. A rash of deaths scatters the map of southern Finland: "Limiting the amount of traffic appears to be an unrealistic option to reduce owl collisions, but perhaps it would be possible to change drivers' attitudes such that they would reduce speed at high-risk areas," Jari suggests.

But the odds did not look good. With milder winters (and the lack of protecting snow) and changes in farming practices in southern and western Finland, where the Eagle Owl has its stronghold, small mammal habitats have declined and the traditional vole cycles, in which the population peaks every three to four years, have almost vanished. The unpredictable conditions for owls in the countryside might explain why some years ago a pair took up residence on the top of the modern glass-and-steel Helsinki shopping centre, and they bred, producing three chicks. This I thought was a good sign. Surely in spite of everything they were adapting well to living alongside us?

Jari explained, "It was a disaster. People liked them, they became like a local mascot, but there were so many dangers for them. Such a large raptor does not fare well so close to dense human population; the dangers are too many. Power lines and traffic mostly, but also disease. The male died of a herpes virus and to be honest I'm pleased that they've gone. It wasn't good for them to be here. The chicks were not safe and they caused such problems: I lost count of how many times they wandered away from their ledge and fell out of the nest and the emergency services had to be called to pick them off the street and put them back."

"What did they feed on, in the middle of the city?" I asked, thinking of the Exeter Eagle Owl.

"They had plenty to eat—probably fed on the local rabbits. And they can become quite resistant to vermin poison: the Eagle Owls that live near urban areas in other parts of Finland, close to rubbish tips, feed on rats that have eaten poison."

I wondered, did that cause fatality?

"No, they seemed from the toxicology tests to be largely unaffected. Every waste-disposal site probably had a pair of

Eagle Owls. There was a limitless supply of *Rattus norvegicus* for them there. But now there are fewer open waste sites: where in the 1990s there were more than a thousand, now there are less than one hundred. EU directives dictate how we dispose of waste and we don't often stop to think how this affects the dependent or adapted wildlife. Now that organic waste is on the decline, sites are more sterile, and alongside these changes, the vermin species, the gulls, and the owls have declined as well." In consequence, the Eagle Owls have come even closer to human settlements, to quarries, and even to towns. It reminded me of what has happened in Britain with urban gulls.

Out in the woods, where I'd be going with Jere, clear-cut areas of forest make ideal sites for the owls, as they often prefer fewer trees and open spaces that are easier to hunt in. But these can quickly regrow and become unsuitable, forcing the owls out again. The owls are site-loyal but also very sensitive, so could this aspect put stress on their breeding? I wondered. Jari passed me some of his studies to read later. These suggested that the owls, who may have a territory of 14 square kilometres, may move a few kilometres to nest elsewhere within their territory, but this is hard to prove. "We need more ringing data. But the owls are clever and they remember being trapped. Once an owl has been caught you will not get it again," Jari laughed. "They remember everything. When the female is on her eggs she is hyper-vigilant and knows her immediate environment intimately. They form a sound map of their territory, using mostly their hearing but also their eyesight, and notice if anything at all changes, even at night—and they have very good night vision—so their powers of observation are prodigious. Coupled with this they are highly sensitive, but this can actually make it easier to find fledglings to ring: the parents make a big fuss if anyone approaches their vicinity and their nervous reactions give away the nest site."

Normally nest sites can be located by Jari and his team through a variety of clues, including feathers and pellets, but the adults will often give the chicks away by reacting strongly to any intruder. "They might perform threat displays, so ringers and researchers can locate them by their particular nervous call, a kind of whistling, and they may even perform a broken-wing act, a total giveaway that there are young nearby," Jari said.

The next day Jari took me down to the vaults of the museum. Here we could look more closely at the owl collection. He showed me the way the owl's wing moults and how we can try to divine its age (Eagle Owls have four or five different age classes from nestling to senior) through its feather moults; in older birds we can begin to age them by which primary flight feathers are missing or have grown back in and look slightly different. Jari displayed those thoughtful silences as he showed me the wings, running his fingers along the fourteenth and fifteenth flight feathers of one that has been preserved fully extended; some of the feathers looked subtly darker, less faded, perhaps newer.

"It's hard to say," he concluded. "An older bird, yes, mature but of indeterminate age; not clear exactly with this specimen." On the way back we passed the mammal vaults and Jari saw me looking at the labels: *Gulo gulo*. Wolverine. I had always wanted to see a wolverine. This might be my only chance.

"Just let me know if there's anything else you'd like to see," Jari offered, noticing my sightline.

"Don't get me started."

"That sounds like an invitation." Jari cheerily slid open a door to reveal an Aladdin's cave of furs. "In you go. Have a look."

As I stepped in, a heap of exuberantly long spotted tails tumbled around my shoes. These were not from Finland. I ran my hands along the snow leopards. Shot amongst high mountainscapes far from here: Siberia, Afghanistan, Tibet, and Bhutan. Along with the Eagle Owls, these large predators now suffer the same threats: conflict with humans, poaching, loss of prey, and climate disruption. I closed my eyes amongst twenty hung-up leopards, blinded by their fur, their bouquets of claws, their memory of high Himalayas and men stalking, booted, tweed-clad, armed with rifles.

Jari quietly opened the next sliding door: rows and rows of wolf. Now as we looked my chest felt heavy. Jari stood beside me as we witnessed the shadowy-black pelts, our eyes slowly ranging over the silvers and greys and even the white furs. After the snow leopard room, and the wolf room, it was the shine of the wolverine pelts that took my breath away; they were as bright as if they had been caught just yesterday, a rich, gleaming mahogany with swirls of chocolate-brown and black. I reached out to touch the famous ice-proof fur. Then the lynx, the colour of oatmeal, with its dangle of chunky snowshoe paws that had once padded stealthily over long-melted winter wastes.

Jari had been so kind, so generous with his time, so honest and revealing about his work at the museum. Back at my hotel I showered the dusty film of formaldehyde from my skin, and gave myself some time for silence, lying on my bed a while with my owl notes. A watery square of city light poured in and warmed me, the captured glowing brightness of the undying midnight sun.

GETTING THE TRAIN in a country where you only speak three words and two phrases of the language was always going to be a risk. (I queued for half an hour to ask for my ticket only to be told by a perplexed official that no, this was a bank, and the tickets were over there on the other side.) But I had to go north if I wanted to meet Jere. He had promised to meet me off the train and take me to find Eagle Owls.

In his day job, Jere is a lumberjack. When Jari had told me this it made me feel safe; I would not be plunging into the wild backwoods with any old person. Jere would know his way, he would know the dangers. When we met I could tell he was as fit and fearless as a young mountain goat, but in the boiling heat of midsummer, he would expect me to keep up, no excuses. It was stiflingly hot when we eventually set off in Jere's rattly car, and the midday sun was relentless. We drove with the windows down and soon we left the dazzle of the main road to rumble along a leafy dirt track. Is this a farm track, I wondered, or were all of the roads gravel in this part of Finland?

"All the roads are like this," Jere said, surprised at my question. We pulled up on a verge and piled quietly out. "The roads are like this because in winter they have to survive the snow."

I tried to imagine how it might be here, in this bird-thronged, singing, green, sweltering glade, how harsh it might be in the middle of winter. Dark all day long, water frozen, pine-scented trees laden with ice. For the owls, hunting is good even in those days of twenty hours of darkness—even when there is only the tiniest bit of twilight; with their acute hearing they still can hear the voles scrabbling and nibbling in their tunnels beneath the snow.

The first nest site was in a bright clearing, a ferny, bramble-covered area with many tree stumps; a clear-felled part of forest that the owls like, Jere told me, speaking softly so as not to disturb the owls. "You'll need to put on those long trousers you brought," he added, tucking the ankles of his lumberjack trousers tightly into the tops of his tall lace-up boots; if there were going to be bloodthirsty insects, they were likely to be right here.

There was no path: Jere took off straight into the middle of this rock-strewn wilderness; I waded in his footsteps, struggling to keep up. As we strode through the jungle of ferns, bilberry, and willowherb, spiders and ants and flies skittered away, midges flew up, and I sprayed a fresh layer of insect repellent over my face and arms. We came upon a flattened grassy area with a strong whiff rising from it, as if an animal had been rolling there. I'd seen patches like this at home, where deer sleep, but this was much, much larger.

"Moose," Jere said, his grey eyes staring into the shadows between the trees. "We probably frightened it away. They don't like people when they have young."

The moose-patch was still warm. I followed Jere's gaze into the trees thinking of the bulk of a female moose; at a leggy 2 metres tall and weighing a hefty 400 kilos, moose are the largest in the deer family and one of the biggest mammals in Europe. I did not fancy coming face to face with a protective moose mother and her jagged, prehistoric antlers.

Jere led me to a boulder with feathers scattered beneath it and, oddly, one abandoned white egg, about the size of a goose's, my first sight of an Eagle Owl egg. Jere searched around amongst brambles and pine needles, and looked concerned. "I think this nest has been abandoned. Don't worry, chicks guaranteed at the next site."

Off he loped, his wiry frame agile and light-footed. The owls are very sensitive when they are nesting and will quickly abandon a nest if anything disturbs them.

Jere's next site was a long walk through fields where we startled a velvet-antlered young buck. As we moved quietly up into more woods we spotted a movement on a tree trunk; a magnificent black woodpecker (a first for me! tick!), its streak of red showing as a bright ruby cap against its coal-dark plumage and the rough bark of a tall pine.

Deeper into the trees and then I found myself teetering along the side of a cliff that plunged down to a mud-brown lake a hundred feet below. Fortunately the sides of this cliff were covered in spindly trees and rocks, enabling us to clamber along. We came to a ledge that was covered in owl feathers, a predated Long-eared Owl, and even the remains of a hedgehog in some pellets, the whole thing eaten, spines and all! The Eagle Owl had made easy work of this prickly meal! Respect.

As I said, Jere had stamina, and next we found ourselves scrambling up the side of a quarry. "I've taken you to some beautiful places," Jere said. "This one, not so beautiful." He scampered up the side of a cliff which had perilous cracks in it. They looked like the inside wall of my mum's house that time it needed underpinning. Huge loose boulders crumbled and teetered as if they could crack off and fall at any minute.

"I'm coming up a different way! That doesn't look safe!" I decided. When I reached the peak I saw Jere standing up, smiling, already holding two chicks like a pair of twin babies, one in each arm. As I approached, one managed to disengage itself and skittered away. Not quite fledged at eight weeks, it ran clumsily with hunched, part-adult wings, and ended up scrambling all the way into a shallow lake at the bottom of the cliff.

"Hold this!" Jere sprang into emergency mode. He thrust the other owlet into my hands. Suddenly I was holding the most ferocious and unwilling baby I have ever seen. I stood very still, trying to exude calm and authority in this precarious but highly responsible position. While Jere was chasing the stray baby, I snuggled my owl tightly into the crook of my arm, gripping its legs and using my front to block its wings from opening. It was warm, sweaty, and heavy, about the size of a Jack Russell terrier, just as strong and much more dangerous-looking. As long as I could keep its wings safely folded by its sides we'd be fine. We stared into one another's eyes. I did my best to exude motherly rather than unfriendly vibes, but it clapped its beak threateningly, glared, and hissed like a viper. I tried not to flinch, holding the thick, twiggy ankles firmly together as I had learned to do with the Barn Owls back at home, but this baby seemed to be in possession of more ideas on how to fight back than the owls I had got to know. All it wanted was to sink some of its deadly toolkit into any part of my flesh. Nevertheless, it was impossibly downy still, its floaty beige covering like mohair, soft and clammy in my hands. Tiny wisps of down were detaching themselves and floating up to my face, tickling my nose and eyes, and with no hands free there was nothing I could do. With very few adult primary feathers coming in at the tips of its wings it could not fly yet, and eyed me angrily, not taking its orange glare away for a minute, like a gremlin that has not quite come into its full power but knows it won't be long.

Below, I could hear Jere lifting the escaped chick from the water and climbing back up to us. But oh dear, now we had attracted the attention of the parents. Like the ominous line in the film *Jurassic Park*, where there's a baby, there's always a mother not far away. And this mother could not have been more Jurassic. She swooped over us, her massive wingspan all velocity and threat; ear tufts laid flat, she had perfect aim, whooshing, primary flight feathers splayed, warning us, her anxious yelping cry echoing around the quarry, her beak snapping. Nearly noiseless in her flight, her upper coverts densely dark brown, with her soft wingbeats the light fell beige and gold through her feathers. She swooped back again, this time on Jere, skimming over the top of his hat in a final warning fly-by. We placed the ringed chicks safely back on their ledge and the mother owl glided away, landing in a tall pine a few yards distant. From where we stood, I could see her heavily streaked front and barred tail. She perched there, anxious, ear tufts more erect in alarm, waiting for us to depart.

Slightly nervous, I asked Jere whether he'd ever been hurt by an owl.

"Yes, once or twice."

One time, he told me, he went to fit a radio tracking transmitter to some Eagle Owls on his own at night. This seemed daredevil, but not out of character. Jere was clearly experienced and he knew what he was doing, but even the best of us can misjudge. He waited for dusk, set up the mist net, and waited, and when the owl came it was a big female. She was caught by the wing and furious, flapping and struggling; it was then that he made his mistake. In order to disentangle her he held her by the free wing and instantly her talons sank into him; one set deep in his arm, the other locked in his thigh.

"It was a mess. Blood everywhere. You can't force the bird to let go. I just had to release the wing, bleed, and wait. It was incredibly painful."

"Is that the only time?"

"Another time I was ringing some chicks and a mad male with one eye, who was huge, punched me in the back by flying in from behind—he hit me so hard and his aim was great, he knocked me right over."

Our final chick of the day was harder to find. But I discovered that once Jere had got started, he wouldn't give in easily. We walked a good distance into the woods; the reindeer moss and lichen crinkled and crunched, dry as biscuit beneath our feet. Jere searched for the signs: the faecal posts and plucking sites that he knew would eventually lead us to our quarry. There was no path so we wended our way into the trees, but Jere knew the woods well, I was sure. Even so, this place was hard to navigate. Hilly, with deep tree-covered ravines, and in places difficult to traverse, with brambles, bilberry, and broom everywhere presenting barriers to wade through or find a way around. I saw crested tits (tick!) whittering together in the high pine branches and wondered at the thick spongelike carpet that crisped and crackled beneath us. Our footfall made it impossible to be silent, and together we sounded like giants crunching through heaps of cornflakes.

Jere scampered down a cliff again, and I waited in a clearing; partly I was afraid to wander away from it as I would surely get lost, but it also meant that I could see any animals coming. For what seemed like half an hour I stood, alone in the sunlight of the glade, amongst the hot stillness, gazing at the magnificence of these woods. Jere had gone so far that I could no longer see him, and when I peered into the ravine into which he was last seen clambering there was no sign of him. Suddenly these dry woods seemed less friendly: all around viridian saplings thrust upward toward the light, bilberry leaves lay thick on low-slung bushes, the sun battered everything: lichen, moss, pines, and earth. There was not a breath of wind, the forest was crinkle-dry; smells of pine and drought rose in the heat; my water had run out and I had not paid attention to any water source or even about the way back to the track. I was alone and unprepared; a mixture of fear and wonder began to rise up my legs. My ancestors knew how to survive here; I did not. So quickly disorientated, I wouldn't have stood a chance! Just as my heartbeat began to up its tempo, Jere sprouted elf-like from the rim of a cliff, grinning proud as a new dad, carrying a whopping and very snappy young female owl. Those huge eyes! They burned like torches. Then there were her amazing white scaly feet. They were huge. And tipped with a savage cluster of sabre-like talons. She stretched them out in front of her body, grasping, hissing.

"Do you want to hold her?" Jere asked, a slight giggle in his voice as we both marvelled at this fierce wonder-baby of the woods. She was barely a fledgling at only eight weeks old, but she could have done some serious damage if mishandled. I gripped her as firmly as I could, and snuggled her into the crook of my arm, where she vibrated with energy and alarm. In a week or two she would be away, flying into her new life of slaughtering voles, rabbits, owls, crows, and hedgehogs.

A woodpecker cried suddenly, indicating the return of the parents. All around us, a flurry of alarm jittered through the branches. One of the parents was close; I felt the back of me prickle. Would they go for us? Perhaps not in the daytime. But we couldn't see them coming in these thick woods; only the birds knew where they were and made a fine show of pointing that out.

As I looked up and scanned into the branches above us, something mottled, ear tufts silhouetted, stared distrustfully down at us. It was the male; slightly smaller than the female, but no less dangerous. He exuded threat, his huge claws gripping the branch. I could even see his soft white eyelids. He clacked his beak and I thought of the snapped spines of rabbits, foxes, other birds of prey, all of which might fight back—but none of which would stand a chance against this supreme predator and its talons.

"This pair may have been nesting here for fifteen or even twenty springs," Jere told me, "and these are great parents." The Eagle Owl can be long-lived in spite of its vulnerability. They can live for twenty years in the wild, or even longer, and maybe twice that in captivity. All that experience forms something akin to wisdom, but not the human sort. It is owl knowledge: how to hunt and feed; how to attract and keep a mate; how to be vigilant; how to defend a territory, protect a family. When to be still, and when to fly. I understand, now, how the owl might have absorbed both ideas, wisdom and evil, in the human mind. Had the natural evolutionary requirement to protect its young been misconstrued as aggression or evil by our forebears? It would not hesitate to strike if it felt the need, and yet we both knew this would be a last resort. It is not wise for a predator to risk injury.

I WATCHED THE glare, the restrained potential of menace. Its amber-orange eyes smouldered.

Jere placed the precious cargo snugly back into her mossy cavity in the shade of pine saplings and we withdrew before she could lunge at his leather boots. Above us, the parent looked no less enraged. Tiny dust motes and wisps of owl down floated up through the warm air at our retreat, trailing behind us as we moved away into the lichen-clad woods.

I MADE IT to Vincenzo's patch in Spain in the end, or near enough. It was October, and he wasn't there, but his owls were. In one swoop I had travelled from the Eagle Owls' northern-most reaches to the southern, and in Extremadura, at the Monfragüe National Park nature reserve, my guide Martin Kelsey said we'd only have to wait. I'd come all the way to see the national park, set within a very special larger Biosphere Reserve, an area of forests, gorges, lakes, and savannah with a rocky Mediterranean landscape. Not only did this place provide a rich habitat for Eagle Owls and Spanish imperial eagles but also something very special: a rare population of Europe's largest carrion-feeding raptor: the black vulture. Extremadura, a sparsely populated area more than twice the size of Wales, presents a vast habitat for vultures; the human population of 1 million coexists with the wildlife through traditional, low-impact agriculture.

The Biosphere Reserve around Monfragüe is an import-ant buffer zone encircling the entire national park. Rich in patchwork habitats for mammals, birds, and insects, the sun-blasted land of the Biosphere is scattered with meadows, wild olive, holm, and cork oaks that sustain the rural community and the wildlife alike. A never-ending whispering carpet, the autumnal grasslands appeared to be made of withered gold, a mass of crisp, sculptural grasses and filigree thistles that fragmented underfoot: cardoon thistles, herbs, wild carrot, silvery broom, and wisps of willow, and when I looked closer into the woven tawny-blond thatch, dotted all through were the delicate white bells of autumn snowflakes. We found lizards, tiny green geckos; the crisp shed skin of a Montpellier snake; praying mantis, a host of dragonflies, tiny white butterflies, and a hunting tiger spider. But over and above that, drifting in and out of the national park and over the sweeping pastures of the Biosphere, ignoring the human lines and boundaries, on invisible updraughts of warm air circled the vultures.

With their spine-tingling wingspans of nearly 3 metres these are one of Europe's rarest, and hugest, birds of prey. They soared high above us, massive wings bowing under their own weight, gliding almost as if in slow motion. Our necks ached in awe and amazement.

Human activity in Extremadura has benefited top predators like the Eagle Owl and the vulture. With livestock grazing on the vast *dehesas*, the open oak pastures, and on the large hunting estates in winter, animals roam freely; the meadows are packed with rabbits and small rodents, and scattered with remains, especially from deer and boar that are readily consumed by the vultures. The two raptors inhabit different ecological niches, the owls here nesting in the plentiful cliffs and sometimes very tall buildings, and the black vultures in tall trees. The Eagle Owl will prey on just about anything live; the black vultures evolved to feed on small prey and carrion such as rabbits, while griffon vultures, also to be found here, can pour in from high crags to disintegrate a deer carcass in

minutes. The black vultures will feed on the scattered mor-
sels that the griffons leave. Each one fits into its own cavity
in the ecosystem. Because of increased livestock and hunting there has been a dramatic surge in the population size
of the black vultures, categorised as near-threatened in other
parts of the world, and in forty years they have increased from
about ninety to over nine hundred pairs in Extremadura. In
the Monfragüe National Park alone there are over three
hundred pairs, creating the world's highest density of this
endangered bird.

After months of drought, the landscape of sun-blasted
pasture was speckled deep green with evergreen oaks. These
cork and holm oak pastures thrive by the Monfragüe syn-
cline, crumpled ridges of 500-million-year-old quartzites
that form silver-green crags thrust skyward. We walked
from the village of Serradilla towards Mirabel, where white-
washed terracotta-tiled homes nestled beneath a ruined castle perched on beetling cliffs. The wildlife does well here, but
the surrounding human settlements are declining as the 50
per cent unemployed population of young people leaves to
find work. With their allotments, Iberian pigs, chickens, and
curious donkeys, the towns had a nearly forgotten feel. But
the rich birdlife (we saw flocks of Spanish sparrows, crested
larks, and many other finches; black redstarts and a hoopoe
flew up as we passed), including such rarities as the Eagle
Owls and vultures, present the region with an exciting natural capital of wonders, and vast potential in terms of birding tourism. If only areas like Monfragüe and the Biosphere
Reserve with their tiny unspoiled villages and traditional
settlements like Serradilla and Mirabel were more widely
known about, more birders would come, and it would inject
a much-needed economic boost of eco-tourism into the fal-
tering local economy.

All around, the cork oak forests thronged with birds; these gnarly trees stood out from the holm oaks with their flayed red hides, as if they were sore after the cork bark had been carefully stripped. But it is all done sensitively, so that the tree can sustain itself and recover its protective coating. We walked to the castle of Mirabel, then down through the cork oak groves, and proud among them stood a "singular" tree, a veteran with its very own information board. This was the Padre Santo (Holy Father) oak, estimated to be nine hundred years old. It had witnessed the whole history of the castle above it, its trunk moulded by generations of cork harvesting. Reddened to the reach of the corking blade, the trunk's forked branches became fissured higher up and its nooks and crannies were feathered with a thousand years of lichen.

The multiplicity of bird voices in these groves is what makes them so unique and special, and it stays with me still. The high twittering calls of a million birds, resounding about the trees and over the sun-gilded herbs and grass, reminds of a lost time, before so many species were threatened. But the highlight was to come. As we waited by the Tiétar river at dusk, Martin brought us to see what I had been hoping for. He said we'd know where the owls were by the call. By the tall cliffs of the river we focused our telescopes, scanned, watched, waited. As the hours passed, the sun went down. We waited. And waited. The gentle evening slid its shadows down the valley and over the bend in the river, and our sense of hearing began to take precedence. Bats flitted around our heads, their high-pitched piping, their echolocation call felt close to our faces, and was as disconcerting as it was invisible.

Búho real, the Spanish call it. The royal owl. A small group of local people gathered together with us, and they watched us as we watched.

"Buuu-hu," we heard just as the light had almost entirely disappeared. It came from somewhere up on the ridge, high above the river.

"El búho!" the Spanish people called excitedly, as if in reply. *El búho!* The owl! We fixed our telescopes on the cliffs above the water and tried to focus on her, searching as they asked: "Donde esta el búho?" Where is she? Where is the owl?

In the dark we could not tell whether this was *Bubo bubo*, or *Bubo bubo hispanus*, the paler version of the nominate species, one of twenty subspecies of this super-predator. But there she was, tucked inside a crook in the cliff, a shadow within a shadow.

The owl called softly at first, breathy and unsure, as if this was just a whisper on waking. Dusk was falling around us, and invisible amongst the quartzite rock face and the tangle of stunted oaks and broom she was muffled, as if calling from inside a crevasse or the knotty branches of a tree.

"Buuu-hu?" the melancholy call came again. Its deep, plaintive note tumbled from the rocks and down to the water. Every two minutes or so, regular now, as if the voice was pulling a shawl of darkness over the ravine and veiling our eyes.

"Buuu-hu." Louder now. Even the river was losing its light, and this time a shoal of goose pimples swam along my arms. My earsight became more and more acute as the darkness deepened.

A fox shrieked, answered by a voice that might have been its echo, a rival, or a mate. A stag bellowed; this was the rut, and as well as the dark, the cooler night temperature brought something feral, a scent of something other, a musky surge, perhaps the stags' testosterone. And rising from the flanks of the valley where the male deer searched came a scent from the does hidden in nearby scrubland and fields.

Then the owl swooped, reflected in the barest glimmer in the river's surface. "Buuu-hu." There she was, an owl silhouette flying up to perch on the crest of the ridge; hefty, backlit by the indigo glow in the sky, glimmering, a jut of rock where there was no rock.

Her head turned, her tall ear tufts starkly outlined. I could just make out the pale throat patch and the ear tufts, not quite erect, drooping at an angle. Where was the male? There was no answer to her call.

"Buuuu-hu." She shuffled her position, tensed her body, wings at the ready, shoulders taut. She was preparing to take off, about to fly. We held our breath. Then her wings opened and like a giant moth she glided away into the black, swooped around, and reappeared on the skyline. As she called, her whole body was held at an angle of 45 degrees. *I am here—where are you? I am here—where are you?* she seemed to say.

She held her head forward, throat puffed and ruffled. Her plaintive voice became more forceful and urgent now.

"Buuuu-hu." Her head turned this way and that, ear tufts up as she searched. One last call in the dark, but her soft booming was unanswered: "Buuuu-hu." *I am here, where are you?*

Nothing came back to her out of the dark. The night was wrapped around her. Scents of pine and broom lay in silky layers, softening the quiet, hushing our feet, our breath. The shallows riffled and the ridge was silent. Between the rough bushes and over the shrubs the owl's voice vanished into the night:

I am here—where are you? I am here—where are you?

In the end it wasn't the size of the Eagle Owl that had astounded me, but its vulnerability. There was something terribly lonely about the solitary boom of its call. I had come so far to find that it seemed as if these fearsome creatures need something none of us can really do without: family. Although solitary for much of the time, they shared that with us. Without family, we are nothing.

Glaucidium passerinum

PYGMY OWL

And sweetest in the gale is heard;
And sore must be the storm
That could abash the little bird
That kept so many warm.

—EMILY DICKINSON,
"'Hope' is the thing with feathers"

I WAS NOT ENTIRELY READY FOR THE SCALE OF MY next owl, especially after studying what was reputed to be the biggest owl in the world. But sometimes it is the small things that can touch the heart the most powerfully.

The smallest owl in the world (by weight) is the Elf Owl. I couldn't travel to Texas or Mexico to see it, so sadly that was out. I would never see its elfin yellow eyes peering out of what must be the best place in the world for a nest: a tiny borehole high up in a giant cactus. But there was something nearly as good, and like so many of the wonders I'd seen on my owl quest, this one had not been in the original plan. All this time I had been thinking that *Athene noctua*, the Little Owl, was the smallest owl I would ever see. But I was taken by surprise. When you tell people that you are interested in owls it is not long before they tap very quickly into the idea, and begin to send you interesting things.

The mystery package arrived from my owl-loving friend Christine in France. Although she had on one occasion given me a glow-in-the-dark owl lamp, I always opened her gifts with anticipation of something good. Without wanting to seem churlish, I have to admit to a slowly expanding roomful of owl things: candles, cups, cards, pictures, Christmas decorations, tiles, coasters, ornaments, statuettes, etc. Really I was happy with wild owls, especially as most of the owl gifts have not much use beyond being an attractive in-the-moment gift idea. I was increasingly uncomfortable with the way man-made tributes to this creature were piling up in my office. It seemed as though the whole world was commercialising something that didn't want to be commercialised. Going to see them in the wild as part of an eco-tourism trip was one thing, but this endless objectifying fetish that was commodifying the owl into cute faces on cups and candles was not sitting comfortably.

This owl gift, however, was more thoughtful than most. It was a thank-you for the wedding present I had given Christine and Marianne. I had got them a delicate, hand-carved Finnish "fanbird": two birds in flight, joined together beak to beak, as a mobile to hang in their window. Sometimes it is the small gestures that create ripples in life, and this one was about to unleash a capacious bow wave. I had told Christine that the British owls would be quite enough to satisfy me and my readers and I didn't need any extra French species, thank you very much. But then I had been tempted to Serbia, to Finland, and to Spain, and soon after that a steady stream of new photographic owl cards, books, and other information arrived as my French friend relentlessly persuaded me to visit. She wanted me to see the species of owl we did not have over here in England. Did I know of the Scops Owl, by the way? Or the Tengmalm's Owl? Very old friends know exactly which buttons to press.

In truth I had been ignoring a whole group of owls that I thought were beyond my reach, not being native to the UK, but it turned out they were less out of reach than I had imagined. In Europe we have thirteen resident, native species. I had only seen half of them. Why stop there? With the visit to Serbia, the strange and unexplained appearance of the Exeter Eagle Owl, and then the Finland journey, my world was slowly becoming an owl vortex. "Beware of what you invite into your life," one shamanic friend said to me over a cup of tea in the Thrive café in Totnes. "What do you think owl energy brings?"

"I don't know."

"Exactly."

"Maybe something predator-ish?"

"It's more than that. They're stealthy, solitary, reluctant to show themselves. You can't ever know what kind of thing Owl might bring, what truths it might reveal."

It was the provoking way she said it that made me decide to find out. First I looked on an owl spirit-animal website, and that explained some of the things "Owl" can mean in your life. Whether the advice was directly connected with owls or not, it seemed to be wise:

> You may need to remove yourself from the noise of life and become the still, silent observer. After slowing down and becoming stable you will be amazed by the wealth of information and meaning that surrounds you. It may be bringing you the ability to see what others may miss. Open your eyes and truly examine how things are, you will be surprised that suddenly you can see things that are normally hidden from view—like the motives of those around you. You'll see into the shadows. External appearances will give way to the truth and meaning hidden beneath.

I liked this, but I also began to feel unsettled as more and more owls crowded in on my life. "I see your English owls," Christine must have said to herself in a kind of spell under her breath, wrapping my present and popping it in the post, "and I raise you with our French owls." Now I viewed her as saying all this in a sly French accent, her eyes narrowed as if instigating some deep magic.

I unwrapped the present, fought through the impossibly tight cellophane packaging, and slipped what turned out to be a new DVD straight into the machine. It was an owl documentary film, entirely narrated in French. I paused it and went to get myself a cup of tea and my trusty old Robert French dictionary. My undergraduate degree had been in French but I would have to pay careful attention to catch all the ornithological vocabulary. I checked the cover of the DVD. On it was an owl that looked like a Little Owl, *une chevêche*, but it was not. It was far littler. And angrier-looking. It had even bushier and more formidable eyebrows than *Athene noctua*. I ran to get my copy of Heimo Mikkola's formidable *Owls of the World*. No, a very different bird from *la chevêche*, the Little Owl; this was *la chevêchette*. That sounded like an extra-little owl. To you and me it is known as *Glaucidium passerinum*, the Eurasian Pygmy Owl.

A Pygmy Owl? I didn't know such a thing existed. I flipped through Mikkola's pages and a whole world of Pygmy Owls opened up. There were twenty species of this tiny beast. Beyond Europe, from the Pearl-spotted Pygmy to the Ferruginous Pygmy, through Cuban to Andean types, this thrush-sized cutie was spread all over the Americas. And all of them, in Mikkola's photographic guide, had those same furious yellow eyes. My mind boggled at the mysteries of evolution. I pressed play and the story of this tiny owl whirred into its gorgeous soundtrack.

Shot entirely on location in the Vercors Plateau bordering the Alps of south-eastern France, the film opened with aerial shots and panoramas of a wilderness area I had never heard of. Amongst an enticing anthemic theme tune it zoomed down to the pine forest, and closer in still, to an ornithologist's-eye view of the tiny Pygmy Owl perched on a twig. Framed amongst the soft needles of a spruce tree, its pure lemon eyes glistened as it warmed itself in the sun. As the camera lovingly lingered, the minute owl stretched out one small, blunt wing to make a perfect fan of its barred flight feathers. The sunlight fell through its plumage, and then it flexed its short tail and puffed out its silky plumage into an appealing miniature pear shape. Then an extreme close-up of its austere face revealed a yellow, hooked bill, as sharp and fit-for-purpose as that of any larger raptor. This owl was no shrinking violet. It was a compact, sparrow-sized little toughie. There was no discernible facial disc but its beak was bewhiskered by tiny facial feathers emanating from white brows and "eye bows." The speckled forehead revealed itself, a kind of flattened, glittery toupee, and when the head swivelled I could see an ingenious design on the hind neck, of dark eye patches with white surrounds, called an "occipital" or "false" face—an evolutionary trick designed to deter predators. The heavily white-streaked breast and belly gave its whole form a "cloaked" appearance as if it were wrapped in a generous, home-knitted body warmer.

Weighing in at only 60 to 80 grams, the Eurasian Pygmy Owl is unique in its lightning flight, ferocious hunting, and wispily intimidating eyebrows. The irascible expression, perfectly encircled by grey-brown pale-speckled plumage, has evolved to vanish into the resin-scented boughs and sifting light of mountainous spruce forests and glaciated grassy clearings. This bird is a relic of the Ice Age. During de-glaciation when the ice began to melt and forest spread over the mountains, colonising the area with sparse tree-covered slopes and leaving valleys with clearings and areas of exposed limestone, the upland-loving Pygmy Owl profited from the variety in the forest landscape. It thrived on the small prey available, exploiting the great spotted woodpeckers whose nest cavities it depended upon to breed. Here was a diminutive raptor turbo-charged with the dynamite of a top predator.

The film continued. The camera panned in from a geo map to the precise location on the edge of the Alps—so now I knew exactly where it was—then showed a view of the magnificent limestone cliffs, a vast extrusion that forms 40 kilometres of impenetrable wall along the edge of the plateau that protects this area, the largest natural reserve in France. For scientists here the Pygmy Owl is an indicator of the health of the mountain forest. How it chooses its territory, how it lives—these questions and more formed the subject of a survey and study carried out by one man, commissioned by the LPO (the Ligue pour la Protection des Oiseaux, the French equivalent of the UK's RSPB and BTO). The expert presenter, the Pygmy Owl Man, was Gilles Trochard, an experienced naturalist of thirty years. Here was a professional who apparently had spent years of his life trudging about after the tiny owls in the snows and blistering heat of these mountains.

The first objective was to locate breeding pairs of this tiny owl (an owl, my new hero Gilles pointed out in the voice-over, that most of the general public do not even know exists). Gilles arrived at a cabin enshrouded in snow and ice, the place he was to be based during the months of his study. And while he shovelled his way into the cabin, hefting the snowdrifts out of the way, he explained that temperatures this winter had been as low as minus 35 degrees Celsius.

Delicate winged things formed a gathering in my stomach. This discreet, furtive owl and its wild forest landscape of upland taiga forest in southern France all suddenly seemed within reach. I didn't stand a chance, and Christine knew it. I had to go there. I had to see this owl. I had to meet this person. This would involve more travel. And a new expert. An expert on an owl so delightful and so tiny that the Eagle Owl could swallow it in one gulp, or, as Gilles was later to quip with twinkling eyes: "Il pourrait l'écraser comme une compote de pomme!"—he could squash him like a pot of apple puree.

No, there was nothing to be done: I wanted to find this tiny owl, meet its lone advocate, and learn about the strange and mysterious life of a new, little-known predatory bird. I felt sure that Pygmy Owl Man Gilles would help me.

All this time I had been content with the owls that I had so far found. That is, until I set eyes upon this little film star, *la discrète chevêchette*. Here was an owl that could flatten its head feathers and do an accurate impression of a goshawk, whilst inhabiting a body around one-tenth of the size. *La chevêchette*, as it is known in France, the "little Little Owl," can hunt and kill birds which are far bigger than itself. Here was a predator that would fit inside a coffee cup but could fight woodpeckers for their nests with all the va-va-voom of a double espresso.

Jenny walked into the room while I was formulating a plan in my head.

"Mum, are you OK? This is the third time you've watched that film."

"Never mind that, look at this!" I made her sit down and watch a part with me: Jenny patiently sat on the edge of the sofa, and admitted that the Vercors Plateau did look lovely, but the persistent whistling the owl made grated after a while and she drifted off, leaving me alone with my new crush.

"The best time to find where the owl will nest is in the spring," Gilles said from beneath his snow hood. "And it's simply the sound of the call that will give him away, far better than any GPS." Gilles used a secret weapon, a special whistle named an ocarina, to lure the owl, but its use was only permitted for scientific research. The only way I too could see this owl would be to accompany Gilles on one of his forays.

I had to find out what Jenny's opinion was about one more thing. I called her back. I couldn't see this owl in Britain, so would have to go and visit this man; what did she think of him? Did she think Gilles would be a good guide to all things pygmy? Or would he be a prima donna? There was something delicate about his expression and body language. Would he be precious with his knowledge? I asked Jenny, trusting the clear-sighted experience of her years, her highly critical eye, and most of all, her plain-speaking.

"I don't know why you think he'd be difficult. I have yet to meet a Frenchman who isn't ... stylish," she said, searching for that last adjective carefully. "I think you shouldn't worry. Since he's made this film, and loves wildlife as much as that, he must be a good guy."

I went back to the film feeling happier. Perched at the summit of a dead spruce, the Pygmy Owl was perfectly disguised—it could have been a blob of the grey-green lichen that was slathered over the trees and streaking every branch and twig.

As the name suggests, the Pygmy Owl is the tiniest of all the European owls. It has a small head (which explains the pear shape) and no ear tufts, with a less defined facial disc than many other owls. This may be because this is a daylight- and crepuscular-hunting owl and it does not need the massive sound receptacle many owls have; it can rely more on eyesight than hearing. It flies in rapid bursts, and when it lands, it cocks its relatively long tail upwards, like a wren. It flicks this from side to side when perched, as if agitated by a fit of nerves. In the winter, it is easier to see around human settlements because it leaves its breeding grounds in the mountains and comes down to hunt garden birds. It flies noisily down from its lookouts at the tops of small trees and pounces on its prey in flight, like a shrike. But this was the friendly owl depicted in so many of the Hieronymus Bosch paintings. In French folklore, for people it is considered a benevolent owl, one that brings good luck to travellers. Its sweet, piping call would accompany pilgrims on their journeys.

I still went online to do a bit of checking—I won't say stalking—about Gilles. To my delight, my sleuthing quickly came up with a wildlife tour company with Gilles's name attached. It turned out that he did week-long tours of the very place in the film! A whoosh of adrenaline flooded me. A group (of which, potentially, I could be a part) would be taken to see the very locations, the very owls starring in that film! I couldn't believe my luck, and immediately checked out the price. It was quite a lot. But that didn't matter. Some things are meant to be, and anyway, I had a credit card. I allowed myself one more watch of the DVD, revising some of the specialist ornithological vocabulary in French.

In fact, now there was a reason, I'll admit that I watched the film again and again, learning every bit of the vocabulary, until I could perfectly pronounce *pelotes de rejection* (owl pellets), *nichoir* (nest box), and *logeoscope* (there is no translation of this invention, but the closest I can think of is "nest viewer"). I learned to say them accurately enough to hold my own, I hoped, amongst a group of French twitchers. They would have high standards and I wanted to blend in. The *logeoscope* was in fact Gilles's own invention for spying on the tiny owl in its nest: it consisted of a stealth viewer attached to a pole made out of collapsible fishing rods that extended up to 9.5 metres long, and was wired up to a laptop. With this, the inhabitants of any nest could be safely observed with minimum disturbance. Using it, Gilles found that the owls usually laid between four and six eggs, but occasionally even up to seven, although not all would fledge.

The film placed Gilles somewhere on the spectrum between obsessively committed loner and serious naturalist. It showed him cross-country skiing stylishly through the mountains in his sunglasses and outdoor stealth gear, carrying his special gadgetry like an ornithological James Bond. Amongst the gravelly French narration and rousing musical soundtrack, I clicked send, and off into the stratosphere went my more than pygmy-sized deposit for the owl trip. Soon I too would be sliding gracefully upon cross-country skis over the snowy plateau, helping Gilles with his *logeoscope*. All I wanted was to learn from him, exchange ideas about owl conservation and the attitudes of the conservationists and government authorities. Were the French as protective and knowledgeable about their owls as the British? Did they too have owl-aholics?

I sat waiting anxiously for the return email. Then I ordered myself the French version of my *Collins Bird Guide*. I would revise and learn as many French bird names as I could. The first good sign was the quick reply I got from Gilles's colleague and partner in business, Pierre Boutonnet. Pierre had started the tour company himself and had soon roped in his expert naturalist friend Gilles, who was equally devoted and experienced in guiding groups. I was delighted to find out that with his good level of English he already had the otter book that I had written during my obsessive four-year quest that took me all over the British Isles in search of my musteline quarry. If Pierre, Gilles's colleague, had read my book that was a very good start. We could almost be friends. Pierre sent through the *fiche technique* that contained all the details of the trip: we were promised all eight species of owl that were present in the Vercors and Drôme region: the Barn, Tawny, Long-eared, Little, Tengmalm's, Scops, Pygmy, and Eagle Owls.

MY OWL QUEST was changing, spreading its wings. When I had first set out to write this book, I had envisaged covering the five (or six) native British species, and had planned to stay within the confines of the British Isles, thereby avoiding too much travel. But this level-headed plan had already fallen by the wayside and my horizons had widened, what with my trips to Serbia and Finland. I now found myself tantalisingly within reach of seeing all of the European species. The Ural Owl I had seen in Finland, and the trip to Vercors would bump the owl count up to nine, leaving only three species unsighted: the Hawk Owl, the Great Grey Owl, and the Snowy Owl. I was learning something about myself here. The burning need to know more about these difficult-to-know species was what kept me going. Now that it had deepened and widened it felt unstoppable. I was drawn to the endless challenge of finding out something that resists being found out about; it was the same with my first love, *Lutra lutra*, the Eurasian otter. A wealth of information and meaning would surround me, the owl oracle had said. I would be able to see what others might miss. I couldn't wait.

The spectacular Vercors Plateau and its wild, forested landscape would make up for any frustrations and discomforts of the long journey to get there. And, after my experience with David and Milan in Serbia, I knew I would end up making some new friends. I now knew about the "Force." I knew the bond, the birdy camaraderie born of a deep common interest that ornithology types always share regardless of borders and language barriers. I was starting to know the lengths people would go to in order to tick off a bird. I suspected that these new people in France would be actual Real Twitchers, with telescopes (which I did not have) and lists (of foreign and unknown birds). This was the next level of birdwatching, charged with a degree of gravitas beyond my wandering quest.

Now, I have to make it clear that I didn't ever in a million years think of myself as a twitcher. I'll even admit to some negative feelings towards this tribe of obsessive bird-addicts, especially after my experience of their habit of needing to "tick." It seemed to me that chasing rare and unusual birds to tick them off a list in a kind of ritual frenzy was silly. During the years we had spent living on the aptly named Isles of Scilly in the late 1990s we had experienced twitchers for the first time, and I had been taken by surprise. I knew the word, but not fully what it meant. We had gone there to take up my first job as a teacher in the secondary school, and our first autumn there as a young family started with some violent storms. The tourist season was over and with the start of October and the Very Bad Weather there arrived strange camouflaged clusters of blokes. They were dressed in greens and browns, each of them bulging with binoculars, no-nonsense boots, long-lens telescopes, and proper head-to-foot waterproofing.

We had been looking forward to relishing our splendid isolation on our new island home, and had begun to enjoy the novelty of increasingly extreme winds, violent rain squalls, and shocking waves. We soon realised that we couldn't even go off-island, and the jolly flat-bottomed ferry, the *Scillonian*, ceased to arrive from the mainland. But we were happy. We had each other. We could beachcomb in peace and relish the tranquillity of winter by the Atlantic. But instead of the delights of peaceful isolation, along with the Very Bad Weather came wave after wave of these odd-bod hordes. We asked around: What was going on? What was this invasion of blokey bird-nerds? How long would they be staying? Would I ever be able to pee in a hedge in private again?

Lining up in crowds and gazing into pittosporum hedges, flower fields, and rocky promontories, these people were looking for disorientated and migrating birds. It was all about a list—certain rare birds needed to be ticked off, and then they would all go away.

Since we couldn't go anywhere, and actually there was not much else to do apart from gazing at the odd washed-up dolphin, we decided to join in. Why not profit from the close-up views of bee-eaters, snow buntings, spotless starlings, and other unusual rarities? Soon, our heads began to swivel and bob along with these camouflaged enthusiasts. As the Scilly hotels, B & Bs, pub gardens, and any spare piece of ground swelled with welly-booted feet it felt as though our tiny islands would sink under their weight. At the most intense flurries, people were trampling over private gardens and blocking the (very sparse) traffic. In every bush, hedge, and roadside tuffet at least sixteen watchers rustled quietly beneath their coating of camouflage windproofs. They spoke excitedly into walkie-talkies (this was just before mobile phones took the world by its horns); we'd find them in front of our house, staking out the slipway to the beach. None of the locals seemed to mind, so we didn't either.

When we left, five years later, my bird knowledge had improved vastly. But soon, work and mainland life made sure that any serious twitching faded to a distant memory, and we put it all behind us. But when my mischievous friend from France sent me the film of the Pygmy Owls of the high Vercors Plateau, I felt that whoosh of bird-love once more. I had not thought twitching would re-enter my life so suddenly.

IT WAS RAINING warm May rain in Geneva when I arrived. Waiting to collect me with a comradely lift-share were fellow owl-ists Guy and Sandra, who fitted me carefully into their car amongst their long lenses, camo gear, and camera equipment. As we took the motorway and zoomed across the border into France my heart melted into the meadows bordered with poppies, pine-forest-smothered mountains whose peaks were hidden in mist. Comfortably snuggled in the back seat I spotted black kites. "They're quite common here," Guy, a Swiss native, explained as we gazed at them circling over the fields.

At the rendezvous in Valence the sun was beginning to come out and the warm ground steamed. We parked and stood by the railway track to wait for Gilles and the others from the group. Skylarks circled overhead, and from the sun-washed fields came aromatic scents of chamomile, honeysuckle, and wild thyme. All at the same time, we heard the familiar *ki-kiki-ki* of a bird of prey and scrabbled to get our binoculars: "Un faucon crécerelle!" Guy said, and in a flash got out his telescope. I know all these bird names in French because of Christine, I thought to myself. She and I would go walking together when we were in our late teens and early twenties and I lived with her in the Loire Valley. She was as interested in nature and birds as I, and taught me all their names in French as we walked. *Rouge-gorge, mésange bleue, pic vert, corbeau, héron cendré, chouette hulotte*: I remembered all of them. *Crécerelle*: easy to hear where our English name for the kestrel comes from. So many of our bird names have French origins, in large part due to the Normans' conquest of our islands and our absorption of their lovely language. We watched as the kestrel pair fed their two young, wheeling around the tracks and fields. There was plenty of feeding for them around the station with its mouse-rich scrubby banks and railway sidings.

Then at last Gilles pulled up in his silvery Dacia Duster and leant out of the window to say a professional *bonjour*. He was wearing sunglasses and the outdoor guiding gear, just as in the film.

That evening, we all assembled. Thierry, Evelyne, and Valérie were an awesome threesome of friends who had gathered from distant parts of northern France, the Vosges mountains, and a tiny island off Brittany; they admitted to me that they allowed themselves one big birdwatching trip away from their families each year. Soon I was in the club: Next year, I could go with them if I'd like to? As I write this now, they're all coming to stay with me in England and we're very excited to be going birdwatching—guess where? In the Isles of Scilly. From Switzerland there were Guy and Sandra of the heavily laden Mercedes. There was another Thierry from the north who walked with a stick and yet still managed to bring a bundle of photographic gadgetry and a special parabolic shotgun listening device, and his affectionate young wife Sophie. And finally Danielle, the only other "single" on the trip, who had left her husband at home as well, somewhere around the Belgian border near Arras.

We were to drive everywhere in a sleek safari-style convoy of three cars. On the second day, Evelyne grabbed me and ordered me to ride with them. Thierry, she said, whose car it was, would be needing to practise his English. We took it in turns to sit next to him in the front. To my delight, the formality most French people would abide by of using the polite form of address, *vous*, appeared to be absent from the start and everyone was already applying the more informal *tu*. I concluded that this must be because we were all birders, and therefore in the same club. That formality dispensed with, and now that we had eaten our three-course meal, Gilles was itching to take us out into the field. He tried to distract us from dessert, but the others objected—being French, missing dessert would be an outrage, and Gilles was made to eat a bowl of fresh strawberries like the rest of us. Then we drove out over the plains of the Rhône Valley to fossick amongst the farmsteads for the first on our owl list—not the Pygmy yet, but *Athene noctua*, the Little Owl.

The sky was grey and heavy with rain. Gilles was lugubrious, his face lined with anxiety. "It never rains like this so near to summer," he complained. Fat drops fell all around. Mist rose in columns between the hills, and more downpours bulged in dark grey clouds on the horizon. It had been a very bad start for all birdlife this spring, he explained: the unseasonal rain was finishing off fledglings just as they left their nests. It was not good.

The Little Owl, however, can hunt in the rain, unlike Barn Owls who become rapidly waterlogged, cannot fly, and can die of cold in bad weather. "The Barn Owls are nearly all gone in this area," Gilles said. "We put up Barn Owl nest boxes but the owls didn't even breed this year. I only know of one or two pairs. There are many roads all over the plains here," he explained. "It's not like the mountains where there is just one road. Here there are many dangers for Barn Owls: they fly low and people drive fast, plus the farmers don't make it easy to put up nest boxes."

Quite soon Gilles found us a Little Owl: he knew where they would be, and using his owl app he played the melancholy tone of the Little Owl call; we waited, and then suddenly there it was, on cue. Shaped like a small pear perched on the apex of a roof, the feisty little character surveyed the intruders to its territory. The atmosphere lifted, and Gilles became happier. The first target species: ticked.

All around, between the sandy, cobbled houses draped in roses and vines, amongst the woodpiles and vegetable gardens, house martins and swallows skimmed the ground, catching flies and midges. The semi-rural, agricultural landscape must have a perfect patchwork for Little Owls: mature trees; good nesting sites in old buildings, woodpiles, and brushwood; hedges and meadows providing plenty of insects and small mammals. Then, just as the sun was going down, an even better encounter: Thierry spotted it first, a small silhouette on a branch—and for ten minutes we watched another Little Owl hunting from the low bough of an ornamental pine in somebody's back garden. It stared at us for a moment at first, and through the scope I saw it blink its heavily feathered lids over two pale yellow eyes. When it got back to the serious business of scanning the ground it dropped repeatedly, as if catching some small insect or invertebrate prey.

"Most of the time, people don't know they're here," Gilles said. "It's not like in England. Your RSPB is huge, filled with bird lovers. All of them standing up for birds and their habitats. You have petitions and campaigns. We don't have anything like that here."

I felt a mixture of pride and concern all at once.

"You have a million members," Gilles went on. "We've got just a few thousand in the LPO." The French bird conservation organisation was created in 1912 in protest about regular massacres of puffins on the north coast of Brittany. Each year the local railway company traditionally organised safaris to shoot the puffins, and this was the catalyst for an enthusiast, Lieutenant Hemery, to lose his temper and try to stand up for the birds. He created a league for their protection and ever since the logo has been a pair of puffins. So far it has only forty-five thousand members, whereas the RSPB in Britain has over a million, two hundred thousand of whom are young people.

"We're decades behind the British. And in the provinces, people like to shoot birds; here, hunting wildlife is important to people, and *les ornithos* are very unpopular, a rarity themselves."

"We shoot birds as well in Britain," I offered, thinking of grouse and other game-bird shooting.

"No, it's different. It's worse here—it's more widespread, more popular," Gilles argued. "We shoot *any bird*, not just game, sometimes even if they're protected."

I was going to bring up the issue of the hen harrier, a protected bird that is often persecuted in Britain, but was upstaged by the arrival of a rain-soaked Little Owl. Perched raggedly on a pine branch, it was determinedly hunting something in the grass between the trees. As we watched, the Little Owl dropped like a stone, down onto something in the long grass, then flew directly with its prey dangling—it turned out to be feeding on earthworms that had risen to the surface during the rain. It flew around the barn and darted skilfully inside the broken window of an outhouse. No sooner had it delivered its wriggly cargo than it reappeared and repeated the whole process. "They have adaptations for these conditions such as waterproofing, and short wings for flying through trees and clearings like this," Gilles pointed out. "They hunt even if the weather is bad, not like Barn Owls. But still, it must be hard work in this rain," Gilles said. "Look, it's drenched." It had young to feed, we concluded, and the weather was no impediment. Little Owl ticked, we moved on.

I couldn't believe birdwatchers were not liked.

"I can't leave my bird book on show on the seat of the car in the countryside: people would slash my tyres," Thierry said.

"It's true. My friends have had their car scratched and the windows broken," Evelyne said.

Gilles nodded grimly.

We drove on through purple mountains of vetch at the roadside; scarlet poppies shone amongst vast twists of prickly thistle and tall grass heavy with seed. All around, the scent of hay and honeysuckle, the relentless, rasping song of crickets, and overhead, skylarks wheeled and sang. Suddenly Gilles stamped his foot on the brake.

"Pie grièche écorcheur!"

This caused a flurry of excitement—no time-wasting, but the professional birding sort of flurry: pull over safely, equipment up, lenses/eyes to three o'clock. Here was a bird name that was only vague in my French memory. A shrike, was it? *Grièche*: shrike. Sounded very similar. I'd never seen one in the UK, which is not surprising since this species has declined dramatically and is now virtually extinct in Britain. But the name is striking enough to say it all: *écorcher* in English means "to skin alive." In England we call it the red-backed shrike, or the butcher bird, and its taxonomic name is *Lanius collurio*, *lanius* being the Latin for "butcher." This is a bloodthirsty predator, a shrike that impales its victims in a larder of thorns to store them. When I saw it through the scope I knew it was indeed a shrike: wheatear-like, but definitely not a wheatear. There was a smart pair of them, tense, jerky: hunting insects by dropping down into the grass. I had never expected to see one, but then why would I? We were here for the owls.

I looked at my fellow groupies whose hungry eyes were now glued to their binoculars. Valérie was hastily setting up her scope and framing the bird meticulously in the lens, Thierry and Sophie capturing it on film. Thanks to all this I could savour the amazing markings, the vivid chestnut back, grey head and nape, and the black, bandit-style mask. I noted the thick, black, hooked bill and the grasping claws, but most of all, the sunset-pink-tinged breast and belly, smooth and pale as candyfloss. Tick! I was hooked.

It turned out Jenny was right. The minute I met Gilles I knew he was going to dispel any worries: beneath the serious, knowledgeable surface of the professional naturalist guide was a human whose warmth was so infectious that after a few days I would not want to leave. Obsessively committed like all the best birdwatchers, Gilles loved people as well as birds. He turned out to be an expert's expert, and was thoroughly communicative and generous with his knowledge. Although he appeared to be totally obsessed with his subject, encyclopedic in fact, and would pause to deliver a lecture in detail at any question big or small, he was typically French about some things. For example, mealtimes. At table, the rigours of ticking birds were put behind us, and like most French he liked nothing more after a long day's work than to drink wine and get down to the serious business of eating while discussing a range of topics. These times, when we were not looking at birds through binoculars, were the moments we spent bonding as a group. There was an unspoken camaraderie, a professional respect and understanding amongst the group, but over meals this was intensified.

In France consuming good food and good wine, and sharing laughter, are taken as seriously as politics, work, and education, in fact more so. One evening, the subject of Britishness came up, and I knew it would only be a matter of time before someone mentioned what the French consider to be the lowest common denominator of British culture. During my time with Christine I'd noticed that the French were fascinated with one particular 1970s slapstick comedy series. You know the one, packed full of bawdy double entendres and starring a particularly silly comic. This very silliness had been hugely popular in France. In my mind I began to count down from ten to one. At six, Gilles, sitting opposite me, tried to catch my eye. Sliding his fork mischievously beneath the last mouthful of his meaty main course (made of something exquisite including dark sauce and some kind of pâté), a giggle rumbled up. "J'adorais regarder le *Benny Hill Show*," he admitted.

"That was not one of our best exports," I pointed out sternly.

Gilles's eyes were now wrinkled with jollity, but the conversation turned to wider things British.

"And Madame Thatcher? *La guerre des Malouines* . . . The Falklands War."

"Not good either." Sage and sympathetic nodding rippled around the table, indicating that we were all of an age to remember. Again, now we were on to politics, I knew what contemporary item was looming next.

"And what about Brexit?"

The referendum was just days away. All eyes rounded on me. Suddenly a wave of something like grief welled up in my chest. I was being asked to explain something to my new friends that was beyond words; a pending calamity of separation, a rending from my lovely friends, the old ones and these new, like an unwanted but unavoidable divorce. I didn't know where to begin.

"But what do you think will happen?" everybody pressed anxiously. "Which way are people going to vote?"

The air was stiff with concern and the small vortex that had opened up somewhere around my solar plexus now deepened into a chasm—for my French friends, an adopted family of sorts, for the bonds of all the shared European history. In that moment I felt the memory of the wars of the twentieth century and their aftermath—the closeness we shared postwar, and ever since—the common aims of peace and reconciliation. It was one of those moments when we find that we have so much in common, in our blood and in our genes; how could we ever be anything but together? I reached for my glass.

"I don't know. I think it will be very close. People have been very confused and misinformed . . . I'm worried. We're like a dysfunctional family in Europe, aren't we?" I said, swallowing hard. "We love to hate one another, but really, it's love."

Thoughtful and gloomy nods passed around the table, the atmosphere thick with melancholy.

"I think people are going to vote based on something that's all wrong."

It was the same in France. The immigration hysteria, the scapegoating and faulty economic advice flying around, for us from figures such as Nigel Farage and Boris Johnson. The French were experiencing the same from the likes of Marine Le Pen and the Front National. I didn't think it was going to go well for the Europhiles. France was in a similar political turmoil that nobody was enjoying. We were together on this.

"No, whatever happens, we're like brothers, our two countries," Thierry said kindly, seeing my watery eyes. He slopped more red wine into my glass. "We love to fight over things, but when there's a problem, we're right there, together, always."

Thierry raised his glass warmly, his brown eyes downcast and emotional. The others joined us and Thierry's fork appeared on my plate to help with the spare rib that I couldn't finish.

We wiped our plates with bread, the dessert slipped down in a flash, and with that, the evening's outing began. We went out to find Barn Owls, and to listen for the wheezing cry of Long-eared Owlets, but were distracted by *Bufo calamita*, natterjack toads! It started with the serenading song of toads, or *le crapaud calamite* in French. In sombre mood I thought that was a prophetic name, perhaps meaning "the toad of calamity." Although the heavy rain that night seemed calamitous (along with the impending Brexit), in fact it meant no such thing. As we stood in the rain and listened, from somewhere low down at the edge of the field a chorus of voices started up. "Our sense of hearing is so much better in the dark," Gilles explained, "when we're not distracted." All at once, many voices rose, and they spread, discordant, urgent, like an out-of-tune Mexican wave travelling rapidly along the ditch until they were a throng that battered our ears.

I looked up the translation later: the Latin name comes from the Greek *kalamos*, meaning "reeds," referring obviously to the creature's habitat. The toad of the reeds. In Britain they are so very rare, hanging on in pockets and puddles on reedy dunes and rare heaths, but here there must have been hundreds, if not thousands. The wheezes of the Long-eared young took second place, I'm afraid, and after we had played a game of hide-and-seek with them amongst the veiling leaves and twigs of a row of lime trees (it was impossible to see them, even though they were so close by), we withdrew, our spirits dampened in an increasing deluge of rain. But the rain, if it kept the owls hidden, to my delight brought the toads out even more. As we drove away, in the yellow of the car headlamps they crossed the road, like nuggets of gold scattered in our beam. Gilles drove slowly and weaved around them, but at my gasp, he put his foot on the brake and leapt out to move them off the road. Just in front of our wheels a large specimen glared up, and he clasped it tightly in his hands and thrust it in through the car window, right up under my nose. Nubbed with emerald green all along the back, it was gem-like, a colour I had never thought possible in nature, and its eyes were molten bronze. Through the window with that bright amphibian came the smell of rain, moss, and algae; the fresh, wet odour penetrated my nose so powerfully that it stayed with me all night.

The next day it was the almighty song of nightingales drifting through the open car window. I put my head out to listen. They were belting it out so loud, their song resonated as we drove, the varied pitch and melody so powerful I could catch it each time we passed one in a thicket, ringing out above the car engines, above the wind, and even above our conversation.

"Do you want to stop?" Gilles said, noticing my head leaning out of the window. "We'll stop and listen to them."

The convoy ground to a halt and we all got out and stood amongst the ash and hazel thickets by the side of the road, our ears absorbed by the glorious tunes of the nightingales. I felt my stomach go into free-fall at the enchantment of it. This plain brown bird utters its dizzying song from cover so we couldn't see them, but so powerful is its song that it does not need to show itself or display. Scientists have shown that the complex, resonant tunes have such force that they affect the female bird's brain. The male's impressive vocal range can produce up to 1,160 syllables (compared to the skylark's 341) and the females are not duped—song conveys a very honest message about the capacities of the singer, and the more operatic this crooner is, the more elaborate his songs, the more likely he is to charm and seduce the female. They were certainly charming me. We stood immobile and listened, all of us, as the miraculous music resonated, tingling through our every sense.

"I think the English name is better than the French—*le rossignol*," Gilles said finally. "It sings like the storm at night: *night-in-gale*."

When you go to a different country and start to break down language barriers, a whole new form of poetry can spring up. In bending and twisting expression, playing with words and phrases to meet and connect up the disconnections, you can find new imaginative words, hidden onomatopoeias. Think about the onomatopoeia in owl calls: our *too-wit too-woo* that the Tawny duo makes in English turns out even better in French. The Tawny Owl is *la chouette hulotte*, with a beautiful sound sense to the name that echoes the bird's call. But there is also a children's song in France that replicates the *too-wit too-woo* duet. However, this simple song also proliferates a misunderstanding about owls. It is more complicated than the British misunderstanding, where we simply conflate the male and female call-and-response into a single cry of "*too-wit too-woo*"; in France it is a muddle of not only gender but also species. In the French language there are two words for "owl," the masculine *hibou* and the feminine *chouette*, and in the song the "male" owl, *le hibou*, takes a romantic turn with the "female" owl, *la chouette*:

> Hou hou, fait le hibou
> chouette, chouette, se dit la chouette,
> voilà un bel ami, un bel oiseau de nuit.
>
> Hou hou, fait le hibou,
> chouette, chouette, se dit la chouette,
> allons nous marier ce soir dans la forêt.

The song begins with the male hoot, then the female hoot, and then they make friends, finishing on the line: "Let's go and get married in the forest." But the misconception here is that *une chouette* is a female *hibou*. It isn't. Unbeknownst to generations of French schoolchildren, in reality the two owls will never be able to be together. Where both words mean a generic owl, they're not just a different gender, in fact they are separated by genetics and taxonomy. The two names represent visual differences and show that the two are different species. The *hibous* are the group of owls with ear tufts, and the *chouettes* are the tuft-less owls, so sorry, children, as biology would have it, sadly they could never get married.

That sorted out, we drove up a sinuous single-track road into the Vercors plateau, and followed joyfully at Gilles's heels as he strode through narrow paths deep into the mountain forest. Today, at last, we would finally see Pygmy Owls. It was spring so most of the owls would be feeding young, and the adult owls would be more easily visible, busily commuting along predictable routes with a cargo of decapitated voles and slaughtered songbirds to sustain the broody females and their hungry progeny.

Having seen Gilles's film, I recognised the location. I knew that due to his detailed survey he would know every nest hole, every breeding pair for the whole area. Pausing only to listen to the song of warblers, to point out a black woodpecker or a bullfinch, Gilles explained about the complex and highly protected ecosystem of the area. No interference is allowed, no agriculture, and no tree felling. Any tree that falls is left, and nature is allowed to make its own way. There are no roads—only subtle walking trails wend their way through parts of the park, but they are rarely used, and vehicles are not allowed at all. In winter, the only access is on foot, then on cross-country skis. In summer, the sparse network of paths that cross the forest are mainly used by animals, and the only human habitation is a shepherd's hut or two. The whole reserve is just about as pristine as it is possible to be, and highly precious because of that.

We watched our steps in this fragile habitat, careful to leave only the lightest of footprints. At given points, in order to attract the owl so we could see it, Gilles sounded the special staccato call through a high, resonant flute called an ocarina, an ancient instrument that would originally have been made of wood, clay, or even chamois horn. The exact note to play on an ocarina is a high whistle of F, or "Fa," that mimics the male's unique territorial cry.

We assembled in a mossy clearing, all of us settling quietly into the green pool of leaves and lichens, listening to the breathing of the air through the trees. Why is it possible to feel so calm in such a wild, remote place? There is something enchanting about the way light and colour work on the senses. The green shade and shafts of warmth both calm you and leave you alert to every small sound. Pine branches sifted sunlight, wood ants trickled, bird wings flitted. Our breath slowed into the trance that the forest invites. Gilles put his lips to the ocarina and whistled. We waited.

Then suddenly a flicker on a branch, a scuttle of tiny talons and he was there. The local male had leapt into our space and our hearts leapt with him. I wanted to shout with delight, so perfect and so improbable was this tiny owl. Perched with concentrated outrage on a branch above our heads, ignoring us, he had presented himself to investigate the call of the perceived intruder. His head spun around, searching. Our long lenses had time to capture the speckled charm of his miniature pear shape; the long barred tail twitching with compressed anger, the head revolving what appeared to be a fantastic 360 degrees as he scanned furiously, trying to locate the imposter. As he turned, we could see the false face, the pair of white-rimmed patches on the rear of his scalp, giving the unsettling impression that we were being spied on from every angle.

Pygmy Owls are highly vocal, and if the male feels threatened he will increase his calls—which now he did, with a kind of *peeu—peeu—peeu*, a whistle uttered regularly until the unwanted visitor has been intimidated enough to withdraw. I noticed that this territorial call resembled the monotone call of the bullfinch, and the female's was a little softer and higher. As we had seen, the male could easily be attracted, and was a pugilistic little fellow. "Sometimes," Gilles said, "he can even be lured into attacking a human. But we won't try that." When threatened by competitors the male will display by calling, but he might also alter his plumage; puffing up like a loosely ruffled pompom he'll try to intimidate owl-intruders. The feathers also loosen and puff out in this way when the owl is dozing or sunbathing.

Very little had been known about the Pygmy Owl before Gilles's study. Even hikers, stopping in their tracks to listen to its strange, monotone whistle, had not seen it, so quick and cryptic an owl it is. Often perched at the vantage point at the very top of a spruce tree, this tiny owl is the size of a pine cone. You need to follow the call, and then deploy binoculars or a scope to pick it out. When this owl finally flew, I noticed it fleeted along with the same swooping flight as a woodpecker. And like the woodpecker it needs to nest in holes in trees. The Pygmy Owl requires a very specific habitat—open spruce forest, with a patchwork of clearings and old deadwood where greater spotted woodpeckers leave handy nest holes that it can occupy. The diameter of the hole is what is important: on average this is roughly circular, and at around 4.5 centimetres the narrow entrance is what the owl depends upon: it is tight enough to prevent predators like the pine marten and other birds of prey entering. Without the great spotted and green woodpeckers, there would be no Pygmy Owl.

As we watched, the owl flew off to search for more prey for his nest-bound mate. We waited, again in silence, and then we were breathless as he returned minutes later with a decapitated vole clenched tightly in his long claws. He perched, and called softly, with that same staccato, piping whistle and then a kind of gentle "bibbling" as if to persuade her to come out. With a smaller, higher voice, the female replied, slightly muffled from within the nest hole. Would we see her? We waited on tenterhooks, and then with another leap of the heart we saw her feathered face appear at the entrance to the nest hole. There she was, expectant, hungry, and ready to receive her delivery. She looked slightly grubby and grey around the edges, a little bedraggled, even. Not surprising, I suppose, if you're stuck all day on eggs while your mate brings you food parcels. She came out, wriggling herself head first, then wings and feet through the narrow hole, flew to a nearby twig, and fluffed out in full view. The male, waiting with his offering, brought the vole to her whole, and then, wondrously, instead of eating the vole herself, back she went into the nest, taking the vole meal out of sight. A small commotion from inside confirmed it. There were chicks! The male flitted away once more. Oh, how I would have loved to see the owlets, but they remained safely tucked in their cavity, veiled from our view.

I was struck by how close we were to the nest, and yet the owls had totally ignored us. More than any other owl we had seen, it was as if our presence was irrelevant and we were not a threat. Perhaps they did not even know what we were— just more harmless earthbound mammals like the deer or wild boar that they would have been used to seeing fossicking around on the forest floor. And so no notice was taken of us and we withdrew, leaving only our footprints behind.

How far would the male go to find food? I wondered. Gilles explained that a pair of Pygmy Owls might occupy a territory of 1 to 1.4 square kilometres; the male calls to mark the edge of his boundary, which itself will be divided into roosting area, nesting area, and hunting area. The small territory explained the fast arrival of our male: he had no difficulty hearing our whistle and arrived almost immediately.

As we quietly withdrew to go and find Tengmalm's Owls, Gilles explained more about his study. The coniferous forests of the plateau, at 1,300 to 1,500 metres above sea level, are an isolated pocket of habitat left behind after the last period of glaciation. The Eurasian Pygmy Owl is considered to be a relic of the glacial age. During the last Ice Age, many species adapted to the conditions and thrived in this part of France as the tundra and taiga conditions suited them. When the glaciers receded, many species followed, except for some isolated pockets like this, where cold, mountain habitat remained. On the high plateaus of the Vercors region, the Pygmy Owls found themselves cut off, but they were well adapted and easily thrived here, in spite of their small size. They are more diurnal than the other owls that share their territory; the more nocturnal Tawny, Tengmalm's, and Long-eared can be found here as well, and feed on the same prey so could be arch-competitors, but since the Pygmy is diurnal it has more of a chance to avoid its enemies. The Pygmy can hunt by sight in the snow, find shelter amongst the mature pines, and has very weatherproof plumage; it is also found in the European taiga or "snow forest," which is part of the world's second-largest biome after the oceans. It wraps the planet in a wide northerly belt, in Europe covering much of Sweden, Finland, and Norway and stretching over some of the higher mountains of central Europe, continuing over Eastern Europe and Siberia to northern Mongolia and Hokkaido. In its American reaches it is known as boreal forest, and here it covers vast areas of Canada. So taiga and boreal were the same eco-region, just with different names. In these regions, the climate is sub-Arctic, and there is a very large temperature range between the seasons.

This Pygmy Owl is a true wilderness bird, then, and interestingly, because of the isolation of the owl's territory in France, very little attention was paid to it here. The sedentary population was only discovered to be breeding on the plateau in 2009 when Gilles was commissioned to undertake his three-year study. Now thirteen occupied nests have been identified so far, all located using the ocarina lure. Gilles noted that only the mating call can truly be imitated with the ocarina, and this has the desired effect, quickly attracting belligerent males to arrive, plumage puffed up and head feathers formed into a rectangular shape, while the head turns, rapidly and repeatedly searching for the intruding male. With radio tracking (and it's no easy task to fit a device to such a tiny raptor), the size of the males' territories was discovered, along with close observation of its breeding and nesting habits. Gilles noted that during the breeding season, the most mating calls were heard at dawn and dusk, in March and April. Incubation was in May, and locating the inhabited nests enabled him to close in on the nest sites and complete his study. Gilles has observed that, unusually in owls, the female always clears out the nest after around five days, as the fur and prey remains (usually voles, but also small birds or reptiles), pellets, and faeces have built up to such a degree that they can begin to attract parasites or might stifle the cavity of the nest. These field signs can then be used as proof of nesting. After fledging, the pair share caring for the young, but after fifteen days it is only the male who carries on feeding them.

Most importantly, these half-pint-sized owls are an indicator species, and one that in this uniquely protected area is not threatened by any human impact. The success of these birds in their untouched environment shows just what we humans can do when we protect an area properly, hand in hand with nature. The presence of this unique little tribe of the forest proves that for now, the richly interlinked ecosystem of the forest, from the mycelium in the earth and the wood ants nesting in the fallen pine needles, to the lichens and the woodpeckers, is in the best of health.

Back in my comfortable room at the auberge I looked over my finds: pine cones, Pygmy Owl pellets, a woodpecker feather. I wrapped the delicate objects as carefully as treasure, and stowed them safe in my case to bring home.

I returned to what seemed like the end of the world, or my part of the world, at least. The Brexit vote left the nation shocked and I consoled myself with the friendships I had built across the Channel, bonds that no political decision could harm. And the tiny Pygmy Owl became for me, in that moment, a heart-warming symbol of hope in a storm, a "King of Birds" as in the words of singer Karine Polwart:

At Ludgate Hill
where the towers of smoke and mirrors bruise the
sky the pilgrims huddle in
as the tiny King of Birds begins to cry
the people start to sing
to light glory in the dark
to ring the bell
and to breathe hope in every heart

—"KING OF BIRDS"

With thanks to Karine Polwart and Hegri Music

Bubo scandiacus

SNOWY OWL

A crystal note alighting
on the Cornish tundra,
you bring news
of the next glacial blowing.
Coded in your feathers,
an address
with no letters and no numbers.
Moon fatale.
You spread your wings
so there's no shade
between your feathers.
I press my cheek against the edges
 of your flight feathers
and feel like my heart's breaking.

—ROSEMARIE CORLETT, "Snowy Owl"

IN THE SPRING OF 2017 A SNOWY OWL CAME TO Orkney. It was a female, and I learned about her visit too late. By the time I could have been on the train and boat, and completed my 700-mile journey, she could have flown the 400 miles back to Norway, or elsewhere. Soon enough she was long gone; but not before some astute and enthusiastic Orcadians had taken several lovely photos of her perched comfortably on a gnarly dry-stone wall and flying low, catching the evening sunlight on her bright wings as she quartered the grassy fields for lemmings. There are no lemmings on Orkney, and so the owl quickly moved on.

The Snowy's breeding grounds are found scattered over the northern Arctic tundra, and so she may well have felt at home in this windswept outcrop in the North Atlantic. Snowy Owls mostly live north of the timber line in treeless wastes: in Europe they have been found in the mountainous regions of Norway and Swedish Lapland, and sometimes northern Finland. A vagrant pair once bred on Fetlar, Shetland. They are still occasionally seen in the northern isles, but only as visitors, and never stopping to breed.

How I longed to see one. To look into the Snowy Owl's fierce gold eyes must be like gazing into the spirit of the Arctic. The more I found out about the birds, the more the longing grew. The Snowy and the Great Grey were now my twin grails, the unreachable ones, and along with the Hawk Owl in Finland, they formed the tundra trinity that had got away.

But for now, Jenny was about to sit her A levels, then Rick was thinking of changing jobs, and worst of all his mother Wendy had been taken seriously ill. Life for a while would be about hunkering down, caring, consolidating, staying at home. I told myself that I would see the remaining owls one day. They would be a cool glow on my horizon, something to hope for next year, an aurora borealis of sorts. Twinkling like a star in the dark, Gilles had said that he wanted me to help him formulate a northern owls and other birds trip to Finland. I could go along as the English speaker, a role I would have loved, but with so many other challenges coming all at once, the idea had to be packed away, and the owls could wait.

The Snowy Owl is very different from all the other owls I'd seen. It is circumpolar in its range, highly nomadic, and hard to pinpoint outside breeding times. With no possibility of new travels, I went to the library to find out more. This way, when I did find one, it would be an informed view.

Early surveys carried out in the 1990s in Arctic Russia enabled scientists to create snapshot estimates of the total world Snowy Owl population. But even with estimates there were problems, as the population varies spatially and temporally: Eugene Potapov and Richard Sale in their beautiful Poyser Monograph on the Snowy Owl suggest that "estimating its size is akin to standing beneath a locust swarm and counting insects, but with no knowledge of how long ago the front of the swarm passed, or how far away the swarm's rear is."

However, the advantage comes at breeding time, at which point the owls must slow down, and will choose a location based on the abundance of small rodents. We do know that this species of owl is thought to form variable "breeding pockets" across the global tundra region, and within that, pairs might have a breeding territory of 25 square kilometres depending on the population cycle and availability of their

main food source, the lemming. A rough "guesstimate" (Potapov and Sale again) has put numbers at around thirteen thousand pairs worldwide, on average, but these can double after a
series of good lemming seasons, and equally might dip steeply
after a deep lemming population depression. Because of the
lemming cycles, the Snowy Owl often performs vast migrations across sparsely populated areas, making individuals hard
to find and the population extremely difficult to count.

Looking at these details more closely, I felt this owl must be
even closer to the essence of wildness than all my other owls.
At around 70 centimetres tall, the dense, compact Snowy is
designed for survival in extreme cold. Its insulation, the soft,
pure white plumage, is designed for long periods standing on
the snow. It has the most densely feathered feet and toes of
any owl, even having plumage between the toes, and close up
they look as if they are sporting an elegant pair of furry ski
boots. But the perfect plumage is not simply for warmth and
camouflage. It might also be useful for sexual signalling, and
can be dotted with dusky patterning; the females are more
darkly barred, with charcoal-black feather tips. Both sexes have
a faintly visible facial disc topped with invisible greyish ear
tufts, and a yellow bill set beneath an extravagant white mous-
tache of vibrissae—I assumed these sensitive bristles evolved
as protective insulation to prevent the bird's nostrils freezing
over during the Arctic winter, but they are in fact employed to
detect information about the prey it has just caught by gently
brushing it in order to "smell" it! Like many owls, Snowies have
very poor close-up vision, as their sight has evolved especially
to watch things at long range across the rolling tundra, such as
their main predator the Arctic fox, or their main winter prey
items, the willow grouse and the ptarmigan.

In spite of the owl's furry ski boots, ornithologists know
that when winter sets in and ice takes hold of the northern

landscape the Snowies begin their migration south. An airport does not seem like a prime owl location, but for several years Logan Airport in Boston, Massachusetts, was chosen by many of these birds as an overwintering spot. In spite of the jet engines, people, and pollution, the owls came to the grassy fields of the airport, proving that once habituated, an owl can put up with an awful lot of noise and disruption. They were attracted to the short-mown, tundra-like grassland, and the abundance of rodents and birds.

Between 1981 and 1993 many of the owls were carefully captured and colour-marked to find out about their movements and if they were a risk to the air traffic. They were marked on the head with an ink that lasted three months, allowing them to be identified at a distance without capturing them, then they were ringed and released. Now their north–south movements could be monitored. Arriving in November, they often stayed until late spring, and one owl repeatedly returned each year for a decade, another for sixteen years. Over time, 385 owls were trapped and ringed, and it was noted that no two had exactly the same plumage. They had individual personalities, it was found, and roosted on the ground just outside the airfield during the day, becoming active and returning to hunt on the airfield at dusk, as they prefer to be primarily nocturnal. They liked to sit on an elevated perch with a viewpoint, and would hunt like a falcon, often pursuing and catching birds in flight. Pellet analysis showed their remarkably catholic taste, from fish and birds to other raptors, including other owls. Predictably, with the fast-moving jets and blinding lights at night, eventually one owl became entangled in an engine turbine and nearly caused an accident. It was decided that to avoid danger to all, the owls should be captured and released at a safer site, but a huge amount had already been learned from the owls of Logan Airport.

MOST COMMONLY FOUND in northerly climes, such as Canada, Alaska, and northern Russia, the Snowy Owl seldom makes it further south. However, it is also a nomadic bird, and I did find that its wanderings have been occasionally known to take it as far south as Hawaii. One arrived at an airport there, too, and had to be removed for safety reasons. So I knew that this owl could achieve spectacular southerly journeys and could easily cross to the UK, however, and I couldn't quite believe it would ever be found here in the British Isles, and certainly not any further south than Orkney, surely? But when a Snowy Owl was reported in West Penwith, Cornwall, a few miles from where Rick's mother Wendy lived, my heart gave a small flip and a surge of hopeful adrenaline charged into my veins. Could this possibly be true? "I remember when I was very small," Wendy told me with interest, "that one day at school we were told a Snowy Owl had landed on the roof and we were to very quietly go out and look at it."

This must have been during the Second World War, while Wendy was still in junior school. I was encouraged. There seemed to be a historical precedent. A quick search found other equally astonishing local sightings of this Arctic bird in West Penwith over the years. A wild Snowy had appeared in the St. Just area in 2008 causing much excitement, and hordes of twitchers swarmed in from all over Britain. In 2010 one was seen again, and in 2011. As recently as 2013 Snowies had been sighted here, all focused around the same area of west Cornwall. My mind computed this. The reported sightings, confirmed year on year, were verified as true.

To see one of these Arctic birds would be like meeting a deity of the north, an icon of desolate, boggy, lichen-clad plains, forest edges, rocky promontories, and shores edged with sea ice. What could have happened to bring it here? I thought nothing like this usually came our way, and certainly not at Easter time. A phone call to a Cornish cousin, Lisa, a keen birdwatcher, quickly confirmed the presence of the Snowy Owl in West Penwith. "A beautiful male, pure white," she said. "I saw it while walking the dogs." Females are flecked with black, I remembered, but males sport no more than a few charcoal flecks which often fade with age.

The evidence was stacking up. After all, these birds have often been known to travel vast distances over water during what are called "irruptions," mass migrations from the Arctic. For many years these invasions puzzled scientists and birders. These are familiar winter birds in southern Canada and the fields of the northern United States, but the arrival of hundreds of owls in places like Alberta and Montreal in Canada was something of a mystery. From the 1940s studies had begun to survey the movements of the owls. Hunters, trappers, taxidermists, and amateurs who completed Christmas bird counts helped to gather data.

Scientific interest about the causes and the ecological impacts of the Snowies' movements increased. During an irruption they travel in loose groups, called "boids," flying westwards as well as southwards, and the data gathered indicated that they were driven by climatic conditions and food availability. Just as lynx had been shown to be influenced by the movements and abundance of hares, the owls were shown to be following prey. Generally they need large rodents like lemmings as their main food, and when times are good lemmings make up 90 per cent of their diet, but if the lemming population runs out, the birds will move on to search for grouse and ptarmigan, and if they fly to the edges of the sea ice, they will feed on water birds such as eider and gulls. In North America, they are attracted south to arable winter fields, and during irruptions they have occasionally been found as far south as California, and one was even seen in Bermuda.

Satellite and telemetry have shown that the owls avoid thick forest during the winter migration. This may be because of the risk of predation by Eagle Owls in Europe and Great horned Owls in North America. Like all owl species they have the same plumage in winter as summer, so their pure white feathers are highly visible in areas without snow. Snowy Owl corpses have been found in America predated by golden eagle, and in a gruesome twist, only the protein-rich brain had been eaten. Telemetry research shows that they always cross forest as quickly as possibly whilst migrating, preferring to stay on vantage points in open fields and clear-cut forest.

Why Snowies migrate and how they choose where to go is complex. Their movements are thought to be due to a combination of winter lemming availability, snow thickness, and, crucially, the movements of other Snowies. When they are breeding at the end of the winter and into the early spring, the owls seem to behave gregariously, and often follow where they notice others flying, as if sensing there might be some feeding that way. In the breeding grounds location is at a premium; the first to arrive will pick the best spots, and the later owls the less good ones, and so on. So where a pair is found breeding, there will likely be another pair nearby. Often during migration, they'll find a good perch, stay a few days, or a few weeks at most, startling and enchanting local residents lucky enough to see them, and then they'll move on until they find suitable breeding places. In Europe, it is a little different, and the owls appear to move around far less; although not so much is known about these owls, it is thought that usually they are more sedentary than their transatlantic cousins.

In the last hundred years, only twenty-nine Snowy Owls have been ringed in the United Kingdom and Ireland, but over four hundred accepted records of sightings exist. I watched Twitter. On this particular occasion, at first none of the local bird groups or rare-bird alert forums in England had mentioned a Snowy in Cornwall. Unusual blow-ins of this sort normally cause their own kind of perfect storm. Surely there would have been a vortex of attention on social media. There appeared to be nothing yet.

But then the morning after the Cornwall owl call from cousin Lisa, somebody else had seen the owl, taken a picture, confirmed it was a Snowy, and alerted Twitter. Joining the rush, Rick and I bundled ourselves into the car and drove a frantic two hours on no breakfast to the location of the sighting. The Snowy had been spotted at St. Just, right at the far end of Cornwall, close to Land's End. I was tense, and worried that in this position right on the tip of the peninsula, jutting out into the Atlantic, harried by gulls, it would not stay long.

At St. Just we burst excitedly into Warren's Bakery to buy a breakfast of hot, freshly baked pasties to fortify ourselves. Everyone local here knew exactly what was happening, so we asked the baker about the owl. Yes, a wild Snowy had indeed been seen on the edge of the village, she told us. We walked into the sleepy square and found more people to ask. One by one, all of the locals we met confirmed it. Photographic evidence on Twitter revealed the bird taking refuge, hunkered low against a granite wall looking a little bedraggled. As well as the striking curve of its ivory head, its implacable golden gaze looked weary. The perfect white plumage with just a very few faint grey flecks on its back and wings showed it was indeed a male. Its heftily feathered feet perched cool as melting snowdrifts amongst the sunshine and gorse of the Cornish peninsula. Snowy Owls roost on or close to the ground, often preferring rock-strewn areas which provide vantage points to look out for wolves on the tundra. No predators like that here, but plenty of locals had seen it, and some twitchers had appeared and photographed the owl.

We took a left at the clock tower, hurried past the baker's factory, and arrived at the spot. No owl. Perhaps it had got fed up with the pestering paparazzi, or perhaps it had realised its mistake and simply moved on. Snowy Owls do this. They effortlessly drift, just not normally in this part of the planet. Later though, the owl was seen posing by a popular Cornish landmark, an early Bronze Age holed stone, the Mên-an-Tol. (If you pass through the hole nine times you can be cured of rickets, legend has it, and when Benji was a toddler we had done the same for him in the hope of curing his infantile eczema.) The stone was reputed to harbour a potent piskie and it could return changeling children to their mothers. Now it was gifted with a visitation from a Snowy Owl. It is hard to go anywhere in this part of Cornwall and not feel infused with its mysteries.

From the misty cliff top at Cape Cornwall we saw gannets spearing down into the blue depths to catch fish, and fulmars wheeled around precarious nesting sites. But the wild essence of sea ice, the neighbour of the Inuit, narwhal, and polar bear: Where was he? By the end of the day we had developed "owl neck" from craning our heads upwards and around to search the rocks and cliffs for our Snowy. We scoured the boulder-strewn camouflage of the Bronze Age field patterns and tors of Nancledra, Towednack, and Zennor. As we moved back and forth through the rocks, thickets, and furze, every bright stone and white gull caught the sun and flared into an owl shape.

Withy nooks of pollen-rich pussy willow, bright gorse, wind-whipped hazel, and battered daffodil fields yielded nothing, but I began to see how the grizzled moorland and rocky tussocks of this place mimicked the raised bogs and marshes of the tundra and might attract a voyaging Snowy Owl. We flushed a sparrowhawk from the high-walled lane and I saw my first swallow of the year. I'm not sure if it was the bite of the wind or being so tired that brought wetness to my eyes just then. I thought of the vast distances travelled by these nomadic birds, and of their lonely isolation. If people do witness them in the wild here in Europe, it is only rare and fleetingly, cryptic clues to the restless wanderings of a creature that seems always just beyond our grasp.

At Towednack church I walked up to the top of the hill, following cousin Lisa's description of seeing the owl hunting in the fields below. I sat on the rocks and looked over the landscape of West Penwith. This landscape must be the closest thing to the tundra an Arctic bird could wish for: undulating, sparsely populated moorland, sporadic granite outcrops and rodent-filled dry-stone walls; many cliff-dwelling seabirds and hundreds of unwary rabbits to feed on. If I were a Snowy Owl, I would be wondering where the lemmings were, and why the permafrost had melted, but I'd make do with the rabbits burrowed into the soft peat. The local herring gulls, however, always on the alert for a good brawl, had put up an effective reception for this impressive predator. The owl must have thought the same, because the next thing we knew, it had taken off and flown the twenty-eight miles out to sea, west to the Isles of Scilly, where it turned up on the tiny islands of Tresco and Bryher! Internet bird forums were all talking about it. The discussions from the Canadian and American members were the most informed and revealing. One said:

> Snowies are perfectly capable of crossing huge distances of open water when they irrupt. They have been recorded in Bermuda before, and one even made it to Hawaii somehow during the winter of 'ii–'i2. This year is shaping up to be another big one for Snowy owls, and they've been turning up

all over. There were even a few on a big offshore
drilling vessel in the northeast last week.

But birders on the international forum were concerned for
the UK bird, which was obviously lost: "The last Snowy to
make it to Bermuda began feasting on the endangered cahow
petrels and had to be collected. History may well repeat itself."

And then finally, the theory that I thought the most amaz-
ing, and when you think about it, perhaps the most plausible:
"It's not uncommon for Snowy Owls to land on ships near the
Canadian coast and they may travel some distances that way."
Aha, I thought. If the owl had not flown all the way across the
North Sea from Norway or Sweden, it explained a lot. It is
sometimes presumed that the few Snowy Owls that arrive as
far south as this one are ship-assisted—perhaps arriving with
timber cargo ships from Quebec. Though in the case of our
Cornish owl this was just speculation, and nothing could be
proven, it seemed the most likely explanation. Perhaps it had
been searching for sea ice that had never materialised, and had
landed on a ship to rest.

Another knowledgeable American birder supported this
idea:

> If there is not a noticeable influx of Snowy owls
> in the lower 48 states of the US then I'm also
> skeptical that this bird arrived at all naturally.
> Though it depends how you treat "ship assisted"
> species—some say that it's not a big deal if the bird
> is not fed on the ship and has survived the trip on
> its own; others say that you shouldn't count the
> migration as natural if it is more or less clear that
> the bird is ship assisted—like for example the Iago
> sparrows (endemic to Cape Verde islands) arriving

in the Netherlands—how did they get there? They
hopped off the research ship *Plancius*.

There we had it; the Snowy had probably landed on a cargo
ship and been taken much further south than it intended.
Although, with the only eyewitness being the owl, we could
never be entirely sure. This year, 2017, there had already been
several confirmed sightings of wild Snowy Owls arriving on
Orkney and in the West of Ireland in Galway and Mayo.

When it was time to leave, setting off from the highest
place on the Isle of Bryher, Watch Point, where it had been
last seen, the errant Snowy Owl must have flown out over
the tall rocks of Shipman Head, heading north-north-west.
Gliding over the foam and froth of Hell Bay, out toward the
vast undulating landscape of the Atlantic, perhaps the expanse
of sea below formed the memory of the tundra in its mind.
Home. Or if not home, something like it, with its spume-
capped plains and crevasses. Heading to who knows where,
the owl must have gone out over the vast, watery plain, disorientated, following pathways in its head, drawn by magnetite or
the remembered scent of ice. It might have made it. Or, never
finding its lost edge of sea ice, it might have ditched into the
waves. Some find their way home, and some do not. Nobody
will know. Nobody will have seen. But somewhere, a small raft
of white feathers might have vanished in a crest of foam.

SNOWY OWLS WERE ONCE prevalent all across Europe.
Their remains have been found on archaeological sites as
far south as Gibraltar, suggesting that the tundra and taiga
ecological zones reached to the Mediterranean area during
glacial periods. This visible owl has attracted human attention
since prehistoric times and in the Trois-Frères cave in Ariège,
France, a well-observed image of a Snowy Owl pair and their

fledgling chick have been etched. The image artfully captures the family resting on the ground, as they are known to do at breeding times. At other sites in south-west France, many accumulated Snowy Owl bones have been found, and these have been worked and modified with flint tools. Wing bones had been fashioned into tubular pieces of smoothly finished bone, and might have been used as whistles, blowpipes for painting, or as flutes.

It is thought that during the glacial period, when wintry conditions hit, the birds descended from the high plateaus to shelter. In the open river valleys and on the plains, the owls would have formed aggregations on or close to the ground, as they are seen to do today, and they must have been easy prey for Palaeolithic people. One site in particular has the bones of at least twenty-five males and sixty-five females, outnumbering the bones of all other bird remains found at the site. Workings on them suggest that the owls were not only used as food but that possibly the skins of these owls were removed carefully and prized as a valuable resource. They may potentially have been for ritual performance. One notable painting at the Trois-Frères cave, dated to around 13,000 BC, suggests this. The famous painting, named *The Sorcerer*, depicts a male figure dressed in a shamanic "master of the animals" costume, with a wolf's tail, antlers on the head, and an owl facial mask. Perhaps the glamour of the Snowy Owl created a natural empathetic relationship between our species. In view of the piles of Snowy bones, there seems to have been a prolonged fixation amongst early peoples of south-west France with the magical Snowy Owl.

In the absence of any resident in Britain, if I wanted to find out more about the elusive Snowy Owl and its circumpolar habitat today I should probably go to Barrow, Alaska. Here for many generations the birds have not only been in close contact with Inuit people, but recently have been extensively studied in their Arctic breeding grounds.

In the native Inupiaq language, Barrow, Alaska, is called Utqiagvik, which translated means roughly "the place where Snowy Owls are hunted." Whereas in Europe this rare and vulnerable bird is now protected, and they rarely come into contact with people any longer, this is not the case in Alaska. Here, a certain number of birds may be shot each year, and they may be used for clothing, or their wings used for traditional household items like dusters and brooms, or made into ceremonial or decorative items like jewellery by the local people. But there are also many local myths and stories about the Snowy Owl. Inuit legend tells of a young girl who was one day turned into an owl with a long pointed bill. Terrified and panicking, she flew straight into a tall cliff, and accidentally flattened her face and beak. That, the story goes, is how owls have stayed ever since.

Mythographer Joseph Campbell, in *The Power of Myth*, suggests that as well as helping our ancestors to make sense of the world and create answers to puzzling questions, these myths can simply reveal wonder. They allow us to be amazed and enchanted with the natural world and also with ourselves. They present the possibility of connection, transformation, and change, and help us to be better humans, aware of the mystique of our history and our potential. As Campbell suggests, they represent possibility, and might enliven our idea of "how to live a human life under any circumstances." Owls had certainly accompanied me through many circumstances in my own life over the past years. But my situation was now dictating that my journey take a break; a trip to Alaska would be pushing it too far. I saw it as a pause, however, not a full stop. One day I would go and see Snowy Owls quartering the tundra.

And what of the Snowy's threats? In my owl journey I had found a creature increasingly and consistently pressured by human activity and climate disruption. The Snowy Owl was no exception, in fact as a specialist Arctic species it seemed much more in danger than some of the others. If the pressure continues unchecked, this owl's habitat is set to become increasingly fragmented. The conservation status of a species is set by the International Union for Conservation of Nature (IUCN) and currently the status given for the Snowy Owl is "least concern," basically because the species occupies such a large, undeveloped, remote territory and there is so little information on long-term population changes. "Despite the least concern status," Potapov and Sale suggest, "there are threats, some of them historical, some set to appear in the future, which makes the species potentially vulnerable on this unstable planet." These two scientists, paying close attention to changes in land use and the effects of exploitation of oil and gas, are worried about something currently very pressing. With even one more degree of climate warming, if the northern ice melts and only islands on which the bedrock stands above sea level remain as refuges, less than one third of their breeding range will be available to the owls: "This is an extreme scenario but accelerating global warming might mean that this occurs within 100 years."

Other spectres haunt the Snowy's existence, putting further pressure on its survival. Historically, Arctic fox and other predator trapping was found to interfere with the already unpredictable lemming cycles, and although the fur trade has now diminished, there is still "bycatch" from trapping. At one time thousands of Snowy Owls were trapped in Russia. In North America, it was for trophy hunting, and in Canada the owls were considered a plump and delicious dish. In Finland, eggs were collected by the hundreds. Recently, collisions with man-made structures have been a threat, but since the Snowy Owl dwells in very sparsely inhabited places you would not consider this to be a common problem; or at least, if it is, it must go unreported. However, with increasing fossil fuel exploration, as well as the very dangerous uranium ore mining amongst the owl's breeding territories, it is being exposed to new and lethal dangers. Its future is far from secure. Suddenly it feels as if this little-seen but precious owl, seated on high promontories on the tundra, might see its own demise. Would its ability to travel and adapt save it, or could it disappear along with the melting ice sheets?

The Snowy Owl's eye is one of the most highly developed of all owls', as it needs to track distant prey in the extremes of the polar night and the slanting low sun of the spring. But bring an owl out of the Arctic and it is immediately vulnerable. It adapted to a habitat where microbes are not prevalent, and outside a cold environment its eyes are susceptible to infection and blindness. Its specialism, along with the fact that it needs lemmings to survive, may mean that as the climate is further disrupted and the tundra scrub moves north into the plains, this special owl will be seriously under threat and could eventually disappear. It is a haunting thought, that *Bubo scandiacus*, the ghost of the tundra, could melt from the landscape and fade away altogether.

Epilogue

AS WE RETURNED HOME AFTER OUR UNSUCCESSFUL
race to Cornwall, thoughts came to me in mounting drifts.
The owl, especially this Snowy, had proved itself to be a keen-
sighted and resilient creature. Now that my domestic life had
taken some difficult turns, I was having to be clear-sighted,
strong, and independent, and I felt Owl-like, just as my friend
had predicted. How clear-sighted we would need to be, to
save these creatures! Instead of blinding and caging our magnificent wildlife, we needed to step away from our rampant
materialism and think to the future.

That night, instead of the Snowy Owl, a soft, silent reminder
came. With a crystalline-clear sky an unseasonal dusting of
frost arrived and we awoke to a fragile carpet of white.

At first light Benji and I were up and out: snow is increasingly rare where we live in Devon, and Dartmoor had a covering, so breathing in the ice-scent and glitter, warmly wrapped,
we declared it a "snow day." I packed our emergency foil wraps

and weatherproof shelter and we drove up into the blue skies and biting winds of Dartmoor.

While many animals hunker down at this time—mice, moles, and earthworms dig themselves in deeper—cossetted in our centrally heated homes, we need contact with the raw edge, risk, and struggle that snow brings. Not only this, but we need contact with the wonder and transformation of snow. It struck me that the vanished Snowy Owl was like climate change; often, unseasonal warmth was robbing us, impoverishing us, of something beautiful and vital. Suddenly it all felt vividly clear; the lost owl was like a monument to lost snow. Snow can make the world seem suddenly rich; it fires us up, sharpens our emotions, and (if we can manage the slipperiness and cold) fills us with glee as our bodies remember what they were made for and what they are capable of. Thousands of years ago our ancestors braved snow and ice and made huge migrations, just like the Snowy Owls. Now for a moment I felt the Snowy there under my skin.

As if in pilgrimage we headed out into our fine layer of snow. We slinked over the ice-slipped roads that flank the edge of the moor, bounced over a cattle grid, and skidded to a halt by a stand of beeches. No shelter here: the wind bellowed in the bare twigs and the trunks were sprayed foamy white all down their northerly sides. We crunched through a magic carpet of ice crystals towards the high vantage point of Buckland Beacon. This bulbous granite formation is one of the many tors that scatter this part of the moor and its horizontal wrinkles make excellent finger-holds if you enjoy climbing. In 1928 two slabs were painstakingly engraved with a set of the Ten Commandments; today these were unreadable, blanketed along with the winter-spindled heather. Only the larger, tougher birds were calling: the gravel-rasp of crows and distant, stately *cronk cronk* of ravens echoed on the wind.

Their shadows cast blue patterns against the snow. A solitary herring gull, blown in from the south coast, seemed to be playing on the freezing cauldron of air.

Benji noticed them first: the tracks were pockmarked everywhere, the long-legged prints of hares, the large hind paws set ahead of the forepaws. Some human prints led to a wreath lain for the full moon (people are like that in Devon), and a mischievous snow sculptor had left us the best for last: not a full snowman, but pertinent parts of him, brazenly pointing to the sky.

With heart-rending speed, by the afternoon it was all over. The thick hawthorn and beech hedges tinkled with drips and the roads ran with streams of snowmelt. We were still tingling with a whole season in one day when we were gifted with a new surprise: a russet knot tumbled in front of us, untied itself, and shot across the road. The word formed in my mouth before I had time to think. Stoat. The long body snaked like a little flame with a smouldering tip—the stoat's distinctive black-tipped tail. This feature, as well as its slightly longer length than the tinier weasel, confirmed its identity as one of Britain's most voracious predators. The incisor teeth of this compact and muscular stealth-machine have evolved to fit perfectly between the upper vertebrae of a rabbit, enabling it to dislocate the neck in one quick bite. Even worse if you are a rabbit, the stoat deliberately performs a capoeira-like dance so fascinating that you forget your fear and cannot resist lingering a few doomed moments.

This stoat was doing nothing but streaking away from us along the tarmac. As well as its creamy throat and underbelly I felt sure that some of its fur was flecked with white. Perhaps a residual winter coat? In the north they routinely grow snowy "ermine" coats in winter to help them be camouflaged. But climate warming is causing these more northerly mustelids the same problems as other snow-animals: and it isn't just the stoat who is suffering. Without regular snow, winter-white snow hares now stand out against the khaki and brown Cairngorm mountainsides and can be easily picked out by predators. Ermine stoats can also be seen by their prey as well as predators. If climate warming continues to eliminate prolonged snows from our winter season, what will become of us all, humans and animals?

A new flurry arrived and we tipped our heads back, eyes closed. I opened my mouth wide to catch the powdery flakes as they fell. I could barely feel them as they melted on my tongue.

WENDY DIED IN her sleep as I was finishing my story. With typical generosity, at the venerable age of ninety, her heart failed, sparing herself and us the worst of a slow drawn-out decline into spreading cancer. When your family has been shaken and re-orientated, some things settle down, and new things arrive. Benji and I still have three European owls to see: the Snowy, the Hawk Owl, and the elusive Great Grey: all of these we can see as captives in our local zoo, but it is the wild where they reside for me, and I know I will not be satisfied until we have at least been in search. When an email from an owl guide in northern Finland popped into my inbox, inviting me to go and see the northern owls that I had missed on my odyssey, I knew this journey was not quite over. In the New Year I would take Benji to see them in the wild. Hawk Owls were performing a record-breaking irruption—a southerly migration in search of food—due to very cold conditions, while *Strix nebulosa*, the Great Grey Owls, were hunting regularly, my contact told me. Both these owls could usually be watched from secret tracks and special hides deep in the forest of northern Finland. Very occasionally, a

Snowy is seen in northern Lapland. These owls were a possibility; perhaps they could be within reach. The tough cookies I hadn't yet seen in their natural habitat: we would make a trip to Lapland, travelling by train, hiring an eco-cabin, and getting a guide to show us the Great Grey and the Hawk Owl hunting; perhaps there would be the possibility of a Snowy Owl. This trip will wait for when Benji is better, and I'll take him with me. He does seem a little better. Something has shifted; he's seen a new specialist and touch wood, for now he's getting stronger and more confident in himself. As Emily Dickinson says:

> "Hope" is the thing with feathers
> That perches in the soul,
> And sings the tune without the words,
> And never stops at all.

ONE WINTER NIGHT after Christmas I had finished writing my pages. The owl book was written. But I woke shivering in the early hours. The feather duvet had fallen away and in through the window came white moonlight; for a moment I felt freighted with fear. Heart thumping, I looked to Rick and his face was pale. I reached out but he was warm, and there were his shoulders, muscular, vulnerable, and the shoulder blades wingless and human. There was the steady beating pulse, along with the pulse of my own. I thought of the snowy tundra, the long migrations of the Snowy Owls, the long life-paired journeys of other migrants, and the distances of the terns, redwings, albatrosses, and firecrests, the journeys so many make to stay alive. I thought of the journey we were still on as a family. Like the birds, we belong to a fragile, fragmented world.

The memory of the owl's scratchy calls pressed into my inner ear. The field outside on the edge of town threw a pale mist over the new estate that had replaced the meadow. Once wings had lit the tall grass that grew there, the screech of an owl had ripped the air. I thought I wouldn't have a chance of seeing them any more as they quartered the field, their low flight no longer brushing the grass. But amongst the newly built landscape of houses, a host of native trees were growing. Around the mature oak, a protecting layer of young trees had been planted, brand-new lungs for the new estate. An apple orchard, some hazel and field maples, as well as English oaks, viburnums, and wild cherry trees. At the edge of the houses, as the roots delved down, minute fissures and cracks were already there in the new concrete. Everywhere, seeds had finely sown themselves, and in spring the green tips of grasses and weeds would find their way back, an unstoppable prairie, rising, soon to be swallow-skimmed, buzzing, and by then, instead of an owl, a small new dog would curl comfortingly around our bare feet, and we'd realise our entire world was re-growing and re-orienting, as if:

> *The end of all our exploring*
> *Will be to arrive where we started*
> *And know the place for the first time.*

—T. S. ELIOT, "Little Gidding"

Flowers and Owls
with some debt to W. H. Auden

—VI GALE

About these they weren't all wrong either,
those minor masters and unsung scholars who
tramped the old world countryside
with rucksack and staff, resting
face down in sweet meadow grass,
sleeping under stars and hoots
at the forest's edge.

We're taken by their work—
often anonymous, inaccurate, anthropomorphic—
herbarium and bestiary, song and myth,
carved foliage and replicated bird.
We can almost hear them as they
munched coarse bread at noon
and pondered: Why aren't
there owls in Iceland? How
do flowers bloom in permafrost?
Are these sooty emissaries
from the Nether World?
And why in Heaven's Order such diversity:
great, small, speckled and barred—
graveyard haunter, messenger of doom,
horned dark bird of poetry and death.
How to turn his evil into magic?

Make a potion of it: owl's broth
for whooping cough, raw owl's egg
down the drunk—he'll sober up for life.
Nail the spread wings to any shed,
save it from lightning and hail.
Tawny, spotted, stippled, and dappled
like fish in the brook. This bird's wise
and deep as words in a book.

Owl-light. Owl's claw. Owl's clover.
Ours are the heavy questions. Will history
hold us up? Will exploration save this earth?
We signal other galaxies, probe the ocean floors,
perfect our own destruction. And breathe
a moment from that simpler time when men
were sometimes wrong in fact, but right
in principle. They dealt with fear,
noted, took delight, pressed on.

ACKNOWLEDGMENTS

A NATURE BOOK like this is always part of a long conversation and my gratitude goes to all those writers, ornithologists, academics, conservationists, poets and critics who have contributed to my understanding, challenged me, sparked ideas, and offered inspiration and direction. They are too many to mention. Among those to thank who were most formative, in no special order, are: Masie Cochran, Beth Steidle, Craig Popelars, and the Tin House team; my wonderful agent Clare Conville; all my friends and colleagues at Plymouth University and at the *Times* newspaper; my family: Rick, Benji and Jenny, and my dogs Barney and Dill, for reminding me to go outside and be more creaturely when I seemed tied to my desk. And for encouragement, music and wisdom: Laura Traister, Karine Polwart, David Lindo, Robert Macfarlane, Mark Cocker, Martin Kelsey, John Lister-Kaye, Hugh Warwick, David and Frances Ramsden and all at the Barn Owl Trust UK; Gilles Trochard, Christine Bettahar, Stephen Powles; Shirley, Oliver and Jonathan Darlington, Paul Riddle, Milan Ruzic, Heimo Mikkola, Mike Toms, Emily Joachim, Jari Valkama, Jere Toivola, Vincenzo Penteriani, Eloise Malone, and Anita

Morris. For their wonderful contributions of poetry: Vi Gale, Caroline Carver, Kenneth Steven, Jennifer Hunt, and Rose Corlett. And most of all the owls who put up with being bothered, ringed, handled, stared at or intruded upon: you truly opened my eyes.

READINGS

Abram, David. *Becoming Animal: An Earthly Cosmology.* New York: Pantheon, 2010.

Abram, David. *The Spell of the Sensuous.* New York: Vintage, 1996.

Addison, Josephine, and Cherry Hillhouse. *Treasury of Birdlore.* London: Carlton Publishing Group, 1998.

Angell, Tony. *The House of Owls.* New Haven, CT: Yale University Press, 2015.

Audubon, John James. *Birds of America* (1838). London: Natural History Museum, 2012.

———. *The Audubon Reader.* New York: Everyman's Library. Alfred A. Knopf, 2006.

Barnes, Simon. *How to Be Wild.* London: Short Books, 2007.

Berger, John. *Why Look at Animals?* London: Penguin, 2009.

Berry, Liz. *Black Country.* London: Chatto & Windus, 2014.

Birkhead, Tim. *Bird Sense: What It's Like to Be a Bird.* London: Bloomsbury, 2013.

Birkhead, Tim, Jo Wimpenny, and Bob Montgomerie. *Ten Thousand Birds: Ornithology since Darwin.* Princeton, NJ: Princeton University Press, 2014.

Boot, Kelvin. *The Nocturnal Naturalist.* Newton Abbot, UK: David & Charles, 1985.

Bradley, Martin. *From Dusk till Dawn.* Dibden Purlieu, UK: Skyhunter Books, 2015.

Calvez, Leigh. *The Hidden Lives of Owls.* Seattle: Sasquatch Books, 2016.

Campbell, Joseph. *The Power of Myth.* New York: Bantam Doubleday, 1989.

Charbonneau-Lassay, Louis. *Le Bestiare du Christ* (1940). Paris: Albin Michel, 2006.

———. *The Bestiary of Christ* (abridged). New York: Penguin, 1991.

Chauvet, Jean-Marie. *Dawn of Art: The Chauvet Cave.* London: Harry N. Abrams, 1996.

Clare, John. *John Clare, Poems Selected by Paul Farley.* London: Faber & Faber, 2011.

Cocker, Mark. *Birders: Tales of a Tribe.* London: Vintage, 2002.

———. *Birds and People.* London: Jonathan Cape, 2013.

Constantine, David, and Bernard O'Donaghue, eds. *The Oxford Poets Anthology.* Manchester, UK: Carcanet, 2007.

Crumley, Jim. *Brother Nature.* Caithness, UK: Whittles Publishing, 2007.

———. *Barn Owl, Encounters in the Wild.* Glasgow: Saraband, 2016.

Dante, Alighieri. *The Divine Comedy* (1320). London: Penguin Classics, 2012.

Daston, Lorraine, and Gregg Mitmann, eds. *Thinking with Animals: New Perspectives on Anthropomorphism.* New York: Columbia University Press, 2005.

Davidson, Peter. *The Last of the Light.* London: Reaktion Books, 2016.

Dickinson, Emily. *The Complete Poems.* Faber & Faber, 2016.

Dooley, Maura. *The Silvering.* Hexham, UK: Bloodaxe Books, 2016.

Eliot, T. S. *Four Quartets* (1942). London: Faber & Faber, 2009.

Etienne, Pascal. *La Chouette Chevêche.* Collection Parthénope. Mèze, France: Biotope Editions, 2012.

Finch, Robert, and John Elder, eds. *The Norton Book of Nature Writing.* New York: W. W. Norton, 1990.

Fitter, Richard, ed, *The Reader's Digest Book of British Birds.* London: Drive Publications for the Automobile Association, 1969.

Gale, Vi. *Odd Flowers and Short-Eared Owls.* Portland, OR: Prescott Street Press, 1984.

Gantz, Jeffrey, trans. *The Mabinogion.* London: Penguin, 1976.

Gosney, Dave. *Finding Birds in Lapland.* Sheffield, UK: Easybirder, 2010.

———. *Finding Birds in South Finland.* Sheffield, UK: Easybirder, 2010.

Grahame, Kenneth. *The Wind in the Willows.* Bath: North Parade Publishing, 2017.

Greenoak, Francesca. *All the Birds of the Air.* London: Andre Deutsch, 1979.

Halpern, Daniel, and Dan Frank, eds. *The Picador Nature Reader*. London: Picador, 1996.

Harding, Stephan. *Animate Earth*. Dartington, UK: Green Books, 2006.

Harraway, Donna. *The Companion Species Manifesto*. Chicago: University of Chicago Press, 2003.

Harting, James Edmund. *The Ornithology of Shakespeare*. Woking, UK: Gresham Books, 1978.

Hegel, G. W. F. *Philosophy of Right* (1820). Translated by S. W. Dyde. Cambridge: Cambridge University Press, 1991

Henderson, Caspar. *The Book of Barely Imagined Beings: A 21st Century Bestiary*. London: Granta, 2012.

Hosking, Eric. *An Eye for a Bird: The Autobiography of a Bird Photographer*. London: Arrow Books Ltd, 1973.

Hudson, W. H. *A Shepherd's Life*. London: Futura, 1910.

Irving, Kirsten, and Jon Stone, eds. *Birdbook: Towns, Parks, Gardens and Woodland*. London: Sidekick Books, 2011.

Jung, Karl. *Selected Letters of CG Jung*, Princeton, NJ: Princeton Legacy Library, 1909–1961.

Kabat-Zinn, Jon. *Coming to Our Senses*. New York: Hyperion, 2005.

Konig, Claus, Friedhelm Weick, and Jan-Hedrick Becking. *Owls of the World*. London: Christopher Helm, 2008.

Leopold, Aldo. *A Sand County Almanac*. Oxford: Oxford University Press, 1949.

Longfellow, Henry. *The Song of Hiawatha*. New York: Hurst, New York, 1898.

Louv, Richard. *Last Child in the Woods*. London: Atlantic Books, 2010.

MacCurrach, Robert. *In the Bend of the River: Finding Vojvodina*. London: Book Stream, 2010.

Maloof, Joan. *Teaching the Trees: Lessons from the Forest*. Athens: University of Georgia Press, 2007.

Maslow, Jonathan. *The Owl Papers*. London: Penguin, 1983.

Maurus, Hrabanus. *De Rerum Naturis*.

Mead, Chris. *Owls*. Stansted, UK: Whittet Books, 2011.

Mikkola, Heimo. *Owls of the World*. London: Bloomsbury, 2012.

———. *Owls of Europe*. Calton, UK: T. & A. D. Poyser, 1983.

Morris, Anita. *Murray the Smallest Owl*. Liverpool: Beatles, Liverpool & More, 2016.

Morris, Desmond. *Owl*. London: Reaktion Books, 2009.

Muldoon, Paul, ed. *The Faber Book of Beasts*. London: Faber & Faber, 2010.

Mynott, Jeremy. *Birdscapes: Birds in our Imagination and Experience*. Princeton, NJ: Princeton University Press, 2012.

Oliver, Mary. *Owls and Other Fantasies: Poems and Essays*. Boston: Beacon Press, 2006.

Parry-Jones, Jemima. *Understanding Owls*. Newton Abbot, UK: David & Charles, 2001.

Piatti, Celestino. *Le bonheur des chouettes*. Dijon, France: Ane Baté Editions, 2013.

Pliny the Elder, *Natural History*. Rome: AD 77

Potapov, Eugene, and Richard Sale. *The Snowy Owl*. London: T. & A. D. Poyser Publishing, 2012.

Potter, Beatrix. *The Tale of Squirrel Nutkin*. London: Frederick Warne and Co, 1903

Quammen, David. *Monster of God*. New York: W. W. Norton, 2003.

Ramsden, David, Matthew Twiggs, Stuart Baker, Maxine Chavner, Sarah Nelms. *Barn Owl Conservation Handbook*. Exeter: The Barn Owl Trust and Pelagic Publishing, 2012.

Roberts, James. *Owl, Owl, Owl*. Hereford, UK: Zoo Press, 2016.

Rouse, Andy. *Little Owls*. London: Electric Squirrel Publishing, 2013.

Scott, Walter. *The Complete Works of Walter Scott*. London: Wordsworth Editions, 1995.

Shakespeare, William. *Macbeth*. London: Wordsworth Classics, 1992

Smith, Ben. *Sky Burials*. Tonbridge, UK: Worple Press, 2014.

Solnit, Rebecca. *Hope in the Dark, Untold Histories, Wild Possibilities*. Edinburgh: Canongate Books, 2016.

Steven, Kenneth. *The Missing Days*. Edinburgh: Scottish Cultural Press, 1995.

Stocking, George W., Jr., ed. *A Franz Boas Reader: The Shaping of American Anthropology, 1883–1911*. Chicago: University of Chicago Press, 1989.

Strachan, Rob. *Mammal Detective*. Linton, UK: Whittet Books, 1995.

Strycker, Noah. *The Magic and Mystery of Birds*. London: Souvenir Press, 2014.

Svensson, Lars, Killian Mullarney, and Dan Zetterstrom. *Le guide ornitho*. Paris: Delachaux et Niestlé, 2015.

———. *Collins Bird Guide to the Birds of Britain and Europe*. London: Harper Collins, 2009.

Taylor, Iain. *Barn Owls, Predator-Prey Relationships and Conservation.* Cambridge: Cambridge University Press, 1994.

Tipling, David, and Jari Peltomaki. *Owls.* London: Evans Mitchell Books, 2013.

Tegner, Henry. *The Molecatcher Says.* London: The Country Book Club, 1965.

Terman, Max. *Messages from an Owl.* Princeton, NJ: Princeton University Press, 1996.

Thomas, Keith. *Man and the Natural World.* London: Penguin, 1984.

Tomlinson, Jill. *The Owl Who Was Afraid of the Dark.* London: Methuen, 1968.

Toms, Mike. *Owls.* London: William Collins, 2014.

Townsend Warner, Sylvia. *Lolly Willowes.* London: Virago, 2012.

Turner, Jack. *The Abstract Wild.* Tucson: University of Arizona Press, 1996.

Unwin, Mike, and David Tipling. *A Parliament of Owls.* London: William Collins, 2016.

Valkama, Jari, ed. *The Finnish Bird Ringing Atlas, Vols. I & II:* Tampere: Luomus Publishing, Finnish Museum of Natural History, 2014.

Van Grouw, Katrina. *The Unfeathered Bird.* Princeton, NJ: Princeton University Press, 2013.

Verney, Frances Parthenope. *Life and Death of Athena, an Owlet from the Parthenon.* London: Florence Nightingale Museum 1855.

Wheye, Darryl, and Kennedy Wheye. *Humans, Nature and Birds: Science Art from Cave Walls to Computer Screens.* New Haven, CT: Yale University Press, 2008.

Williams, Terry Tempest. *The Secret Language of Snow.* New York: Pantheon, 1984.

———. *Refuge.* London: Vintage, 1992.

———. *When Women Were Birds.* New York: Picador USA, 2012.

Wilson, Edward O. *Biophilia.* Cambridge, MA: Harvard University Press, 1984.

PERMISSIONS

WITH GRATEFUL THANKS to Jonathan Cape and Liz Berry for the use of "Owl"; Faber and Faber for T. S. Eliot's "Little Gidding"; to Kenneth Steven, Rosie Corlett, Caroline Carver, and Jennifer Hunt personally for their poems; Karine Polwart and Hedri Music for "King of Birds"; and E. O. Wilson and Harvard University Press for quotation from *Biophilia*.

NATIONAL AND INTERNATIONAL ASSOCIATIONS AND WEBSITES

Royal Society for the Protection of Birds: rspb.org.uk
British Trust for Ornithology: bto.org
Birdlife International: birdlife.org
The Barn Owl Trust: barnowltrust.org.uk
The Barn Owl Centre of Gloucestershire: barnowl.co.uk
Hungry Owl Project: hungryowl.org
The Owl Foundation: theowlfoundation.ca
National Audubon Society: audubon.org
Ligue pour la Protection des Oiseaux: lpo.fr
Bird Protection and Study Society of Serbia: birdlife.org/ europe-and
    -central-asia/partners/serbia-bird-protection
    -and-study-society-serbia
The Hawk and Owl Trust: hawkandowltrust.org
UK Little Owl Project: littleowlproject.uk
Jari Peltomaki bird photography in Finland: jaripeltomaki.com
Burrowing Owl Conservation Network:
    burrowingowlconservation.org
The International Owl Society: international-owl-society. com
The Owl Pages: owlpages.com
The Owls Trust: theowlstrust.org
World Owl Trust: owls.org/
Monfragüe National Park: turismoextremadura.com/en/explora
    /Monfraguee-National-Park/

The Epilepsy Society (UK) and the Epilepsy Foundation (US) have some useful advice about non-epileptic attack disorder. There are also NEAD Facebook groups and PSYCHOGENIC NONEPILEPTIC SEIZURES carer forums and YouTube channels where you can get support for this little-known and isolating condition.

epilepsysociety.org.uk/non-epileptic-seizures
facebook.com/groups/507012559418695